Fix It!™ Grammar

Robin Hood

TEACHER'S MANUAL
LEVEL 3

Pamela White

Fourth Edition, January 2022
Institute for Excellence in Writing, L.L.C.

The purchase of this book allows its owner access to e-audio resource talks by Andrew Pudewa. See blue page for details and download instructions.

ISBN 978-1-62341-362-0

Additional copies of this Teacher's Manual may be purchased from IEW.com/FIX-L3-T

Institute for Excellence in Writing (IEW®)
8799 N. 387 Road
Locust Grove, OK 74352
800.856.5815
info@IEW.com
IEW.com

Printed in Illinois, United States of America

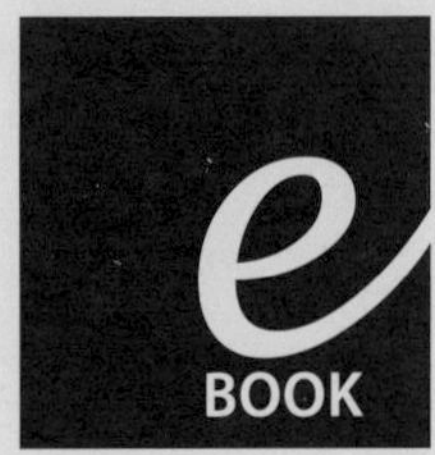

Accessing Your Downloads

The purchase of this book entitles its owner to a free download of the following:

- *Mastery Learning, Ability Development, and Individualized Education* e-audio
- *But, but, but ... What about Grammar?* e-audio
- *Fix It! Grammar: Robin Hood* vocabulary list with definitions
- *Fix It! Grammar Glossary*

To download these e-resources, please follow the directions below:

1. Go to our website: IEW.com
2. Log in to your online customer account. If you do not have an account, you will need to create one.
3. After you are logged in, go to this web page: IEW.com/FIX-E
4. Click the red arrow, and then click the checkboxes next to the names of the files you wish to place in your account.
5. Click the "Add to my files" button.
6. To access your files now and in the future, click on "Your Account" and click on the "Files" tab (one of the gray tabs).
7. Click on each file name to download the files onto your computer.

If you have any difficulty receiving these downloads after going through the steps above, please call 800.856.5815.

Institute for Excellence in Writing
8799 N. 387 Road
Locust Grove, OK 74352

Instructions

The list below shows the components to each *Fix It! Grammar* weekly exercise.

Although **Mark It** is listed before **Fix It**, the student may choose to **Fix It** first and then **Mark It**. This is acceptable because the *Fix It! Grammar* exercises are like a word puzzle. The goal is to complete the lists at the top of the student page for each passage.

Students should discuss their work with the teacher after working through each daily passage. However, older students may work with their teacher on a weekly basis. Students should actively be involved in comparing their work with the Teacher's Manual. The repetition of finding and fixing their own mistakes allows them to recognize and avoid those mistakes in the future.

Fix It! Grammar should be treated as a game. Keep it fun!

Learn It! On the first day of the new Week, read through the Learn It section. Each Learn It covers a concept that the student will practice in future passages. Instructions for marking and fixing passages are included in each Learn It.

Read It! Read the day's passage.

Look up the bolded vocabulary word in a dictionary and pick the definition that fits the context of the story. Maintain a list of vocabulary words and their definitions.

The vocabulary definitions are printed in the Teacher's Manual.

Mark It! Mark the passage using the guide at the top of the daily practice page.

Fix It! Correct the passage using the guide at the top of the daily practice page.

The Teacher's Manual includes detailed explanations for grammar concepts and punctuation in each daily passage.

Rewrite It! After marking, correcting, and discussing the passage with the teacher, copy the corrected passage on the lines provided or into a separate notebook.

- Copy the corrected story, not the editing marks.
- Indent and use capital letters properly.
- Copy the corrected punctuation.

Editing Marks

Mark	Meaning
¶	indent
^	insert
ℊ	delete
t (triple underline)	capitalize
T (slash)	lowercase
∽	reverse order
#	add a space
⁀‿	close the space

Helpful Hints

Use different colors for **Mark It** and **Fix It**.

Appendix I Complete Story Familiarize yourself with the story that you will be editing by reading the complete story found in Appendix I.

Appendix II Collection Pages Look for strong verbs, quality adjectives, and -ly adverbs in this book and write them on the collection pages in Appendix II.

Appendix III Lists Refer to the lists found in Appendix III to quickly identify pronouns, prepositions, verbs, and conjunctions.

Appendix IV Grammar Glossary Reference the Grammar Glossary found in Appendix IV of the Teacher's Manual for more information about the concepts taught in the *Fix It! Grammar* series.

Additional Resource

Fix It! Grammar Cards are an optional product that will enhance the *Fix It! Grammar* learning experience.

Fix It! Grammar Cards

Thirty full color grammar cards highlight key *Fix It! Grammar* concepts for quick and easy reference.

For a more relaxed and entertaining way to drill and review grammar concepts learned, instructions for a download of multiple game ideas are included in the card pack.

Fix It! Grammar Cards are beautifully designed and come in a sturdy card box for easy storage.

IEW.com/FIX-GC

On the chart below *Fix It! Grammar Cards* are listed in the order that the information is taught in this book. Some cards are not introduced until future books.

WEEK	Fix It! Grammar Cards for *Robin Hood* Level 3
1	Editing Marks, Capitalization, Title, Noun, Pronoun, Preposition
2	Subject-Verb Pair, Verb, Linking Verb, Helping Verb, Conjunction, Coordinating Conjunction, Apostrophes
3	Adjective, Dependent Clause
5	Adverb
6	Sentence Openers, Prepositional Phrase
7	#3 -ly Adverb Opener, Number Words and Numerals
8	www Word
9	Indefinite Pronoun
10	Clause
11	Run-On
14	Interjection
15	Indentation, Quotation
25	Commas with Adjectives before a Noun
Not Used	#4 -ing Opener, Comparative and Superlative Adjectives and Adverbs

Scope and Sequence

Week numbers indicate when a concept is introduced or specifically reinforced in a lesson. Once introduced the concept is practiced throughout the book.

Parts of Speech

Week	1	2	3	4	5	6	7	8	9	10	11	12	13	14	15	16	17	18	19	20	21	22	23	24	25	26	27	28	29	30
Noun	1			4							11																				
subject noun		2																													
noun of direct address					5																										
plural noun																				19												
Pronoun |1|																													
personal pronoun |1|																													
subject pronoun		2												14																		
indefinite pronoun									9																						
demonstrative pronoun									9																						
reflexive pronoun																						22									
Preposition	1																				20										
prepositional phrase	1																17			20										
Verb																														
action verb		2		4			7				11																		29	
linking verb		2					7																								29	
helping verb		2					7																								29	
Coordinating Conjunction		2														16					21									
Adjective			3	4							11																				
article adj |1|																													
possessive adj			3																	19												
adj after linking verb			3																												
coordinate adjectives																									25					
cumulative adjectives																										26				
Adverb					5	6	7																									
Interjection														14																	

Capitalization

Week	1	2	3	4	5	6	7	8	9	10	11	12	13	14	15	16	17	18	19	20	21	22	23	24	25	26	27	28	29	30
First Word of Sentence |1|																													
Proper Noun |1|																													
Personal Pronoun I |1|																													
Interjection														14																	
Quotation Marks															15																
Proper Adjective			3																												

Punctuation

Week	1	2	3	4	5	6	7	8	9	10	11	12	13	14	15	16	17	18	19	20	21	22	23	24	25	26	27	28	29	30
End Marks																														
period	1																													
question mark	1																													
exclamation mark	1													14																
w/quotation marks															15															
Commas																														
a and b		2														16					21									
a, b, and c		2														16					21									
MC, cc MC																16					21									
who/which clause			3																											
that clause				4																										
noun of direct address					5																									
#2 prepositional opener						6																								
#3 -ly adverb opener							7																							
adverb clause								8																						
#5 clausal opener												12																		
comma splice													13																	
interjection														14																
quotations															15															
coordinate adjectives																									25					
cumulative adjectives																										26				
Quotation Marks															15													28		
Apostrophes																														
contraction		2																												
possessive adj																			19											

Clauses

Week	1	2	3	4	5	6	7	8	9	10	11	12	13	14	15	16	17	18	19	20	21	22	23	24	25	26	27	28	29	30
Who/Which Clause			3							10	11												23							
That Clause				4						10																				
Adverb Clause								8		10		12								20										
Dependent Clause										10							17													
Main Clause										10							17													

Homophones/Usage

Week	1	2	3	4	5	6	7	8	9	10	11	12	13	14	15	16	17	18	19	20	21	22	23	24	25	26	27	28	29	30
To/Two/Too				4																										
Its/It's					5																									
Your/You're					5																									
There/Their/They're									9																					
Whose/Who's														14																
Then/Than																		18												

Other Concepts

Week	1	2	3	4	5	6	7	8	9	10	11	12	13	14	15	16	17	18	19	20	21	22	23	24	25	26	27	28	29	30
Indentation	1														15															
Numbers							7																							
Subject-Verb Pairs		2																												
Fused Sentence											11		13																	
Comma Splice													13																	
Imperative Sentence														14																

Stylistic Techniques

Week	1	2	3	4	5	6	7	8	9	10	11	12	13	14	15	16	17	18	19	20	21	22	23	24	25	26	27	28	29	30
Strong Verb		2																						24						
Quality Adjective			3																					24						
Who/Which Clause			3								11												23							
-ly Adverb					5								13											24						
Adverb Clause								8																						
#1 Subject Opener						6																								
#2 Prepositional Opener						6																					27			
#3 -ly Adverb Opener							7																							
#5 Clausal Opener												12															27			
#6 Vss Opener													13																	

Vocabulary

1 reigned legendary rambled experienced	2 wrath challenged readily strolled	3 entertaining carefree sociably confronted	4 taunt champion exceptional retorted	5 offense composedly seethed capital	6 impulsively furious toppled tortured
7 accounts slain vowed lavish	8 sheltered displaced famished narrowly	9 greedy devastated fled peasants	10 declared plundered aid earnestly	11 corrupt courageous peril gurgling	12 romped restless directed signal
13 roamed spanned stout quickened	14 rudely confident riled asserted	15 bellowed lethal crimson sparring	16 countered gazed sturdy fashioned	17 towered rival crafted risk	18 goaded victor adept nimbly
19 adversary parried leveled deftly	20 budged battled fatigue privately	21 delivered recovered inflamed counterattacked	22 ridiculous strutted wield echoed	23 rustled steadfast rugged pounced	24 struggled blameless introduced appoint
25 thrashing motley devoted bout	26 instructed paced quiver attentively	27 released impressive notched flawlessly	28 magnificent urged extended snickered	29 howled jubilant quipped guffaw	30 retraced festivity warmly trustworthy

Contents

Weekly Lessons

Appendices

Learn It!

Every word belongs to a word group—a part of speech. There are eight parts of speech: noun, pronoun, verb, preposition, conjunction, adjective, adverb, interjection.

For more information about the parts of speech, see the glossary.

Noun

A **noun** names a person, place, thing, or idea.

A **compound noun** is two or more words combined to form a single noun. This includes proper nouns with two or more words, such as *King Richard.*

Noun Tests:

the ________

two ________

Article Adjective

The **article adjectives** are *a, an, the.* A noun follows an article adjective.

Pronoun

A **pronoun** replaces a noun in order to avoid repetition. It refers back to some person or thing recently mentioned and takes the place of that person or thing.

There are many types of pronouns. **Personal pronouns** take the place of common and proper nouns. Review the personal pronouns in Appendix III.

The noun the pronoun replaces is called the antecedent.

Week 3 students will learn that possessive pronouns like *his* and possessive nouns like *Robin's* function as adjectives.

Preposition

A **preposition** starts a phrase that shows the relationship between a noun or pronoun and another word in the sentence. A prepositional phrase always begins with a preposition and ends with a noun or pronoun. Review the prepositions in Appendix III.

Memorize It! preposition + noun (no verb)

Mark It! Write *n* above each noun. Use a single *n* for a compound noun.
Write *ar* above each article and *pr* above each pronoun.
Underline each prepositional phrase.

Robin Hood (*n*) and his (*pr*) men (*n*) lived <u>in the (*ar*) forest (*n*).</u>

Ask students to identify the nouns, article adjective, pronoun, and prepositional phrase and to explain how the prepositional phrase follows the pattern.

In what? ***forest***
in the forest starts with a preposition (in) and ends with a noun (forest). It has an article in between, but no verb.

Capitalization

Capitalize the first word of a sentence.

Capitalize proper nouns.

Capitalize the personal pronoun *I*.

Fix It! Place three short lines below letters that should be capitalized.

robin lived in sherwood forest. he told his men, "i will hunt with you."

End Mark

Use a period at the end of a statement.

Use a question mark at the end of a question.

Use an exclamation mark at the end of a sentence that expresses strong emotion.

Fix It! Place the correct end mark at the end of each sentence.

Did Robin give up**?** He would never quit**!** He was used to challenges**.**

Indentation

Students will be required to identify where passages should be indented Week 15. Until then, require students to copy the indentation correctly when they rewrite the passage.

Notice that some sentences are indented. An indented sentence means that the sentence begins a new paragraph.

In fiction (stories), there are four reasons to start a new paragraph: new speaker, new topic, new place, new time.

Read It!

in the olden days of england, king richard **reigned** over the land

Mark It!

2 articles (ar)
4 nouns (n)
3 prepositional phrases

Fix It!

4 capitals
1 end mark

reigned
ruled as king or queen

in the olden days of england, king richard **reigned** over the land.

Capitalization	***In*** first word of the sentence ***England***; ***King Richard*** proper noun In this sentence *King Richard* is a compound noun, forming a name for one individual. Because the compound noun forms a proper noun, both words are capitalized.
End Marks	Use a period at the end of a statement.

Rewrite It! In the olden days of England, King Richard reigned over the land.

Read It!	Mark It!	Fix It!
a **legendary** outlaw lived in sherwood forest in central england. his name was robin hood	1 article (ar) 5 nouns (n) 1 pronoun (pr) 2 prepositional phrases	7 capitals 1 end mark

legendary
remarkable enough to be famous

ar n n
a **legendary** outlaw lived in sherwood forest

n pr n n
in central england. his name was robin hood.

Capitalization	***A***; ***His*** first word of the sentence ***Sherwood Forest***; ***England***; ***Robin Hood*** proper noun
End Marks	Use a period at the end of a statement.
Pronoun	***His*** replaces *outlaw's* Week 3 students will learn that a possessive pronoun like *his* is a pronoun that functions as an adjective.

Rewrite It! A legendary outlaw lived in Sherwood Forest in central England. His name was Robin Hood.

Read It!	Mark It!	Fix It!
robin and the loyal men with him **rambled** through the countryside. they hunted in the deep forests	3 articles (ar) 4 nouns (n) 2 pronouns (pr) 3 prepositional phrases	2 capitals 1 end mark

rambled
wandered without specific plan or direction

n ar n pr
robin and the loyal men with him **rambled** through

ar n pr ar n
the countryside. they hunted in the deep forests.

Capitalization	***Robin*** proper noun; first word of the sentence ***They*** first word of the sentence
End Marks	Use a period at the end of a statement.
Pronoun	***him*** replaces *Robin* ***They*** replaces *Robin* and *men*

Rewrite It! Robin and the loyal men with him rambled through the countryside. They hunted in the deep forests.

Read It!	Mark It!	Fix It! Day 4
robin was skilled with the bow. in truth, he was the most **experienced** archer in england	2 articles (ar) 5 nouns (n) 1 pronoun (pr) 3 prepositional phrases	3 capitals 1 end mark

experienced
having expert skill or knowledge

robin was skilled with the bow. in truth, he was the most **experienced** archer in england.

Capitalization	***Robin*** proper noun; first word of the sentence ***In*** first word of the sentence ***England*** proper noun
End Marks	Use a period at the end of a statement.
Pronoun	***he*** replaces *Robin*

Rewrite It! Robin was skilled with the bow. In truth, he was the most experienced archer in England.

Learn It!

Verb

A **verb** shows action, links the subject to another word, or helps another verb. To determine if a word is a verb, use the verb test.

An **action verb** shows action or ownership.

A **linking verb** links the subject to a noun or adjective. The words below are linking verbs.

Memorize It! **am, is, are, was, were, be, being, been**
seem, become, appear, grow, remain
taste, sound, smell, feel, look

A **helping verb** helps an action verb or a linking verb. The helping verb is always followed by another verb. The words below are helping verbs.

Memorize It! **am, is, are, was, were, be, being, been**
have, has, had, do, does, did, may, might, must
can, will, shall, could, would, should

Every verb has a subject. The subject and verb (s v) belong together.

For more information about verbs, see page G-9.

Verb Test:

I ____.

It ____.

Some verbs function as either action or linking verbs.

He *smelled* (action) burned wood.

He *smelled* (linking) awful.

If you can substitute *is* for the verb, it is probably functioning as a linking verb.

Subject

A **subject** is a noun or pronoun that performs a verb action. It tells who or what the clause is about.

Find It! Read the sentence and look for the verb.
Ask, "Who or what ____ (verb)?"

Mark It! Write *v* above each verb and *s* above each subject.

s v v
Robin had practiced archery for many years.

s v
His skills were incredible.

For more information about subjects and s v pairs, see pages G-7, G-17.

Ask students to identify the subjects and verbs.

What is the verb? ***had practiced***

Who had practiced? ***Robin***

What is the verb? ***were***

What were? ***skills***

Strong Verb

A **strong verb** dresses up writing because it creates a strong image or feeling. A strong verb is an action verb, never a linking or helping verb. Look for strong verbs in this book and write them on the Strong Verb collection page, Appendix II.

For more information about coordinating conjunctions, see page G-12.

Conjunction

A conjunction connects words, phrases, or clauses.

A **coordinating conjunction** connects the same type of words, phrases, or clauses.

Memorize It!

F	A	N	B	O	Y	S
for	and	nor	but	or	yet	so

Robin strolled through the forest and whistled happily.

Because the items that the cc connects must be grammatically the same, *and* connects two verbs, *strolled* and *whistled*. It does not connect the noun *forest* and the verb *whistled*.

Comma

A **comma** is used to separate items in a sentence. This week you will learn two comma rules.

Do not use a comma before a coordinating conjunction when it connects two items in a series unless they are main clauses.
PATTERN a and b

Use commas to separate three or more items in a series.
PATTERN a, b, and c

Ask students to identify the coordinating conjunction and explain what it connects.

But connects two adjectives: *brave*, *reckless*. No comma is used. a and b

And connects three verbs: *chose*, *pulled*, *let*. Two commas are used. a, b, and c

Mark It! Write *cc* above each coordinating conjunction.

Fix It! Remove a comma before a coordinating conjunction that connects only two items in a series. Add commas to separate three or more items in a series.

Robin was brave, but reckless. (cc above *but*; comma deleted)

He chose his arrow**,** pulled it back**,** and let it fly. (cc above *and*)

For more information about contractions, see page G-28.

Contraction

A **contraction** combines two words into one. It uses an apostrophe to show where a letter or letters have been removed.

Fix It! Place an apostrophe to show where a letter or letters have been removed.

Ask students to identify what letter has been removed.

The apostrophe shows where the letter *o* has been removed from the phrase *should not*.

Robin decided that he shouldn**'**t give up.

Read It!	Mark It!	Fix It!
why was robin hood an outlaw under the **wrath** of the law? its an interesting story for children and adults	4 articles (ar) 7 nouns (n) 1 pronoun (pr) 1 coordinating conjunction (cc) 3 prepositional phrases 2 subject-verb pairs (s v)	4 capitals 1 end mark 1 apostrophe

wrath
strong anger; punishment as a result of anger

why was robin hood an outlaw under the wrath of the law? it's an interesting story for children and adults.

Capitalization	***Why***; ***It's*** first word of the sentence ***Robin Hood*** proper noun
End Marks	Use a period at the end of a statement.
Pronoun	***It*** replaces *story*
S V Pairs	***Robin Hood was***; ***It's*** The contraction *it's* includes both a subject (it) and a verb (is).
Commas	Do not use a comma to separate two items connected with a coordinating conjunction. **PATTERN a and b** *children* and *adults*
Apostrophes	*It's* is a contraction. Use an apostrophe to show where letters have been removed.

Rewrite It! Why was Robin Hood an outlaw under the wrath of the law? It's an interesting story for children and adults.

Read It!	Mark It!	Fix It!
the sheriff of nottingham had **challenged** the local archers to a shooting match, and even offered a prize	4 articles (ar)	2 capitals
	5 nouns (n)	1 comma
	1 coordinating conjunction (cc)	1 end mark
	2 prepositional phrases	
	1 subject-verb pair (s v)	

challenged
called to a contest of skill or strength

the sheriff of nottingham had **challenged** the local archers to a shooting match, and even offered a prize.

Capitalization	***The*** first word of the sentence ***Nottingham*** proper noun
End Marks	Use a period at the end of a statement.
S V Pairs	***sheriff had challenged, offered*** *Shooting* functions as an adjective that describes *match*. A word that ends in -ing functions as a verb only if it follows a helping verb. (See Week 3 Day 3.)
Commas	Do not use a comma to separate two items connected with a coordinating conjunction. **PATTERN a and b** *challenged* and *offered*

Rewrite It! The sheriff of Nottingham had challenged the local archers to a shooting match and even offered a prize.

Read It!	Mark It!	Fix It!
robin was just eighteen. he **readily** accepted the challenge grabbed his bow and left his hometown	1 article (ar) 4 nouns (n) 3 pronouns (pr) 1 coordinating conjunction (cc) 2 subject-verb pairs (s v)	2 capitals 2 commas 1 end mark

readily
quickly; easily

robin (s, n) was (v) just eighteen. he (s, pr) **readily** accepted (v) the (ar) challenge (n), grabbed (v) his (pr) bow (n), and (cc) left (v) his (pr) hometown (n).

Capitalization	***Robin*** proper noun; first word of the sentence ***He*** first word of the sentence
End Marks	Use a period at the end of a statement.
Pronoun	***He*** replaces *Robin* ***his***; ***his*** replace *Robin's* Week 3 students will learn that a possessive pronoun like *his* is a pronoun that functions as an adjective.
S V Pairs	***Robin was***; ***He accepted, grabbed, left***
Commas	Use commas to separate three or more items in a series connected with a coordinating conjunction. **PATTERN a, b, and c** *accepted*, *grabbed*, and *left*

Rewrite It! Robin was just eighteen. He readily accepted the challenge, grabbed his bow, and left his hometown.

Read It!	Mark It!	Fix It!
robin **strolled** merrily. the trip shouldnt take him more than two, or three days	1 article (ar) 3 nouns (n) 1 pronoun (pr) 1 coordinating conjunction (cc) 2 subject-verb pairs (s v)	2 capitals 1 comma 1 end mark 1 apostrophe

strolled
walked casually

robin **strolled** merrily. the trip shouldn't take him more than two, or three days.

Capitalization	***Robin*** proper noun; first word of the sentence ***The*** first word of the sentence
End Marks	Use a period at the end of a statement.
Pronoun	***him*** replaces *Robin*
S V Pairs	***Robin strolled***; ***trip should take*** The contraction *shouldn't* includes both a helping verb (should) and an adverb (not).
Commas	Do not use a comma to separate two items connected with a coordinating conjunction. **PATTERN a and b** *two* or *three*
Apostrophes	*Shouldn't* is a contraction. Use an apostrophe to show where letters have been removed.

Rewrite It! Robin strolled merrily. The trip shouldn't take him more than two or three days.

Learn It!

Adjective

An **adjective** describes a noun or pronoun.

An adjective tells which one, what kind, how many, or whose.

Memorize It! **which one? what kind? how many? whose?**

Robin crossed the slippery bridge.

An adjective usually comes before the word it describes. The adjective *slippery* describes *bridge*. What kind of bridge? *slippery*

The bridge appeared slippery.

An adjective may follow a linking verb. The linking verb (appeared) links the subject (bridge) to an adjective (slippery). The adjective *slippery* describes *bridge*. What kind of bridge? *slippery*

Robin carried his bow.

Because the possessive pronouns *my, your, his, her, its, our, their* function as adjectives, you will now mark them as adjectives. The pronoun *his* replaces *Robin's* and functions as an adjective. Whose bow? *his*

Find It! Find the nouns and pronouns in the sentence.

Once you find a noun or pronoun, ask the adjective questions to identify the adjectives.

Mark It! Write ***adj*** above each adjective.

adj **adj**
Robin strolled through the quiet woods with his bow.

adj **adj**
Robin's skill in archery was famous.

For more information about adjectives, see page G-14.

Adjective Test:

the____ pen

Students will continue to write ***ar*** above article adjectives.

Ask students to find nouns (or pronouns) and then ask questions to identify adjectives.

What kind of woods? ***quiet***

Whose bow? ***his***
A possessive pronoun like *his* is a pronoun functioning as an adjective in order to show ownership.

Whose skill? ***Robin's***
A possessive noun like *Robin's* is a noun functioning as an adjective in order to show ownership.

What kind of skill? ***famous***
The adjective *famous* follows the linking verb and describes the subject.

Capitalization

Capitalize proper adjectives formed from proper nouns.

The English flag flew at King Richard's castle.

The proper adjective *English* comes from the proper noun *England*, the name of a specific country. The proper adjective *King Richard's* comes from the proper noun *King Richard*, the name of a specific person.

Quality Adjective

A **quality adjective** dresses up writing because it creates a strong image or feeling. A quality adjective is more specific than a weak adjective. A weak adjective is overused, boring, or vague. Look for quality adjectives in this book and write them on the Quality Adjective collection page, Appendix II.

For more information about *who/which* clauses, see page G-39.

Who/Which Clause

A ***who/which* clause** is a group of words that describes the noun it follows. It begins with the word *who* or *which,* a relative pronoun.

> *Who* refers to people, personified animals, and pets.
> *Which* refers to things, animals, and places.

A *who/which* clause is a dependent clause, which means it must be added to a sentence that is already complete.

Ask students to identify the subject and verb in the *who/which* clause and to identify the noun that the clause describes.

Robin eyed the target. ***(sentence)***

Robin, who eyed the target. ***(fragment)***

Robin, who eyed the target, picked up his bow. ***(sentence)***

A *who/which* clause contains a subject and a verb. The subject of most *who/which* clauses is *who* or *which,* but sometimes the subject is another word in the clause.

What is the verb? ***hoped***

Who hoped? ***he***
The relative pronoun *which* replaces the noun *contest.*

which he hoped to win describes *contest.* Commas are used because the *which* clause is nonessential.

Mark It! Place parentheses around the *who/which* clause and write ***w/w*** above the word *who* or *which.* Write ***v*** above each verb and ***s*** above each subject.

Robin thought about the contest, **(**which [w/w] he [s] hoped [v] to win**)**.

The men **(**who [w/w] [s] worked [v] for the king**)** could not be trusted.

What is the verb? ***worked***

Who worked? ***who***
The relative pronoun *who* replaces the noun *men.*

who worked for the king describes *men.* Commas are not used because the *who* clause is essential to the meaning of the sentence by telling which men could not be trusted.

Comma

A **comma** is used to separate items in a sentence. Commas are used to separate the *who/which* clause from the rest of the sentence unless the *who/which* clause changes the meaning of the sentence.

 Place commas around the *who/which* clause if it is nonessential.

 Do not place commas around the *who/which* clause if it is essential (changes the meaning of the sentence).

At this level, help students understand why some *who/which* clauses have commas and some do not.

Require students to copy the commas correctly when they rewrite the passage.

When you rewrite the passages, copy the commas correctly.

Read It!	Mark It!	Fix It! Day 1
robin whistled, and thought about the contest, which would be **entertaining.** he wasnt worried about the other archers	2 articles (ar) 3 nouns (n) 1 pronoun (pr) 3 adjectives (adj) 1 coordinating conjunction (cc) 2 prepositional phrases 1 *who/which* clause (w/w) 3 subject-verb pairs (s v)	2 capitals 1 comma 1 end mark 1 apostrophe

entertaining
amusing; giving pleasure

robin whistled, and thought about the contest, (which would be **entertaining**). he wasn't worried about the other archers.

Capitalization	***Robin*** proper noun; first word of the sentence ***He*** first word of the sentence
End Marks	Use a period at the end of a statement.
Pronoun	***He*** replaces *Robin*
Adjective	What kind of which (contest)? ***entertaining*** The adjective follows the linking verb and describes the subject. What kind of he (Robin)? ***worried*** The adjective follows the linking verb and describes the subject. Which archers? ***other***
W/W Clause	***which would be entertaining*** The *which* clause describes *contest*, the noun it follows.
S V Pairs	***Robin whistled***, ***thought***; ***which would be***; ***He was***
Commas	Do not use a comma to separate two items connected with a coordinating conjunction. **PATTERN a and b** *whistled* and *thought*
Apostrophes	*Wasn't* is a contraction. Use an apostrophe to show where letters have been removed.

Rewrite It! Robin whistled and thought about the contest, which would be entertaining. He wasn't worried about the other archers.

Read It!	Mark It!	Fix It!
the day seemed pleasant and **carefree**. however, robin's mood would soon change	1 article (ar) 2 nouns (n) 3 adjectives (adj) 1 coordinating conjunction (cc) 2 subject-verb pairs (s v)	3 capitals 1 end mark

carefree
without worry

ar s n v adj cc adj
the day seemed pleasant and **carefree**. however,

adj s n v v
robin's mood would soon change.

Capitalization	***The***; ***However*** first word of the sentence ***Robin's*** proper adjective
End Marks	Use a period at the end of a statement.
Adjective	What kind of day? ***pleasant*** and ***carefree*** The adjectives follow the linking verb and describe the subject. Whose mood? ***Robin's***
S V Pairs	***day seemed***; ***mood would change***
Commas	Do not use a comma to separate two items connected with a coordinating conjunction. **PATTERN a and b** *pleasant* and *carefree*

Rewrite It! The day seemed pleasant and carefree. However, Robin's mood would soon change.

Read It!

robin met fifteen foresters who worked for the king. they were sitting beneath a huge oak, and were feasting **sociably**

sociably
in a friendly, agreeable way

Mark It!

2 articles (ar)
4 nouns (n)
1 pronoun (pr)
2 adjectives (adj)
1 coordinating conjunctions (cc)
2 prepositional phrases
1 *who/which* clause (w/w)
3 subject-verb pairs (s v)

Fix It!

2 capitals
1 end mark
1 comma

robin [s n] met [v] fifteen [adj] foresters [n] (who [w/w s] worked [v] for the [ar] king [n]). they [s pr] were [v] sitting [v] beneath a [ar] huge [adj] oak [n], and [cc] were [v] feasting [v] **sociably.**

Capitalization	***Robin*** proper noun; first word of the sentence ***They*** first word of the sentence
End Marks	Use a period at the end of a statement.
Pronoun	***They*** replaces *foresters*
Adjective	How many foresters? ***fifteen*** What kind of oak? ***huge***
W/W Clause	***who worked for the king*** The *who* clause describes *foresters*, the noun it follows.
S V Pairs	***Robin met***; ***who worked***; ***They were sitting***, ***were feasting*** In this sentence *sitting* and *feasting* function as verbs because they follow the helping verb *were*. A word that ends in -ing functions as a verb only if it follows a helping verb.
Commas	Do not use a comma to separate two items connected with a coordinating conjunction. **PATTERN a and b** *were sitting* and *were feasting*

Rewrite It! Robin met fifteen foresters who worked for the king. They were sitting beneath a huge oak and were feasting sociably.

Read It!

a man who had a scar on his face **confronted** robin. he called robin's bow and arrows cheap, and shoddy

confronted
faced boldly and critically

Mark It!

2 articles (ar)
6 nouns (n)
1 pronoun (pr)
4 adjectives (adj)
2 coordinating conjunctions (cc)
1 prepositional phrase
1 *who/which* clause (w/w)
3 subject-verb pairs (s v)

Fix It!

4 capitals
1 comma
1 end mark

a man (who had a scar on his face) **confronted** robin.
he called robin's bow and arrows cheap, and shoddy.

Capitalization	***A***; ***He*** first word of the sentence ***Robin*** proper noun ***Robin's*** proper adjective
End Marks	Use a period at the end of a statement.
Pronoun	***He*** replaces *man*
Adjective	Whose face? ***his*** The possessive pronoun *his* functions as an adjective. Whose bow and arrows? ***Robin's*** What kind of bow and arrows? ***cheap*** and ***shoddy***
W/W Clause	***who had a scar on his face*** The *who* clause describes *man*, the noun it follows.
S V Pairs	***man confronted***; ***who had***; ***He called***
Commas	Do not use a comma to separate two items connected with a coordinating conjunction. **PATTERN a and b** *bows* and *arrows* **PATTERN a and b** *cheap* and *shoddy*

Rewrite It! A man who had a scar on his face confronted Robin. He called Robin's bow and arrows cheap and shoddy.

Learn It!

That Clause

A ***that* clause** is a group of words that begins with the word *that* and contains a subject and a verb. A *that* clause is a dependent clause, which means it must be added to a sentence that is already complete.

For more information about *that* clauses, see page G-41.

Mark It! Place parentheses around the *that* clause and write ***that*** above the word *that*. Write ***v*** above each verb and ***s*** above each subject.

that s v v

Robin knew (that he could win the contest).

Ask students to identify the subject and verb in the *that* clause.

What is the verb? ***could win***

Who could win? ***he***

Comma

A **comma** is used to separate items in a sentence. Because *that* clauses are essential to the sentence, commas are not used with *that* clauses.

That clauses do not take commas.

Homophone

A **homophone** is a word that sounds like another word but is spelled differently and has a different meaning. Correctly use the homophones *to, two,* and *too.*

For more information about homophones, see page G-35.

To is a preposition or part of an infinitive: *to Nottingham* (preposition); *to travel* (infinitive).

Two is a number: *two arrows* (2 arrows).

Too is an adverb meaning also or to an excessive degree: *traveled too; too excited.*

Fix It! Place a line through the incorrect homophone and write the correct word above it.

Robin was headed ~~two~~ *to* Nottingham ~~to~~ *too*. He brought his ~~to~~ *two* straightest arrows.

Think About It!

Many words can be used as different parts of speech. However, a word can perform only one part of speech at a time. For example, *light* can be a noun, adjective, or verb.

Noun: The light hurt my eyes.

In this sentence *light* is a thing.
A noun is a person, place, thing, or idea.

Adjective: The light rain was falling.

In this sentence *light* describes rain. What kind of rain? *light.*
An adjective describes a noun or pronoun.

Verb: The lamps light the room.

In this sentence *light* is a verb. *Light* is the action. What *light* the room? *lamps.*
The subject-verb pair is *lamps light.*

Read It!	Mark It!	Fix It! Day 1
then robin grew angry. no young man likes other men too **taunt** him about his prize possessions	4 nouns (n) 1 pronoun (pr) 6 adjectives (adj) 1 prepositional phrase 2 subject-verb pairs (s v)	3 capitals 1 end mark 1 homophone

taunt
mock

then robin grew angry. no young man likes other men ~~too~~ to **taunt** him about his prize possessions.

(Marked: robin — s, n; grew — v; angry — adj; no — adj; young — adj; man — s, n; likes — v; other — adj; men — n; too → to; him — pr; his — adj; prize — adj; possessions — n; prepositional phrase: about his prize possessions; capitals: then, robin, no.)

This is the last week that a detailed explanation about pronouns is provided.

Capitalization	***Then***; ***No*** first word of the sentence ***Robin*** proper noun
End Marks	Use a period at the end of a statement.
Pronoun	***him*** replaces *man*
Adjective	What kind of Robin? ***angry*** The adjective follows the linking verb and describes the subject. What kind of man? ***young*** Which young man? ***No*** Which men? ***other*** What kind of possessions? ***prize*** Whose prize possessions? ***his*** The possessive pronoun *his* functions as an adjective.
S V Pairs	***Robin grew***; ***man likes***
Homophones	Use ***to***, the infinitive marker. The phrase *to taunt* does not follow the **PATTERN preposition + noun.** When *to* is followed by a verb, it is called an infinitive. Do not mark infinitives as prepositional phrases. Do not mark them as verbs. They function as neither.

Rewrite It! Then Robin grew angry. No young man likes other men to taunt him about his prize possessions.

Read It!	Mark It!	Fix It! Day 2
he boasted that he was as skillful with a bow and arrow as any man. he was headed too nottingham to prove his skill in a **champion** match	2 articles (ar) 6 nouns (n) 3 pronouns (pr) 4 adjectives (adj) 1 coordinating conjunction (cc) 4 prepositional phrases 1 *that* clause (that) 3 subject-verb pairs (s v)	3 capitals 1 end mark 1 homophone

champion
first among all competitors

he boasted (that he was as skillful with a bow and arrow as any man). he was headed ~~too~~ to nottingham to prove his skill in a **champion** match.

Capitalization	***He***; ***He*** first word of the sentence ***Nottingham*** proper noun
End Marks	Use a period at the end of a statement.
Pronoun	***He***; ***he***; ***He*** replace *Robin*
Adjective	What kind of he (Robin)? ***skillful*** The adjective follows the linking verb and describes the subject. Which man? ***any*** Whose skill? ***his*** The possessive pronoun *his* functions as an adjective. What kind of match? ***champion***
Note	As *skillful* is not a prepositional phrase because it does not follow the pattern. **PATTERN preposition + noun (no verb)** *Skillful* is an adjective. *As* is an adverb modifying the adjective *skillful*.
S V Pairs	***He boasted***; ***he was***; ***He was headed*** *To prove* is an infinitive. It does not function as a verb.
Homophones	Use ***to***, the preposition.
Commas	Do not use a comma to separate two items connected with a coordinating conjunction. **PATTERN a and b** *bow* and *arrow*

Rewrite It! He boasted that he was as skillful with a bow and arrow as any man. He was headed to Nottingham to prove his skill in a champion match.

Read It!	Mark It!	Fix It!
he planned to shoot with other archers for the grand prize, which was a barrel of **exceptional** ale, and a new bow **exceptional** unusually excellent; superior	3 articles (ar) 5 nouns (n) 1 pronoun (pr) 4 adjectives (adj) 1 coordinating conjunction (cc) 3 prepositional phrases 1 *who/which* clause (w/w) 2 subject-verb pairs (s v)	1 capital 1 comma 1 end mark

he planned to shoot with other archers for the grand prize, (which was a barrel of **exceptional** ale, and a new bow).

Capitalization	***He*** first word of the sentence
End Marks	Use a period at the end of a statement.
Pronoun	***He*** replaces *Robin*
Adjective	Which archers? ***other*** What kind of prize? ***grand*** What kind of ale? ***exceptional*** What kind of bow? ***new***
W/W Clause	***which was a barrel of exceptional ale and new a bow*** The *which* clause describes *prize*, the noun it follows.
S V Pairs	***He planned***; ***which was*** *To shoot* is an infinitive. It does not function as a verb.
Commas	Do not use a comma to separate two items connected with a coordinating conjunction. **PATTERN a and b** *barrel* and *bow*

Rewrite It! He planned to shoot with other archers for the grand prize, which was a barrel of exceptional ale and a new bow.

Read It!

one forester laughed at him, and **retorted** that he had big words for a little boy! he said that he should drink his ale with milk

retorted
answered angrily

Mark It!

1 article (ar)
5 nouns (n)
4 pronouns (pr)
4 adjectives (adj)
1 coordinating conjunction (cc)
3 prepositional phrases
2 *that* clauses (that)
4 subject-verb pairs (s v)

Fix It!

2 capitals
1 comma
1 end mark

one forester laughed at him, and **retorted** (that he had big words for a little boy)! he said (that he should drink his ale with milk).

Capitalization	***One***; ***He*** first word of the sentence
End Marks	Use a period at the end of a statement.
Pronoun	***him***; ***he*** replace *Robin* ***He*** replaces *forester* ***he*** replaces *Robin*
Adjective	How many foresters? ***one*** What kind of words? ***big*** What kind of boy? ***little*** Whose ale? ***his*** The possessive pronoun *his* functions as an adjective.
S V Pairs	***forester laughed***, ***retorted***; ***he had***; ***He said***; ***he should drink***
Commas	Do not use a comma to separate two items connected with a coordinating conjunction. **PATTERN a and b** *laughed* and *retorted*

Rewrite It! One forester laughed at him and retorted that he had big words for a little boy! He said that he should drink his ale with milk.

Learn It!

Adverb

An **adverb** modifies a verb, an adjective, or another adverb.

An adverb tells how, when, where, why, to what extent.

Memorize It! **how? when? where? why? to what extent?**

An adverb often ends in -ly.

Mark It! Write ***adv*** above each -ly adverb.

adv

The deer carefully hid in a secluded thicket.

For more information about adverbs, see pages G-15, G-37, and G-43.

Ask students to find verbs, adjectives, or adverbs and then ask questions to identify adverbs.

Hid how? ***carefully***
carefully modifies a verb (hid)

-ly Adverb

An **-ly adverb** dresses up writing when it creates a strong image or feeling. Look for -ly adverbs in this book and write them on the -ly Adverb collection page, Appendix II.

Noun of Direct Address

A **noun of direct address** (NDA) is a noun used to refer to someone directly. It names the person spoken to.

It can appear at any natural pause in a quoted sentence.

"Robin**,** tomorrow you will win the contest," his friend said.

"Tomorrow**,** Robin**,** you will win the contest," his friend said.

"Tomorrow you will win the contest**,** Robin," his friend said.

If you remove the NDA from the sentence, you will still have a sentence.

Because a noun can perform only one function in a sentence, a noun of direct address is never the subject of a sentence. In these sentences the noun of direct address is *Robin* because that is the noun used to directly address Robin. The subject is the pronoun *you*.

Comma

A **comma** is used to separate items in a sentence. Commas are used to separate the noun of direct address from the rest of the sentence.

Place commas around a noun of direct address.

Fix It! Add commas to separate the noun of direct address from the sentence.

"Robin**,** you should enter the contest," his friend suggested.

Ask students to identify the noun of direct address.

Robin is the noun of direct address. Place a comma after *Robin*.

Homophone

A **homophone** is a word that sounds like another word but is spelled differently and has a different meaning. Correctly use the homophones *its* and *it's, your* and *you're.*

Its is a possessive pronoun: *its target* (the target belongs to it).

The possessive pronoun *its* tells whose and functions as an adjective.

It's is a contraction: *it's spring* (it is spring).

The contraction *it's* is a shortened form of *it is* and functions as the subject pronoun (it) and verb (is) of the clause.

Your is a possessive pronoun: *your bow* (the bow belongs to you).

The possessive pronoun *your* tells whose and functions as an adjective.

You're is a contraction: *you're right* (you are right).

The contraction *you're* is a shortened form of *you are* and functions as the subject pronoun (you) and verb (are) of the clause.

Fix It! Place a line through the incorrect homophone and write the correct word above it.

It's ***its***
~~Its~~ trying to hide, but ~~it's~~ antlers are showing.

You're ***your***
~~Your~~ on ~~you're~~ way to the archery contest.

Read It!	Mark It!	Fix It!
robin immediately took **offense**, and challenged the forester. "sir do you see the deer at the edge of the wood? i bet you twenty pounds that i can hit it"	4 articles (ar) 8 nouns (n) 5 pronouns (pr) 1 adjective (adj) 1 adverb (adv) 1 coordinating conjunction (cc) 2 prepositional phrases 1 *that* clause (that) 4 subject-verb pairs (s v)	4 capitals 2 commas 1 end mark

offense
resentment or emotional pain

robin immediately took **offense**, and challenged the forester. "sir, do you see the deer at the edge of the wood? i bet you twenty pounds (that i can hit it)."

Capitalization	***Robin*** proper noun; first word of the sentence ***Sir*** first word of the quoted sentence ***I*** personal pronoun I; first word of the sentence ***I*** personal pronoun I
End Marks	Use a period when a quote makes a statement. Place it inside the closing quotation mark.
Adjective	How many pounds? ***twenty***
Adverb	Took offense when? ***immediately***
S V Pairs	***Robin took***, ***challenged***; ***you do see***; ***I bet***; ***I can hit***
Commas	Do not use a comma to separate two items connected with a coordinating conjunction. PATTERN **a and b** *took* and *challenged* Place commas around a noun of direct address (NDA). ***Sir,***

Rewrite It! Robin immediately took offense and challenged the forester. "Sir, do you see the deer at the edge of the wood? I bet you twenty pounds that I can hit it."

Read It!	Mark It!	Fix It! Day 2
composedly robin took his bow in his hand grabbed an arrow from it's pouch and drew the feather to his ear	2 articles (ar) 7 nouns (n) 4 adjectives (adj) 1 adverb (adv) 1 coordinating conjunction (cc) 3 prepositional phrases 1 subject-verb pair (s v)	2 capitals 2 commas 1 end mark 1 homophone

composedly
calmly

adv: composedly; s n: robin; v: took; adj: his; n: bow; in his (adj) hand (n),
v: grabbed; ar: an; n: arrow; from ~~it's~~ its (adj) pouch (n), cc: and; v: drew; ar: the
n: feather; to his (adj) ear (n).

composedly robin took his bow in his hand, grabbed an arrow from ~~it's~~ its pouch, and drew the feather to his ear.

Capitalization	***Composedly*** first word of the sentence ***Robin*** proper noun
End Marks	Use a period at the end of a statement.
Adjective	Whose bow? ***his*** The possessive pronoun *his* functions as an adjective. Whose hand? ***his*** Whose pouch? ***its*** The possessive pronoun *its* functions as an adjective. Whose ear? ***his***
Adverb	Took how? ***Composedly***
S V Pairs	***Robin took, grabbed, drew***
Commas	Use commas to separate three or more items in a series with a coordinating conjunction. **PATTERN a, b, and c** *took*, *grabbed*, and *drew*
Homophones	Use ***its***, the possessive pronoun.

Rewrite It! Composedly Robin took his bow in his hand, grabbed an arrow from its pouch, and drew the feather to his ear.

Read It!	Mark It!	Fix It!
the arrow hit the buck. the foresters **seethed** with rage, especially the man who lost the bet	5 articles (ar) 6 nouns (n) 1 adverb (adv) 1 prepositional phrase 1 *who/which* clause (w/w) 3 subject-verb pairs (s v)	2 capitals 1 end mark

seethed
were angry

the arrow hit the buck. the foresters **seethed** with rage, especially the man (who lost the bet).

Capitalization	***The***; ***The*** first word of the sentence
End Marks	Use a period at the end of a statement.
Adverb	Seethed how? ***especially***
W/W Clause	***who lost the bet*** The *who* clause describes *man*, the noun it follows.
S V Pairs	***arrow hit***; ***foresters seethed***; ***who lost***

Rewrite It! The arrow hit the buck. The foresters seethed with rage, especially the man who lost the bet.

Read It!	Mark It!	Fix It! Day 4
the loser heatedly responded, "fool you killed the king's deer. its a **capital** offense. by law your going to die"	3 articles (ar)	4 capitals
	5 nouns (n)	1 comma
	3 pronouns (pr)	1 end mark
	2 adjectives (adj)	2 homophones
capital punishable by death	1 adverb (adv)	
	1 prepositional phrase	
	4 subject-verb pairs (s v)	

the loser heatedly responded, "fool**,** you killed the king's deer. ~~its~~ It's a **capital** offense. by law ~~your~~ you're going to die**.**"

Capitalization	***The*** first word of the sentence ***Fool***; ***It's***; ***By*** first word of the quoted sentence
End Marks	Use a period when a quote makes a statement. Place it inside the closing quotation mark.
Adjective	Whose deer? ***king's*** What kind of offense? ***capital***
Adverb	Responded how? ***heatedly***
S V Pairs	***loser responded***; ***you killed***; ***It's***; ***you're going*** The contraction *you're* includes both a subject (you) and a helping verb (are). *Going* functions as a verb because it follows the helping verb *are*. A word that ends in -ing functions as a verb only if it follows a helping verb. *To die* is an infinitive. It does not function as a verb.
Commas	Place commas around a noun of direct address (NDA). ***Fool,***
Homophones	Use ***it's***, the contraction for *it is*. Use ***you're***, the contraction for *you are*.

Rewrite It! The loser heatedly responded, "Fool, you killed the king's deer. It's a capital offense. By law you're going to die."

Learn It!

Sentence openers are descriptive words, phrases, and clauses that are added to the beginning of a sentence. Using different sentence openers makes writing more interesting.

In this book you will learn five types of sentence openers—five ways to open or begin a sentence. After you mark a sentence, determine if the sentence begins with an opener that you know. If it does, mark it! Do not mark questions or quoted sentences.

There are six IEW sentence openers. This book will teach five of them.

#1 Subject Opener

A **#1 subject opener** is a sentence that begins with the subject of the sentence. Sometimes, an article or adjective will come before the subject, but the sentence is still a #1 subject opener.

Mark It! Write (1) above the first word of a sentence that starts with a subject opener.

(1) S V
Robin spotted a deer in the field.

(1) S V
The swift deer leaped into the forest.

For more information about the #1 subject and #2 prepositional openers, see page G-42.

After students mark the sentence, ask them to identify the opener.

The first sentence is a #1 subject opener because it begins with the subject of the sentence (Robin).

The second sentence is also a #1 subject opener. It has adjectives (The swift) in front of the subject (deer), but no other words.

#2 Prepositional Opener

A **#2 prepositional opener** is a sentence that begins with a prepositional phrase. The first word in the sentence must be a preposition.

Mark It! Write (2) above the first word of a sentence that starts with a prepositional phrase.

(2)
Along the road Robin walked quickly.

(2)
Along the narrow and winding road, Robin walked quickly.

(2)
Along the narrow and winding road toward Nottingham, Robin walked quickly.

These three sentences are #2 prepositional openers because each begins with a prepositional phrase.

Students will mark every sentence except questions and quoted sentences.

Comma

A **comma** is used to separate items in a sentence.

If a prepositional opener has five words or more, follow it with a comma.

If two or more prepositional phrases open a sentence, follow the last phrase with a comma.

When you rewrite the passages, copy the commas correctly.

A third comma rule states if a prepositional opener functions as a transition, follow it with a comma. In this book students do not need to determine if a prepositional phrase is a transition.

Adverb

An **adverb** modifies a verb, an adjective, or another adverb.

An adverb tells how, when, where, why, to what extent.

Week 5 you learned that an adverb often ends in *-ly*. However, many adverbs do not end in *-ly*. Some common examples include *very, together, never, soon.*

Robin usually had his bow with him.

An adverb often ends in *-ly*.
The adverb *usually* tells when.

Robin always had his bow with him.

Some adverbs do not end in *-ly*.
The adverb *always* tells when.

Robin did not have his bow with him.

The words *yes, no, not, too* function as adverbs.
When you see them, label them adverbs.

Mark It! Write ***adv*** above each adverb

adv *adv*
Robin was very confident as he carefully aimed at the deer.

Read It!

in anger the forester **impulsively** sprang to his feet grabbed his bow and shot an arrow at robin

impulsively
quickly and hastily; acting emotionally

Mark It!

2 articles (ar)
6 nouns (n)
2 adjectives (adj)
1 adverb (adv)
1 coordinating conjunction (cc)
3 prepositional phrases
1 subject-verb pair (s v)
1 opener

Fix It!

2 capitals
2 commas
1 end mark

(2) prepositional

in anger (n) the (ar) forester (s n) **impulsively** (adv) sprang (v) to his (adj) feet (n), grabbed (v) his (adj) bow (n), and (cc) shot (v) an (ar) arrow (n) at robin (n).

Capitalization	***In*** first word of the sentence ***Robin*** proper noun
End Marks	Use a period at the end of a statement.
Adjective	Whose feet? ***his*** The possessive pronoun *his* functions as an adjective. Whose bow? ***his***
Adverb	Sprang how? ***impulsively***
S V Pairs	***forester sprang***, ***grabbed***, ***shot***
Commas	Use commas to separate three or more items in a series connected with a coordinating conjunction. **PATTERN a, b, and c** *sprang*, *grabbed*, and *shot*

Rewrite It!

In anger the forester impulsively sprang to his feet, grabbed his bow, and shot an arrow at Robin.

Read It!

robin hood was fortunate that the arrow barely missed him. without delay the **furious** forester reached for a second arrow

furious
extremely angry

Mark It!

3 articles (ar)
5 nouns (n)
1 pronoun (pr)
3 adjectives (adj)
1 adverb (adv)
2 prepositional phrases
1 *that* clause (that)
3 subject-verb pairs (s v)
2 openers

Fix It!

3 capitals
1 end mark

① subject

robin hood (s, n) was (v) fortunate (adj) (that (that) the (ar) arrow (s, n) barely (adv) missed (v) him (pr)).

② prepositional

without delay (n) the (ar) **furious** (adj) forester (s, n) reached (v) for a (ar) second (adj) arrow (n).

Capitalization	***Robin Hood*** proper noun; first word of the sentence ***Without*** first word of the sentence
End Marks	Use a period at the end of a statement.
Adjective	What kind of Robin Hood? ***fortunate*** The adjective follows the linking verb and describes the subject. What kind of forester? ***furious*** Which arrow? ***second***
Adverb	Missed to what extent? ***barely***
S V Pairs	***Robin Hood was***; ***arrow missed***; ***forester reached***

Rewrite It! Robin Hood was fortunate that the arrow barely missed him. Without delay the furious forester reached for a second arrow.

Read It!

in self-defense young robin shot an arrow, which struck the man. he **toppled** forward with a cry

toppled
fell or tumbled down

Mark It!

3 articles (ar)
5 nouns (n)
1 pronoun (pr)
1 adjective (adj)
1 adverb (adv)
2 prepositional phrases
1 *who/which* clause (w/w)
3 subject-verb pairs (s v)
2 openers

Fix It!

3 capitals
1 end mark

(2) prepositional

in self-defense [n] young [adj] robin [s n] shot [v] an [ar] arrow [n], (which [s w/w] struck [v] the [ar] man [n]). (1) subject he [s pr] **toppled** [v] forward [adv] with a [ar] cry [n].

Capitalization	***In***; ***He*** first word of the sentence ***Robin*** proper noun
End Marks	Use a period at the end of a statement.
Adjective	Which Robin? ***young***
Adverb	Toppled where? ***forward***
W/W Clause	***which struck the man*** The *which* clause describes *arrow*, the noun it follows.
S V Pairs	***Robin shot***; ***which struck***; ***He toppled***

Rewrite It! In self-defense young Robin shot an arrow, which struck the man. He toppled forward with a cry.

Read It!	Mark It!	Fix It! Day 4
robin hood was very upset. it **tortured** his conscience that hed killed a man	1 article (ar)	3 capitals
	3 nouns (n)	1 end mark
	2 pronouns (pr)	1 apostrophe
	2 adjectives (adj)	
tortured severely pained	1 adverb (adv)	
	1 *that* clause (that)	
	3 subject-verb pairs (s v)	
	2 openers	

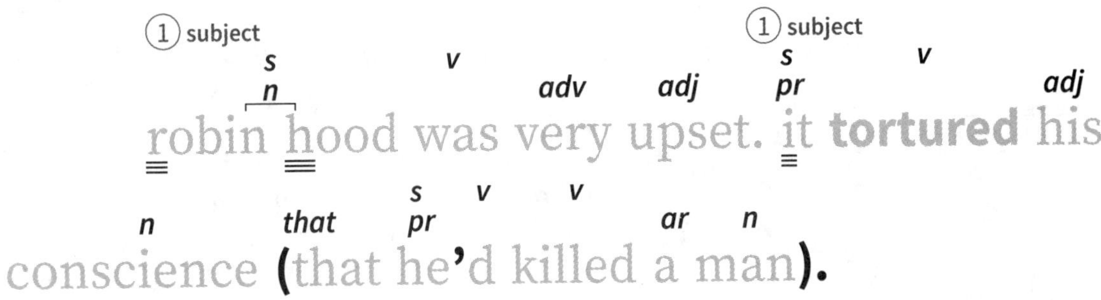

Capitalization	***Robin Hood*** proper noun; first word of the sentence ***It*** first word of the sentence
End Marks	Use a period at the end of a statement.
Adjective	What kind of Robin Hood? ***upset*** The adjective follows the linking verb and describes the subject. Whose conscience? ***his*** The possessive pronoun *his* functions as an adjective.
Adverb	Upset to what extent? ***very***
S V Pairs	***Robin Hood was***; ***It tortured***; ***he'd killed*** The contraction *he'd* includes both a subject (he) and helping verb (had).
Apostrophes	*He'd* is a contraction. Use an apostrophe to show where letters have been removed.

Rewrite It! Robin Hood was very upset. It tortured his conscience that he'd killed a man.

Learn It!

#3 -ly Adverb Opener

A **#3 -ly adverb opener** is a sentence that begins with an -ly adverb.

Mark It! Write ③ above the first word of a sentence that starts with an -ly adverb.

③ *-ly*
Surprisingly, Robin approached the town.

③ *-ly*
Confidently Robin approached the town.

Comma

A **comma** is used to separate items in a sentence. A comma is used to separate an -ly adverb opener from the rest of the sentence when the -ly adverb modifies the sentence.

, Use a comma if an -ly adverb opener modifies the sentence.

 Do not use a comma if an -ly adverb opener modifies the verb.

When you rewrite the passages, copy the commas correctly.

Numbers

Spell out numbers that can be expressed in one or two words, like *twelve* and *one hundred.*

Use a hyphen with numbers from twenty-one to ninety-nine.

Spell out ordinal numbers, like *first* and *second.*

Ordinal numbers tell the order or position in a sequence.

Fix It! Place a line through the incorrect number and write the correct word above it.

nine
Robin had ~~9~~ arrows in his quiver.

For more information about the #3 -ly adverb opener, see page G-43.

After students mark the sentence, ask them to identify the opener.

Both sentences are #3 -ly adverb openers because both begin with an -ly adverb.

Surprisingly is a sentence adverb. It modifies the entire sentence: it was surprising that Robin approached the town. Use a comma.

Confidently modifies the verb: Robin approached in a confident manner. Do not use a comma.

In this book students do not determine if an -ly adverb modifies the sentence and needs a comma. However, discuss comma usage and require students to copy the commas correctly when they rewrite the passages.

Students will mark every sentence opener that they have learned unless it is a question or a quoted sentence.

For more information about numbers, see page G-33.

Think About It!

According to the verb definition, there are three categories of verbs: action, linking, helping. Every clause has an action verb or a linking verb. When a helping verb helps either an action verb or a linking verb, the two verbs together are called the verb phrase.

Action: Robin shot an arrow.

In this sentence *shot* is the action verb. *Shot* is the action that Robin is doing.

Linking: Robin felt upset.

In this sentence *felt* is the linking verb. *Felt* links the subject *Robin* to the adjective *upset*.

Helping + Action: Robin had shot an arrow.

In this sentence *had* is a helping verb helping the action verb *shot*. *Had shot* is the verb phrase.

Helping + Linking: Robin did feel upset.

In this sentence *did* is a helping verb helping the linking verb *feel*. *Did feel* is the verb phrase.

Linking Verbs List

am, is, are, was, were, be, being, been (be verbs)

seem, become, appear, grow, remain

taste, sound, smell, feel, look (verbs dealing with the senses)

The first eight words are called *be* verbs. They appear on both the Linking Verbs and Helping Verbs Lists.

Helping Verbs List

am, is, are, was, were, be, being, been (be verbs)

have, has, had, do, does, did, may, might, must

can, will, shall, could, would, should

Read It!	Mark It!	Fix It!
fearfully robin hood escaped to sherwood forest. he was an outlaw on 2 **accounts**, and could not return home	1 article (ar)	6 capitals
	4 nouns (n)	1 end mark
	1 pronoun (pr)	1 comma
accounts reasons	1 adjective (adj)	1 number
	3 adverbs (adv)	
	1 coordinating conjunction (cc)	
	2 prepositional phrases	
	2 subject-verb pairs (s v)	
	2 openers	

③ -ly adverb

adv (fearfully) · s n (robin hood) · v (escaped) · n (sherwood forest)

fearfully robin hood escaped to sherwood forest.

① subject

s pr (he) · v (was) · ar (an) · n (outlaw) · adj two (2) · n (accounts) · cc (and) · v (could return) · adv (not) · adv (home)

he was an outlaw on ~~2~~ **accounts**, and could not return home.

Capitalization	***Fearfully***; ***He*** first word of the sentence ***Robin Hood***; ***Sherwood Forest*** proper noun
End Marks	Use a period at the end of a statement.
Adjective	How many accounts? ***two***
Adverb	Escaped how? ***Fearfully*** ***not*** functions as an adverb Could return where? ***home***
Note	A word can perform only one part of speech at a time. Although the word *home* usually functions as a noun, in this sentence the word *home* answers the question where. Therefore, in this sentence *home* functions as an adverb.
S V Pairs	***Robin Hood escaped***; ***He was***, ***could return***
Commas	Do not use a comma to separate two items connected with a coordinating conjunction. **PATTERN a and b** *was* and *could return*

Rewrite It! Fearfully Robin Hood escaped to Sherwood Forest. He was an outlaw on two accounts and could not return home.

Read It!	Mark It!	Fix It!
in a single day he had shot a deer that the king reserved for his own table, and had **slain** a man to	4 articles (ar)	1 capital
	5 nouns (n)	1 comma
	1 pronoun (pr)	1 end mark
	3 adjectives (adj)	1 homophone
slain killed	1 adverb (adv)	
	1 coordinating conjunction (cc)	
	2 prepositional phrases	
	1 *that* clause (that)	
	2 subject-verb pairs (s v)	
	1 opener	

(2) prepositional

ar adj n s pr v v ar n that ar s n

in a single day he had shot a deer (that the king

v adj adj n cc v v ar n adv too

reserved for his own table), and had **slain** a man ~~to~~.

Capitalization	***In*** first word of the sentence
End Marks	Use a period at the end of a statement.
Adjective	How many days? ***single*** Whose table? ***own*** Whose own table? ***his*** The possessive pronoun *his* functions as an adjective.
Adverb	***too*** functions as an adverb
S V Pairs	***he had shot***, ***had slain***; ***king reserved***
Commas	Do not use a comma to separate two items connected with a coordinating conjunction. PATTERN **a and b** *had shot* and *had slain*
Homophones	Use ***too***, which means also in this sentence.

Rewrite It! In a single day he had shot a deer that the king reserved for his own table and had slain a man too.

Read It!

the sheriff of nottingham was related to the dead forester. firmly he **vowed** that robin must be punished

vowed
solemnly promised

Mark It!

2 articles (ar)
4 nouns (n)
1 pronoun (pr)
1 adjective (adj)
1 adverb (adv)
2 prepositional phrases
1 *that* clause (that)
3 subject-verb pairs (s v)
2 openers

Fix It!

4 capitals
1 end mark

① subject

ar the s n sheriff of n nottingham v was v related to ar the adj dead n forester. ③ -ly adverb adv firmly s pr he v **vowed** (that that s n robin v must v be v punished).

Capitalization	***The***; ***Firmly*** first word of the sentence ***Nottingham***; ***Robin*** proper noun
End Marks	Use a period at the end of a statement.
Adjective	What kind of forester? ***dead***
Adverb	Vowed how? ***Firmly***
S V Pairs	***sheriff was related***; ***he vowed***; ***Robin must be punished***

Rewrite It! The sheriff of Nottingham was related to the dead forester. Firmly he vowed that Robin must be punished.

Read It!	Mark It!	Fix It! Day 4
within a few days robin heard that a **lavish** reward of 200 pounds would be given two the man who captured him	3 articles (ar)	2 capitals
	5 nouns (n)	1 end mark
lavish	1 pronoun (pr)	1 homophone
extravagant	3 adjectives (adj)	1 number
	3 prepositional phrases	
	1 *who/which* clause (w/w)	
	1 *that* clause (that)	
	3 subject-verb pairs (s v)	
	1 opener	

② prepositional

within a few days robin heard (that a **lavish** reward of ~~200~~ two hundred pounds would be given ~~two~~ to the man) (who captured him).

Capitalization	***Within*** first word of the sentence ***Robin*** proper noun
End Marks	Use a period at the end of a statement.
Adjective	How many days? ***few*** What kind of reward? ***lavish*** How many pounds? ***two hundred***
W/W Clause	***who captured him*** The *who* clause describes *man*, the noun it follows.
Note	Commas are not used because this *who* clause is essential to the meaning of the sentence. It tells which man would receive the reward. Require students to copy the commas correctly when they rewrite the passage.
S V Pairs	***Robin heard***; ***reward would be given***; ***who captured***
Homophones	Use ***to***, the preposition.

Rewrite It! Within a few days Robin heard that a lavish reward of two hundred pounds would be given to the man who captured him.

Learn It!

Adverb Clause

An **adverb clause** is a group of words that begins with a www word and contains a subject and a verb. An adverb clause is a dependent clause, which means it must be added to a sentence that is already complete.

For more information about adverb clauses, see page G-21.

Memorize It! **www word + subject + verb**

Use the acronym *www.asia.b* to remember the eight most common www words.

Memorize It!

w	*w*	*w*	*a*	*s*	*i*	*a*	*b*
when	**while**	**where**	**as**	**since**	**if**	**although**	**because**

Mark It! Place parentheses around the adverb clause and write ***AC*** above the www word. Write *v* above each verb and *s* above each subject.

AC *s* *v*
(Because Robin was now an outlaw), he had to hide
AC *s* *v* *v*
(where the sheriff could not find him).

Ask students to identify the subject and verb in the adverb clause.

What is the verb? ***was***

Who was? ***Robin***

Use a comma after an adverb clause that comes before a main clause. AC, MC

What is the verb? ***could find***

Who could find? ***sheriff***

Do not use a comma before an adverb clause that follows the main clause. MC AC

Comma

A **comma** is used to separate items in a sentence. A comma is used after but not before an adverb clause.

Use a comma after an adverb clause that comes before a main clause.
PATTERN AC, MC

Do not use a comma before an adverb clause.
PATTERN MC AC

When you rewrite the passages, copy the commas correctly.

Think About It!

Many words can be used as different parts of speech. However, a word can perform only one part of speech at a time. For example, *as* can be a preposition that begins a prepositional phrase, and *as* can be a www word that begins an adverb clause.

Prepositional Phrase: As an outlaw Robin hid from the sheriff.

As an outlaw is a prepositional phrase.
PATTERN preposition (As) + noun (outlaw) (no verb)

Adverb Clause: (As he hid in the forest), Robin collected a band of loyal men.

As he hid in the forest is an adverb clause.
PATTERN www word (As) + subject (he) + verb (hid)

Read It!

for an entire year robin **sheltered** in sherwood forest while he met other outlaws, and gained valuable hunting skills

sheltered
hid; found a refuge

Mark It!

1 article (ar)
5 nouns (n)
1 pronoun (pr)
4 adjectives (adj)
1 coordinating conjunction (cc)
2 prepositional phrases
1 adverb clause (AC)
2 subject-verb pairs (s v)
1 opener

Fix It!

4 capitals
1 comma
1 end mark

(2) prepositional

for an entire year robin **sheltered** in sherwood forest (while he met other outlaws, and gained valuable hunting skills).

Capitalization	***For*** first word of the sentence ***Robin***; ***Sherwood Forest*** proper noun
End Marks	Use a period at the end of a statement.
Adjective	Which year? ***entire*** Which outlaws? ***other*** What kind of skills? ***hunting*** What kind of hunting skills? ***valuable***
S V Pairs	***Robin sheltered***; ***he met***, ***gained***
Commas	Do not use a comma to separate two items connected with a coordinating conjunction. **PATTERN a and b** *met* and *gained*

Rewrite It! For an entire year Robin sheltered in Sherwood Forest while he met other outlaws and gained valuable hunting skills.

Read It!	Mark It!	Fix It!
eventually, he gathered a band of loyal men. these good men had been **displaced** for many reasons	1 article (ar) 4 nouns (n) 1 pronoun (pr) 4 adjectives (adj) 1 adverb (adv) 2 prepositional phrases 2 subject-verb pairs (s v) 2 openers	2 capitals 1 end mark

displaced
put out of the usual place; lacking a home

(3) -ly adverb — (1) subject

adv: eventually, s pr: he v: gathered ar: a n: band of adj: loyal n: men. adj: these

eventually, he gathered a band of loyal men. these

adj: good s n: men v: had v: been v: displaced for adj: many n: reasons.

good men had been **displaced** for many reasons.

Capitalization	***Eventually***; ***These*** first word of the sentence
End Marks	Use a period at the end of a statement.
Adjective	What kind of men? ***loyal*** What kind of men? ***good*** Which good men? ***These*** How many reasons? ***many***
Adverb	He gathered a band of loyal men when? ***eventually*** *Eventually* is a sentence adverb. It modifies the entire sentence: It was eventual that he gathered a band of loyal men. For this reason, it doesn't answer a question about the verb but about the entire sentence. It requires a comma.
S V Pairs	***he gathered***; ***men had been displaced***

Rewrite It! Eventually, he gathered a band of loyal men. These good men had been displaced for many reasons.

Read It!	Mark It!	Fix It!
some men, who were **famished**, shot deer because they had to little food	3 nouns (n)	1 capital
	1 pronoun (pr)	1 end mark
	3 adjectives (adj)	1 homophone
	1 adverb (adv)	
	1 *who/which* clause (w/w)	
	1 adverb clause (AC)	
	3 subject-verb pairs (s v)	
	1 opener	

famished
extremely hungry

① subject

some (adj) men (s, n), (who (s, w/w) were (v) **famished** (adj)), shot (v) deer (n) (because (AC) they (s, pr) had (v) ~~to~~ too (adv) little (adj) food (n)).

Capitalization	***Some*** first word of the sentence
End Marks	Use a period at the end of a statement.
Adjective	How many men? ***Some*** What kind of who (men)? ***famished*** The adjective follows the linking verb and describes the subject. How much food? ***little*** *How much* is a form of the adjective question *how many*.
Adverb	***too*** functions as an adverb
W/W Clause	***who were famished*** The *who* clause describes *men*, the noun it follows.
S V Pairs	***men shot***; ***who were***; ***they had***
Homophones	Use ***too***, which means to an excessive degree in this sentence.

Rewrite It! Some men, who were famished, shot deer because they had too little food.

Read It!	Mark It!	Fix It! Day 4
theyd **narrowly** escaped from the foresters when they were hunting the king's deer	2 articles (ar)	1 capital
	2 nouns (n)	1 end mark
	2 pronouns (pr)	1 apostrophe
	1 adjective (adj)	
narrowly barely; almost unsuccessfully	1 adverb (adv)	
	1 prepositional phrase	
	1 adverb clause (AC)	
	2 subject-verb pairs (s v)	
	1 opener	

① subject

they'd **narrowly** escaped from the foresters (when they were hunting the king's deer).

(they'd: s pr v; narrowly: adv; escaped: v; the: ar; foresters: n; when: AC; they: s pr; were: v; hunting: v; the: ar; king's: adj; deer: n)

Capitalization	***They'd*** first word of the sentence
End Marks	Use a period at the end of a statement.
Adjective	Whose deer? ***king's***
Adverb	Escaped how? ***narrowly***
S V Pairs	***They'd escaped***; ***they were hunting*** The contraction *They'd* includes both a subject (They) and a verb (had). *Hunting* functions as a verb because it follows the helping verb *were*. A word that ends in -ing functions as a verb only if it follows a helping verb.
Apostrophes	*They'd* is a contraction. Use an apostrophe to show where letters have been removed.

Rewrite It! They'd narrowly escaped from the foresters when they were hunting the king's deer.

Learn It!

Pronoun

A **pronoun** replaces a noun in order to avoid repetition.

There are many types of pronouns. Week 1 you reviewed **personal pronouns**, which take the place of common and proper nouns.

An **indefinite pronoun** is not definite. It does not refer to any particular person or thing. The words below are indefinite pronouns.

all	both	few	one	own
another	each	many	other	several
any	either	more	others	some
anybody	everybody	most	nobody	somebody
anyone	everyone	much	no one	someone
anything	everything	neither	nothing	something
anywhere	everywhere	none	nowhere	somewhere

A **demonstrative pronoun** points to a particular person or thing. There are only four demonstrative pronouns.

this	that	these	those

For more information about pronouns, see page G-6.

Mark It! Write *pr* above each pronoun.

pr *pr* *pr*
Many had nowhere to go. That was tragic!

Think About It!

Many words can be used as different parts of speech. However, a word can perform only one part of speech at a time. The indefinite and demonstrative pronouns function as pronouns when they take the place of a noun. However, these same words function as adjectives when they come before a noun.

Pronoun: Many had nowhere to go.

In this sentence *Many* is a pronoun because it takes the place of the names of the people who had nowhere to go. *Many* is the subject of the clause.

Adjective: Many families had nowhere to go.

In this sentence *Many* is an adjective because it comes before a noun and tells how many families.

Pronoun: That was tragic.

In this sentence *That* is a pronoun because it takes the place of the explanation of what was tragic. *That* is the subject of the clause.

Adjective: That arrow hit the target.

In this sentence *That* is an adjective because it comes before a noun and tells which arrow.

That Clause: Robin knew (that the poor families needed help).

In this sentence *that* is used to begin a dependent clause. It is followed by a subject and a verb and completes the main clause telling what Robin knew.

When a word on the demonstrative pronoun or indefinite pronoun list comes before a noun, it is an adjective, not a pronoun.

In this book when *that* functions as an adjective or the subject of a clause, it does not begin a *that* clause.

When *that* begins a dependent clause, it follows the pattern that + subject + verb and functions as neither an adjective nor subject of the clause.

Homophone

A **homophone** is a word that sounds like another word but is spelled differently and has a different meaning. Correctly use the homophones *there, their,* and *they're.*

There can function as other parts of speech, but in this book students will only see it as an adverb.

There is an adverb pointing to a place: *over there* (there is the spot).

Their is a possessive pronoun: *their arrows* (the arrows belong to them).

The possessive pronoun *their* tells whose and functions as an adjective.

They're is a contraction: *they're angry* (they are angry).

The contraction *they're* is a shortened form of *they are* and functions as the subject pronoun (they) and verb (are) of the clause.

Fix It! Place a line through the incorrect homophone and write the correct word above it.

their ***there***

The archers raised ~~there~~ bows to shoot the target over ~~their~~.

Read It!	Mark It!	Fix It! Day 1
others, who were strong, and goodhearted, had lost they're farms because the **greedy** king wanted there lands	1 article (ar) 3 nouns (n) 1 pronoun (pr) 5 adjectives (adj) 1 coordinating conjunction (cc) 1 *who/which* clause (w/w) 1 adverb clause (AC) 3 subject-verb pairs (s v) 1 opener	1 capital 1 comma 1 end mark 2 homophones

greedy
wanting too much wealth

① subject

others, (who were strong, and goodhearted), had lost ~~they're~~ their farms (because the **greedy** king wanted ~~there~~ their lands).

Capitalization	***Others*** first word of the sentence
End Marks	Use a period at the end of a statement.
Adjective	The dual adjectives *strong* and *goodhearted* follow the linking verb and describe the subject (who). What kind of who (Others)? ***strong*** and ***goodhearted*** Whose farms? ***their*** The possessive pronoun *their* functions as an adjective. What kind of king? ***greedy*** Whose lands? ***their***
W/W Clause	***who where strong and goodhearted*** The *who* clause describes *others*, the pronoun it follows.
S V Pairs	***Others had lost***; ***who were***; ***king wanted***
Commas	Do not use a comma to separate two items connected with a coordinating conjunction. **PATTERN a and b** *strong* and *goodhearted*
Homophones	Use ***their***; ***their***, the possessive pronoun.

Rewrite It! Others, who were strong and goodhearted, had lost their farms because the greedy king wanted their lands.

Read It!	Mark It!	Fix It! Day 2
tragically, some had been **devastated** by unreasonable taxes that they couldnt pay	1 noun (n) 2 pronouns (pr) 1 adjective (adj) 2 adverbs (adv) 1 prepositional phrase 1 *that* clause (that) 2 subject-verb pairs (s v) 1 opener	1 capital 1 end mark 1 apostrophe

devastated
ruined or destroyed; overwhelmed by grief

(3) -ly adverb

adv: tragically; s pr: some; v: had been devastated; adj: unreasonable

tragically, some had been **devastated** by unreasonable

n: taxes; that; s pr: they; v: could; adv: n't; v: pay

taxes **(**that they couldn**'**t pay**).**

Capitalization	***Tragically*** first word of the sentence
End Marks	Use a period at the end of a statement.
Adjective	What kind of taxes? ***unreasonable***
Adverb	Some had been devastated how? ***Tragically*** *Tragically* is a sentence adverb. It modifies the entire sentence: It was tragic that some had been devastated. For this reason, it doesn't answer a question about the verb but about the entire sentence. It requires a comma. ***n't*** the contraction for *not* functions as an adverb
S V Pairs	***some had been devastated***; ***they could pay***
Apostrophes	*Couldn't* is a contraction. Use an apostrophe to show where letters have been removed.

Rewrite It! Tragically, some had been devastated by unreasonable taxes that they couldn't pay.

Read It!	Mark It!	Fix It!
throughout england poor families **fled** from there homes, and secretly hid in sherwood forest	4 nouns (n)	4 capitals
	2 adjectives (adj)	1 comma
	1 adverb (adv)	1 end mark
	1 coordinating conjunction (cc)	1 homophone
fled ran away	3 prepositional phrases	
	1 subject-verb pair (s v)	
	1 opener	

② prepositional

throughout england poor families **fled** from ~~there~~ their homes, and secretly hid in sherwood forest.

Capitalization	***Throughout*** first word of the sentence ***England***; ***Sherwood Forest*** proper noun
End Marks	Use a period at the end of a statement.
Adjective	What kind of families? ***poor*** Whose homes? ***their*** The possessive pronoun *their* functions as an adjective.
Adverb	Hid how? ***secretly***
S V Pairs	***families fled, hid***
Commas	Do not use a comma to separate two items connected with a coordinating conjunction. **PATTERN a and b** *fled* and *hid*
Homophones	Use ***their***, the possessive pronoun.

Rewrite It! Throughout England poor families fled from their homes and secretly hid in Sherwood Forest.

Read It!	Mark It!	Fix It! Day 4
a band of 45 brave **peasants**, who greatly admired robin hood, chose him to be there leader	1 article (ar)	3 capitals
	4 nouns (n)	1 end mark
	1 pronoun (pr)	1 homophone
	3 adjectives (adj)	1 number
peasants farmers; workers from a low social rank	1 adverb (adv)	
	1 prepositional phrase	
	1 *who/which* clause (w/w)	
	2 subject-verb pairs (s v)	
	1 opener	

(1) subject

a band of ~~45~~ forty-five brave **peasants**, (who greatly admired robin hood), chose him to be ~~there~~ their leader.

Capitalization	***A*** first word of the sentence ***Robin Hood*** proper noun
End Marks	Use a period at the end of a statement.
Adjective	What kind of peasants? ***brave*** How many brave peasants? ***forty-five*** Whose leader? ***their*** The possessive pronoun *their* functions as an adjective.
Adverb	Admired to what extent? ***greatly***
W/W Clause	***who greatly admired Robin Hood*** The *who* clause describes *peasants*, the noun it follows.
S V Pairs	***band chose***; ***who admired*** *To be* is an infinitive. It does not function as a verb.
Homophones	Use ***their***, the possessive pronoun.

Rewrite It! A band of forty-five brave peasants, who greatly admired Robin Hood, chose him to be their leader.

Learn It!

Clause

A **clause** is a group of related words that contains both a subject and a verb.

For more information about clauses, see page G-20.

Dependent Clause

A **dependent clause** is a clause that cannot stand alone as a sentence because it does not express a complete thought. Dependent clauses begin with a word that causes them to be an incomplete thought.

In this book you have learned three types of dependent clauses.

A *who/which* clause begins with *who* or *which*.
A *that* clause begins with *that*.
An adverb clause begins with a www word.

A dependent clause must be added to a main clause.

Main Clause

A **main clause** is a clause because it contains a subject and a verb. A main clause expresses a complete thought, so it can stand alone as a sentence.

Another term for a main clause is an independent clause.

[Families lived in the forest].

Every sentence must have a main clause.

[Families lived in the forest] (because they lost their homes).

In addition to a main clause, a sentence may include one or more dependent clauses.

Mark It! Place square brackets around the main clause *[MC]*.
Write *v* above each verb and *s* above each subject.

s **v**

Usually, **[**Robin practiced archery in the morning**]**.

When you mark the main clause with square brackets, begin with the subject of the main clause. Sometimes, an article or adjectives will come before the subject.

Think About It!

The word *because* usually begins an adverb clause. However, when *because* is followed by *of*, the two words together are a preposition.

Adverb Clause: Robin aimed carefully (because he wanted the prize).

Because he wanted the prize is an adverb clause.
PATTERN www word (because) + subject (he) + verb (wanted)

Prepositional Phrase: Robin aimed carefully because of the prize.

Because of the prize is a prepositional phrase.
PATTERN preposition (because of) + noun (prize) (no verb)

Read It!	Mark It!	Fix It! Day 1
robin's followers **declared** that they would rob everyone who had robbed them	1 noun (n) 3 pronouns (pr) 1 adjective (adj) 1 *who/which* clause (w/w) 1 *that* clause (that) 1 [main clause] 3 subject-verb pairs (s v) 1 opener	1 capital 1 end mark

declared
said something in a strong and confident way

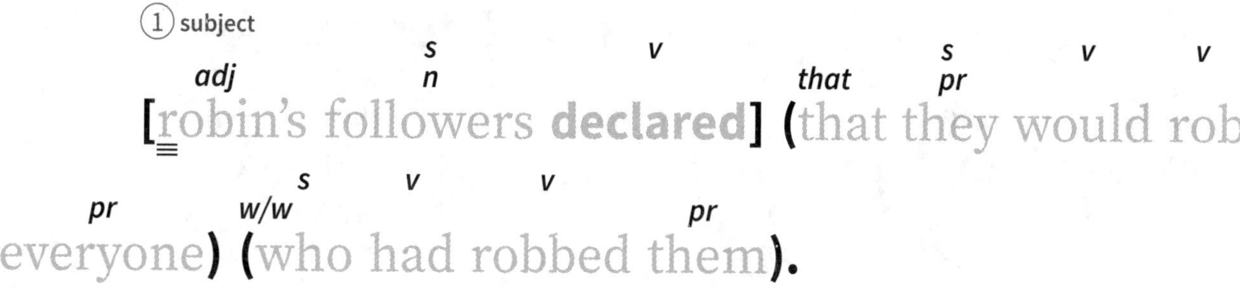

Capitalization	***Robin's*** first word of the sentence
End Marks	Use a period at the end of a statement.
Adjective	Whose followers? ***Robin's***
S V Pairs MC	***followers declared***
that	*that* ***they would rob***
w/w	***who had robbed*** The *who* clause describes *everyone*, the pronoun it follows.

Rewrite It! Robin's followers declared that they would rob everyone who had robbed them.

Read It!	Mark It!	Fix It!
especially if powerful men **plundered** the poor, robin and his men would recapture there goods, and would return them	1 article (ar)	2 capitals
	5 nouns (n)	1 comma
	1 pronoun (pr)	1 end mark
	3 adjectives (adj)	1 homophone
plundered robbed	1 adverb (adv)	
	2 coordinating conjunctions (cc)	
	1 adverb clause (AC)	
	1 [main clause]	
	2 subject-verb pairs (s v)	
	1 opener	

③ -ly adverb

especially (if powerful men **plundered** the poor), [robin and his men would recapture ~~there~~ their goods, and would return them].

Capitalization	***Especially*** first word of the sentence ***Robin*** proper noun
End Marks	Use a period at the end of a statement.
Adjective	What kind of men? ***powerful*** Whose men? ***his*** The possessive pronoun *his* functions as an adjective. Whose goods? ***their*** The possessive pronoun *their* functions as an adjective.
Adverb	Powerful men plundered to what extent? ***especially***
S V Pairs AC	*if **men plundered***
MC	***Robin**, **men would recapture**, **would return***
Commas	Do not use a comma to separate two items connected with a coordinating conjunction. PATTERN **a and b** *Robin* and *men* PATTERN **a and b** *would recapture* and *would return*
Homophones	Use ***their***, the possessive pronoun.

Rewrite It! Especially if powerful men plundered the poor, Robin and his men would recapture their goods and would return them.

Read It!	Mark It!	Fix It!
to those in need, these men would offer **aid**, and protection	4 nouns (n)	1 capital
	1 pronoun	1 comma
	1 adjective (adj)	1 end mark
	1 coordinating conjunction (cc)	
	2 prepositional phrases	
	1 [main clause]	
	1 subject-verb pair (s v)	
	1 opener	

aid
help or support

(2) **prepositional**

to those in need, [these men would offer **aid**, and protection].

(pr: those; n: need; adj: these; s n: men; v: would; v: offer; n: aid; cc: and; n: protection)

Capitalization	***To*** first word of the sentence
End Marks	Use a period at the end of a statement.
Adjective	Which men? ***these***
Note	A word will only perform one part of speech at a time. The words *those* and *these* can function as indefinite pronouns or as adjectives. When the word replaces a noun (*those* replaces *families*), it functions as a pronoun. When the word describes a noun (Which men? *these men*), it functions as an adjective.
S V Pairs MC	***men would offer***
Commas	Do not use a comma to separate two items connected with a coordinating conjunction. **PATTERN a and b** *aid* and *protection*
Note	It is correct to have a comma after *need* because of the advanced comma rule: Use a comma if two + prepositional phrases open a sentence. Put the comma after the last phrase.

Rewrite It! To those in need, these men would offer aid and protection.

Read It!	Mark It!	Fix It!
they **earnestly** swore that they would never harm a maid wife or widow	1 article (ar) 3 nouns (n) 2 pronouns (pr) 2 adverbs (adv) 1 coordinating conjunction (cc) 1 *that* clause (that) 1 [main clause] 2 subject-verb pairs (s v) 1 opener	1 capital 2 commas 1 end mark

Day 4

earnestly
with deep and sincere feeling

① subject

s pr *adv* *v* *that* *s pr* *v* *adv* *v*

[they **earnestly** swore] (that they would never harm

ar *n* *n* *cc* *n*

a maid, wife, or widow).

Capitalization	***They*** first word of the sentence
End Marks	Use a period at the end of a statement.
Adverb	Swore how? ***earnestly*** Harm when? ***never***
S V Pairs MC	***They swore***
that	*that* ***they would harm***
Commas	Use commas to separate three or more items in a series connected with a coordinating conjunction. **PATTERN a, b, and c** *maid*, *wife*, or *widow*

Rewrite It! They earnestly swore that they would never harm a maid, wife, or widow.

Learn It!

Who/Which Clause

A ***who/which* clause** is a dependent clause that begins with the word *who* or *which.*

A *who/which* clause can also begin with the word *whose,* the possessive case of *who* and *which.*

When *whose* begins a *who/which* clause, *whose* will not function as the subject of the clause because *whose* functions as a possessive adjective and shows ownership.

Robin, ~~Robin's~~ whose arrow broke, missed the mark.

The two sentences *Robin missed the mark* and *Robin's arrow broke* have been combined with a *who/which* clause. *Whose* takes the place of the possessive adjective *Robin's.*

Mark It! Place parentheses around the *who/which* clause and write ***w/w*** above the word *who* or *which.* Write ***v*** above each verb and ***s*** above each subject.

s v v
w/w
The men (whose lands were taken) hid in the forest.

For more information about *who/which* clauses, see page G-39.

Ask students to identify the subject and verb in the *whose* clause and to identify the noun that the clause describes.

What is the verb? ***were taken***

What were taken? ***lands***

whose lands were taken describes *men*

whose replaces *men's*

Commas are not used because the *whose* clause is essential to the meaning of the sentence. Only the men whose lands were taken hid in the forest.

Run-On

A **run-on** occurs when a sentence has main clauses that are not connected properly.

A **fused sentence** is two main clauses placed in one sentence without any punctuation between them. This is a common type of run-on error. The easiest way to fix this error is to place a period at the end of each main clause.

Find It! Look for two main clauses that are missing a period between them.

Fix It! Correct a fused sentence by putting a period between the main clauses. Capitalize the first word of the new sentence.

s v v s v
[The men could not pay their taxes]. [they hid in the forest].

For more information about run-ons, see page G-17.

The second kind of run-on is a comma splice. Students will learn about comma splices Week 13.

Think About It!

Many words can be used as different parts of speech. However, a word can perform only one part of speech at a time. For example, *swimming* can be a verb, adjective, or noun.

Verb: Robin was swimming in the river.

In this sentence *swimming* is a verb because it follows the helping verb *was.* A word that ends in -ing functions as a verb only if it follows a helping verb.

Adjective: Robin jumped into the swimming hole.

In this sentence *swimming* describes *hole.* What kind of hole? *swimming.* An adjective describes a noun or pronoun.

Noun: Swimming was Robin's favorite summer activity.

In this sentence *swimming* is a thing. A noun is a person, place, thing, or idea.

Read It!	Mark It!	Fix It!
because of the desperate times, these men, whose families were hungry, stole money from **corrupt** noblemen they gave it to the peasants **corrupt** guilty of dishonest practices, such as bribery	2 articles (ar) 6 nouns (n) 2 pronouns (pr) 4 adjectives (adj) 3 prepositional phrases 1 *who/which* clause (w/w) 2 [main clauses] 3 subject-verb pairs (s v) 2 openers	2 capitals 2 end marks

②prepositional

because of the desperate times, [these men, (whose families were hungry), stole money from **corrupt** noblemen]. [they gave it to the peasants].

(ar: the; adj: desperate; n: times; adj: these; s n: men; w/w: whose; s n: families; v: were; adj: hungry; v: stole; n: money; adj: corrupt; n: noblemen; ① subject; s pr: they; v: gave; pr: it; ar: the; n: peasants)

Capitalization		***Because***;***They*** first word of the sentence
End Marks		This passage contains 2 end marks. There are 2 main clauses. Use a period at the end of a statement.
Adjective		What kind of times? ***desperate*** Which men? ***these*** What kind of families? ***hungry*** The adjective follows the linking verb and describes the subject. What kind of noblemen? ***corrupt***
S V Pairs	MC	***men stole***
	w/w	*whose* ***families were*** The *whose* clause describes *men*, the noun it follows.
	MC	***They gave***

Rewrite It! Because of the desperate times, these men, whose families were hungry, stole money from corrupt noblemen. They gave it to the peasants.

Read It!	Mark It!	Fix It! Day 2
the peasants loved robin, and his merry men they often told tales of there **courageous** deeds	1 article (ar)	3 capitals
	5 nouns (n)	1 comma
	1 pronoun (pr)	2 end marks
	4 adjectives (adj)	1 homophone
courageous brave	1 coordinating conjunction (cc)	
	1 adverb (adv)	
	1 prepositional phrase	
	2 [main clauses]	
	2 subject-verb pairs (s v)	
	2 openers	

(1) subject [the(ar) peasants(s n) loved(v) robin(n), and(cc) his(adj) merry(adj) men(n)].

(1) subject [they(s pr) often(adv) told(v) tales(n) of ~~there~~ their(adj) **courageous**(adj) deeds(n)].

Capitalization	***The***; ***They*** first word of the sentence ***Robin*** proper noun
End Marks	This passage contains 2 end marks. There are 2 main clauses. Use a period at the end of a statement.
Adjective	What kind of men? ***merry*** Whose merry men? ***his*** The possessive pronoun *his* functions as an adjective. What kind of deeds? ***courageous*** Whose courageous deeds? ***their*** The possessive pronoun *their* functions as an adjective.
Adverb	Told tales when? ***often***
S V Pairs	MC ***peasants loved*** MC ***They told***
Commas	Do not use a comma to separate two items connected with a coordinating conjunction. **PATTERN a and b** *Robin* and *men*
Homophones	Use ***their***, the possessive pronoun.

Rewrite It! The peasants loved Robin and his merry men. They often told tales of their courageous deeds.

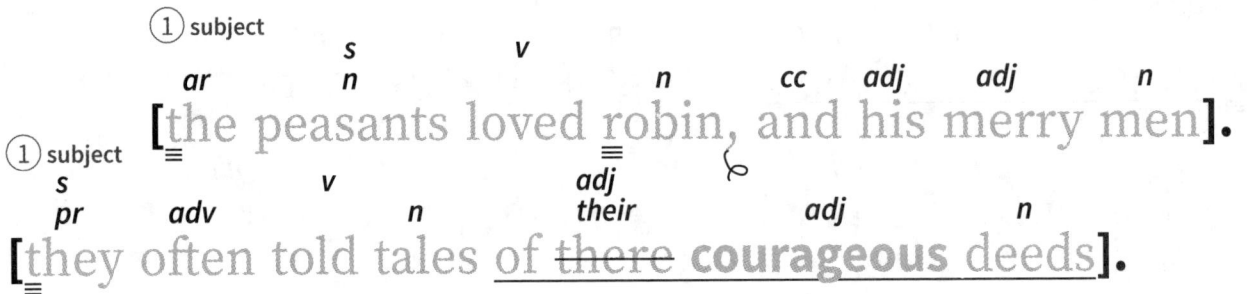

Read It!	Mark It!	Fix It!
repeatedly robin and his men moved there camp because they were always in **peril**	4 nouns (n)	2 capitals
	1 pronoun (pr)	1 end mark
	2 adjectives (adj)	1 homophone
	2 adverbs (adv)	
peril great danger	1 coordinating conjunction (cc)	
	1 prepositional phrase	
	1 adverb clause (AC)	
	1 [main clause]	
	2 subject-verb pairs (s v)	
	1 opener	

③ -ly adverb

adv repeatedly [*s n* robin *cc* and *adj* his *s n* men *v* moved *adj* ~~there~~ their *n* camp]

AC (because *s pr* they *v* were *adv* always in *n* **peril**).

Capitalization		***Repeatedly*** first word of the sentence ***Robin*** proper noun
End Marks		This passage contains 1 end mark. There is 1 main clause. Use a period at the end of a statement.
Adjective		Whose men? ***his*** The possessive pronoun *his* functions as an adjective. Whose camp? ***their*** The possessive pronoun *their* functions as an adjective.
Adverb		Moved how? ***repeatedly*** Were in peril when? ***always***
S V Pairs	MC	***Robin***, ***men moved***
	AC	*because **they were***
Homophones		Use ***their***, the possessive pronoun.
Commas		Do not use a comma to separate two items connected with a coordinating conjunction. **PATTERN a and b** *Robin* and *men*

Rewrite It! Repeatedly Robin and his men moved their camp because they were always in peril.

Read It!	Mark It!	Fix It! Day 4
for entertainment the men enjoyed competitions target practice and fishing in the cold, **gurgling** brook	2 articles (ar) 6 nouns (n) 3 adjectives (adj) 1 coordinating conjunction (cc) 2 prepositional phrases 1 [main clause] 1 subject-verb pair (s v) 1 opener	1 capital 2 commas 1 end mark

gurgling
making irregular bubbling noises

(2) prepositional

for entertainment (n) [the (ar) men (s, n) enjoyed (v) competitions (n), target (adj) practice (n), and (cc) fishing (n) in the (ar) cold (adj), **gurgling** (adj) brook (n)].

Capitalization	***For*** first word of the sentence
End Marks	This passage contains 1 end mark. There is 1 main clause. Use a period at the end of a statement.
Noun	*Fishing* functions as a noun. *Fishing* is one of the things the men enjoyed. A word that ends in -ing functions as a verb only if it follows a helping verb. (See Week 8 Day 4.)
Adjective	What kind of practice? ***target*** What kind of brook? ***cold***, ***gurgling***
S V Pairs MC	***men enjoyed***
Commas	Use commas to separate three or more items in a series connected with a coordinating conjunction. **PATTERN a, b, and c** *competitions*, *practice*, and *fishing*

Rewrite It! For entertainment the men enjoyed competitions, target practice, and fishing in the cold, gurgling brook.

Learn It!

#5 Clausal Opener

A **#5 clausal opener** is a sentence that begins with an adverb clause.

The #5 clausal opener begins with a www word: when, while, where, as, since, if, although, because. It must contain a subject and a verb.

(While the men relaxed)

This is an incorrect sentence fragment. A group of words is not a sentence unless it includes a main clause.

(While the men relaxed), [Robin was restless].

The #5 clausal opener will always have a comma and a main clause after it.

Mark It! Write ⑤ above the first word of a sentence that starts with an adverb clause.

⑤
AC S V
(Since Robin was restless), [he looked for adventure].

For more information about the #5 clausal opener, see page G-45.

After students mark the sentence, ask them to identify the opener.

This sentence is a #5 clausal opener because it begins with an adverb clause.

Comma

A **comma** is used to separate items in a sentence. Week 8 you learned that a comma is used after but not before an adverb clause.

Fix It! Add a comma after an adverb clause.
Remove a comma before an adverb clause.

AC
(While his men rested), [Robin set out].

AC
[Robin left his men], (because he wanted adventure).

Read It!	Mark It!	Fix It!
the children of the merry men **romped** along the bank they laughed, and joked together	3 articles (ar)	2 capitals
	3 nouns (n)	1 comma
	1 pronoun (pr)	2 end marks
	1 adjective (adj)	
romped played roughly and in a lively manner	1 adverb (adv)	
	1 coordinating conjunction (cc)	
	2 prepositional phrases	
	2 [main clauses]	
	2 subject-verb pairs (s v)	
	2 openers	

Day 1

① subject

ar s n ar adj n v ar n

[the children of the merry men **romped** along the bank].

① subject

s pr v cc v adv

[they laughed, and joked together].

Capitalization	***The***; ***They*** first word of the sentence
End Marks	This passage contains 2 end marks. There are 2 main clauses. Use a period at the end of a statement.
Adjective	What kind of men? ***merry***
Adverb	Joked how? ***together***
S V Pairs MC	***children romped***
MC	***they laughed, joked***
Commas	Do not use a comma to separate two items connected with a coordinating conjunction. **PATTERN a and b** *laughed and joked*

Rewrite It! The children of the merry men romped along the bank. They laughed and joked together.

Read It! | **Mark It!** | **Fix It!** Day 2

although everyone seemed happy robin was **restless**. "for 14 days weve enjoyed very little sport my friends," he complained

restless
unable to be at rest; active and uneasy

4 nouns (n)	1 adverb clause (AC)	3 capitals
3 pronouns (pr)	3 [main clauses]	2 commas
5 adjectives (adj)	4 subject-verb pairs (s v)	1 end mark
1 adverb (adv)	1 opener	1 apostrophe
1 prepositional phrase		1 number

⑤ clausal

(although everyone seemed happy), [robin was **restless**]. "for ~~14~~ fourteen days [we've enjoyed very little sport], my friends," [he complained].

Capitalization	***Although*** first word of the sentence ***Robin*** proper noun ***For*** first word of the quoted sentence
End Marks	This passage contains 2 end marks. There are 3 main clauses. The quotation and the attribution belong in the same sentence. Use a period at the end of a statement.
Adjective	What kind of everyone? ***happy*** The adjective follows the linking verb and describes the subject. What kind of Robin? ***restless*** The adjective follows the linking verb and describes the subject. How many days? ***fourteen*** How much sport? ***little*** Whose friends? ***my*** The possessive pronoun *my* functions as an adjective.
Adverb	Little to what extent? ***very***
S V Pairs	AC *although* ***everyone seemed*** MC ***Robin was*** MC ***we've enjoyed*** The contraction *we've* includes both a subject (we) and a helping verb (have). MC ***he complained***
Commas	Use a comma after an adverb clause. PATTERN **AC, MC** Place commas around a noun of direct address (NDA). **, *my friends***
Note	In this sentence *my friends* is the name Robin is using to directly address his men. It is the NDA.
Apostrophes	*We've* is a contraction. Use an apostrophe to show where letters have been removed.

Rewrite It! Although everyone seemed happy, Robin was restless. "For fourteen days we've enjoyed very little sport, my friends," he complained.

Read It!	Mark It!	Fix It! Day 3
"while i journey to nottingham too seek adventures you can wait for me here," robin **directed**	3 nouns (n)	4 capitals
	3 pronouns (pr)	1 comma
	1 adverb (adv)	1 end mark
directed gave commands	2 prepositional phrases	1 homophone
	1 adverb clause (AC)	
	2 [main clauses]	
	3 subject-verb pairs (s v)	

"(while i journey to nottingham ~~too~~ seek adventures),

[you can wait for me here]," [robin **directed**].

Capitalization		***While*** first word of the quoted sentence ***I*** personal pronoun I ***Nottingham***; ***Robin*** proper noun
End Marks		This passage contains 1 end mark. The quotation and the attribution belong in the same sentence. Use a period at the end of a statement.
Adverb		Wait where? ***here***
S V Pairs	AC	*while **I journey***
	MC	***you can wait***
	MC	***Robin directed***
Note		*To seek* is an infinitive. It does not function as a verb.
Commas		Use a comma after an adverb clause. **PATTERN AC, MC**
Homophones		Use ***to***, the infinitive marker.

Rewrite It! "While I journey to Nottingham to seek adventures, you can wait for me here," Robin directed.

Read It!	Mark It!	Fix It!
he told his men that they should come quickly, when they heard his **signal**, which would be 3 short blasts on his bugle	4 nouns (n)	1 capital
	3 pronouns (pr)	1 comma
	5 adjectives (adj)	1 end mark
	1 adverb (adv)	1 number
signal something agreed upon as the sign for needed action	1 prepositional phrase	
	1 *who/which* clause (w/w)	
	1 *that* clause (that)	
	1 adverb clause (AC)	
	1 [main clause]	
	4 subject-verb pairs (s v)	
	1 opener	

① subject

[he told his men] (that they should come quickly,) (when they heard his **signal**), (which would be 3 short blasts on his bugle).

s pr he, *v* told, *adj* his, *n* men; *that* that, *s pr* they, *v* should, *v* come, *adv* quickly; *AC* when, *s pr* they, *v* heard, *adj* his, *n* signal; *w/w* which, *s* which, *v* would, *v* be, *adj* three, *adj* short, *n* blasts, *adj* his, *n* bugle

Capitalization		***He*** first word of the sentence
End Marks		This passage contains 1 end mark. There is 1 main clause. Use a period at the end of a statement.
Adjective		Whose men? ***his*** The possessive pronoun *his* functions as an adjective.
		Whose signal? ***his***
		What kind of blasts? ***short***
		How many short blasts? ***three***
		Whose bugle? ***his***
Adverb		Come how? ***quickly***
S V Pairs	MC	***He told***
	that	*that* ***they should come***
	AC	*when* ***they heard***
	w/w	***which would be*** The *which* clause describes *signal*, the noun it follows.
Commas		Do not put a comma in front of an adverb clause. PATTERN MC AC

Rewrite It! He told his men that they should come quickly when they heard his signal, which would be three short blasts on his bugle.

Learn It!

#6 Vss Opener

A **#6 vss opener** is a very short sentence.

Very short means two to five words. *Sentence* means it must have a main clause.

Robin sought adventure.

This sentence is short because it has three words.
It is a sentence because it has a main clause. It is a #6 vss opener.

Mark It! Write (6) above the first word of a very short sentence.

(6)
S V
[The wet log wobbled].

For more information about the #6 vss opener, see page G-45.

After students mark the sentence, ask them to identify the opener.

This sentence is a #6 vss because it is short (four words) and it has a main clause.

Run-On

A **run-on** occurs when a sentence has main clauses that are not connected properly.

Week 11 you learned that a **fused sentence** is two main clauses placed in one sentence without any punctuation between them. This is one type of run-on error.

A **comma splice** is two main clauses placed in one sentence with only a comma between them. This is a second type of run-on error. The easiest way to fix both of these errors is to place a period at the end of each main clause.

Find It! Look for two main clauses that have only a comma between them.

Fix It! Correct a comma splice by replacing the comma with a period. Capitalize the first word of the new sentence.

S V S V
[Robin noticed a log across a stream],. [the log looked sturdy].

For more information about run-ons, see pages G-17.

For more information about impostor -ly adverbs, see page G-37.

Impostor -ly Adverb

An **impostor -ly adverb** is a word that looks like an adverb because it ends in -ly but is actually an adjective. Although many adverbs end in -ly, some adjectives also end in -ly. If the -ly word describes a noun or pronoun, it is an impostor -ly adverb. Only adjectives describe nouns.

Mark It! Write ***adv*** above each adverb. Write ***adj*** above each adjective.

adj adv adj
The sturdy log safely spanned the chilly stream.

Ask students to identify adjectives and adverbs. If the word ends in -ly, ask if it describes a noun. If it does, it is an adjective.

What kind of log? ***sturdy***
Sturdy answers what kind and describes a noun, so *sturdy* is an adjective.

Spanned how? ***safely***
Safely answers how and modifies a verb, so *safely* is an adverb.

What kind of stream? ***chilly***
Chilly answers what kind and describes a noun, so *chilly* is an adjective. It is an impostor -ly adverb.

Read It!	Mark It!	Fix It!
robin hood **roamed** through the forest, he searched for adventure	1 article (ar)	3 capitals
	3 nouns (n)	1 comma
	1 pronoun (pr)	2 end marks
	2 prepositional phrases	
	2 [main clauses]	
	2 subject-verb pairs (s v)	
	2 openers	

Day 1

roamed
walked or traveled without a fixed purpose or direction

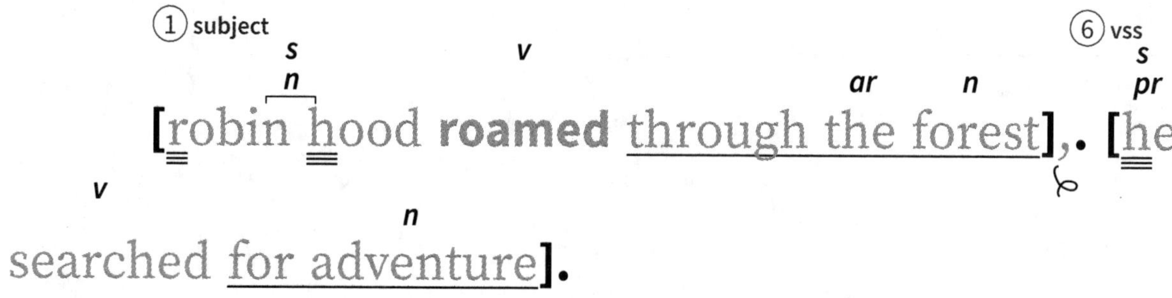

Capitalization		***Robin Hood*** proper noun; first word of the sentence ***He*** first word of the sentence
End Marks		This passage contains 2 end marks. There are 2 main clauses. Use a period at the end of a statement.
S V Pairs	MC MC	***Robin Hood roamed*** ***He searched***
Commas		Do not use a comma to connect two main clauses. MC, MC (comma splice) is always wrong.

Rewrite It! Robin Hood roamed through the forest. He searched for adventure.

Read It!	Mark It!	Fix It! Day 2
at a sharp curve in a path, robin neared a log, which **spanned** a broad pebbly stream, and acted as a narrow bridge	5 articles (ar) 6 nouns (n) 4 adjectives (adj) 1 coordinating conjunction (cc) 3 prepositional phrases 1 *who/which* clause (w/w) 1 [main clause] 2 subject-verb pairs (s v) 1 opener	2 capitals 1 comma 1 end mark

spanned
extended across

② prepositional

at a sharp curve in a path, [robin neared a log], (which **spanned** a broad pebbly stream, and acted as a narrow bridge).

Capitalization	***At*** first word of the sentence ***Robin*** proper noun
End Marks	This passage contains 1 end mark. There is 1 main clause. Use a period at the end of a statement.
Adjective	What kind of curve? ***sharp*** What kind of stream? ***pebbly*** What kind of pebbly stream? ***broad*** What kind of bridge? ***narrow***
S V Pairs MC	***Robin neared***
w/w	***which spanned, acted*** The *which* clause describes *log*, the noun it follows.
Commas	Do not use a comma to separate two items connected with a coordinating conjunction. PATTERN **a and b** *spanned* and *acted*

Rewrite It! At a sharp curve in a path, Robin neared a log, which spanned a broad pebbly stream and acted as a narrow bridge.

Read It!	Mark It!	Fix It!
as he approached the log he noticed a large, **stout** stranger, who was approaching the log from the other side	4 articles (ar) 4 nouns (n) 2 pronouns (pr) 3 adjectives (adj) 1 prepositional phrase 1 *who/which* clause (w/w) 1 adverb clause (AC) 1 [main clause] 3 subject-verb pairs (s v) 1 opener	1 capital 1 comma 1 end mark

stout
heavily built; bold and brave

⑤ clausal

(as he approached the log), [he noticed a large, **stout** stranger], (who was approaching the log from the other side).

Capitalization	***As*** first word of the sentence
End Marks	This passage contains 1 end mark. There is 1 main clause. Use a period at the end of a statement.
Adjective	What kind of stranger? ***large***, ***stout*** Which side? ***other***
S V Pairs AC	*As* ***he approached***
MC	***he noticed***
w/w	***who was approaching*** The *who* clause describes *stranger*, the noun it follows. *Approaching* functions as a verb because it follows the helping verb *was*. A word that ends in -ing functions as a verb only if it follows a helping verb.
Commas	Use a comma after an adverb clause. PATTERN **AC, MC**

Rewrite It! As he approached the log, he noticed a large, stout stranger, who was approaching the log from the other side.

Read It!	Mark It!	Fix It!
robin **quickened** his pace the stranger did to, both wanted to cross	1 article (ar)	3 capitals
	3 nouns (n)	1 comma
	1 pronoun (pr)	3 end marks
	1 adjective (adj)	1 homophone
quickened sped up	1 adverb	
	3 [main clauses]	
	3 subject-verb pairs (s v)	
	3 openers	

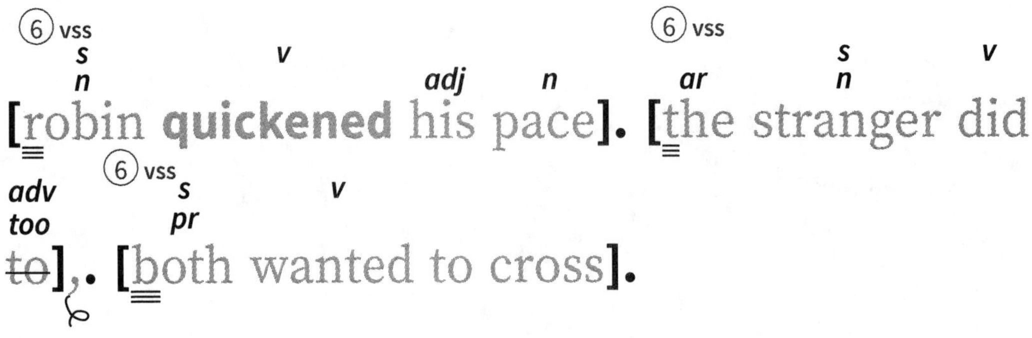

Capitalization		***Robin*** proper noun; first word of the sentence ***The***; ***Both*** first word of the sentence
End Marks		This passage contains 3 end marks. There are 3 main clauses. Use a period at the end of a statement.
Adjective		Whose pace? ***his*** The possessive pronoun *his* functions as an adjective.
Adverb		***too*** functions as an adverb
S V Pairs	MC	***Robin quickened***
	MC	***stranger did***
	MC	***Both wanted***
Note		*To cross* is an infinitive. It does not function as a verb.
Commas		Do not use a comma to connect two main clauses. MC, MC (comma splice) is always wrong.
Homophones		Use ***too***, which means also in this sentence.

Rewrite It! Robin quickened his pace. The stranger did too. Both wanted to cross.

Learn It!

Interjection

An **interjection** expresses an emotion.

For more information about interjections, see page G-15.

Wow**! H**e hit the bull's-eye!

When an interjection expresses a strong emotion, use an exclamation mark. Capitalize the word that follows an exclamation mark.

Hmm**, h**e still has one arrow.

When an interjection does not express a strong emotion, use a comma. Do not capitalize the word that follows a comma.

Capitalization

Capitalize an interjection when it is the first word of a sentence.

Capitalize a word that follows an exclamation mark.

Mark It! Write ***int*** above each interjection.

Fix It! Place a comma or an exclamation mark after each interjection. Place three short lines below letters that should be capitalized.

int
Yikes**!** he killed the king's deer!

Imperative Sentence (Implied Subject)

An **imperative sentence** gives a command or makes a request.

For more information about the imperative mood, see page G-11.

Every verb has a subject, a noun or pronoun that performs the verb action. However, the imperative sentence does not have a written subject. Rather, the subject is implied.

Because commands are always directed toward someone or something, the subject of an imperative sentence is always *you.*

Find It! Read the sentence and look for the verb. Ask, "Who or what ___ (verb)?" If the sentence forms a command, the subject is *you.*

Mark It! Write (you) in parentheses to show the subject. Write ***v*** above each verb and **s** above *you.*

s **v**
(you) Step up to the mark.

Whose can also ask a question, but in this book students will only see it as a word that begins a *who/which* clause.

Homophone

A **homophone** is a word that sounds like another word but is spelled differently and has a different meaning. Correctly use the homophones *whose* and *who's.*

Whose is a possessive pronoun: *whose* arrows (the arrows belong to whom).

The relative pronoun *whose* functions as a possessive adjective and begins a *who/which* clause.

Who's is a contraction: *who's* tired (who is tired).

The contraction *who's* is a shortened form of *who is* and functions as the subject pronoun (who) and verb (is) of the clause

Fix It! Place a line through the incorrect homophone and write the correct word above it.

Whose **Who's**

~~Who's~~ bow is this? ~~Whose~~ ready to shoot next?

Read It!	Mark It!	Fix It! Day 1
"go back sir," demanded robin **rudely**. "the one whose the better man should cross first"	2 articles (ar) 1 pronoun (pr) 3 nouns (n) 3 adverbs (adv) 1 *who/which* clause (w/w) 3 [main clauses] 4 subject-verb pairs (s v)	3 capitals 1 comma 1 end mark 1 homophone

rudely
impolitely

[(you) "Go back], sir," [demanded Robin **rudely**].

"[The one (~~whose~~ who's the better man) should cross first]."

Capitalization	***Go***; ***The*** first word of the quoted sentence ***Robin*** proper noun
End Marks	This passage contains 2 end marks. There are 3 main clauses. The first quotation and the attribution belong in the same sentence. Use a period when a quote makes a statement. Place it inside the closing quotation mark.
Adverb	Go where? ***back*** Demanded how? ***rudely*** Cross when? ***first***
S V Pairs MC	***(you) Go*** The subject of an imperative sentence is always *you*.
MC	***Robin demanded***
MC	***one should cross***
w/w	***who's*** The contraction *who's* includes both a subject (who) and a verb (is). The *who* clause describes *one*, the pronoun it follows.
Commas	Place commas around a noun of direct address (NDA). ***, sir***
Homophones	Use ***who's***, the contraction for *who is*.

Rewrite It! "Go back, sir," demanded Robin rudely. "The one who's the better man should cross first."

Read It!	Mark It!	Fix It!
the **confident** stranger responded, "you go back i am the better man"	2 articles (ar) 2 nouns (n) 2 pronouns (pr) 2 adjectives (adj) 1 adverb (adv) 3 [main clauses] 3 subject-verb pairs (s v) 1 opener	3 capitals 2 end marks

confident
sure of oneself; bold

(1) subject

[the **confident** stranger responded], "[you go back]. [i am the better man]."

Capitalization		***The*** first word of the sentence ***You*** first word of the quoted sentence ***I*** personal pronoun I; first word of the quoted sentence
End Marks		This passage contains 2 end marks. There are 3 main clauses. The attribution and the first sentence of the quotation belong together. Use a period when a quote makes a statement. Place it inside the closing quotation mark.
Adjective		What kind of stranger? ***confident*** What kind of man? ***better***
Adverb		Go where? ***back***
S V Pairs	MC	***stranger responded***
	MC	***You go***
	MC	***I am***

Rewrite It! The confident stranger responded, "You go back. I am the better man."

Read It!	Mark It!	Fix It!
naturally, this **riled** robin, since his merry men always respected him, and obeyed him immediately	2 nouns (n) 3 pronouns (pr) 2 adjectives (adj) 3 adverbs (adv) 1 coordinating conjunction (cc) 1 adverb clause (AC) 1 [main clause] 2 subject-verb pairs (s v) 1 opener	2 capitals 2 commas 1 end mark

Day 3

riled
irritated

③ -ly adverb

naturally, [this **riled** robin], (since his merry men always respected him, and obeyed him immediately).

Capitalization	***Naturally*** first word of the sentence ***Robin*** proper noun
End Marks	This passage contains 1 end mark. There is 1 main clause. Use a period at the end of a statement.
Adjective	What kind of men? ***merry*** Whose merry men? ***his*** The possessive pronoun *his* functions as an adjective.
Adverb	This riled Robin how? ***Naturally*** *Naturally* is a sentence adverb. It modifies the entire sentence: It was natural that this riled Robin. For this reason, it doesn't answer a question about the verb but about the entire sentence. It requires a comma. Respected when? ***always*** Obeyed him when? ***immediately***
S V Pairs MC	***this riled***
AC	*since* ***men respected*, *obeyed***
Commas	Do not put a comma in front of an adverb clause. **PATTERN MC AC** Do not use a comma to separate two items connected with a coordinating conjunction. **PATTERN a and b** *respected* and *obeyed*

Rewrite It! Naturally, this riled Robin since his merry men always respected him and obeyed him immediately.

Read It!

Mark It!

Fix It!

Day 4

"if you dont go back ill fire an arrow at you" **asserted** robin

"hah do you think that im afraid" the other mocked

asserted
stated with force or confidence

Mark It!		Fix It!
2 articles (ar)	1 prepositional phrase	6 capitals
2 nouns (n)	1 *that* clause (that)	1 comma
6 pronouns (pr)	1 adverb clause (AC)	5 end marks
1 adjective (adj)	4 [main clauses]	3 apostrophes
2 adverbs (adv)	6 subject-verb pairs (s v)	
1 interjection (int)		

AC: s pr, v, adv, v, adv; s pr, v, v, ar, n, pr

"(if you don't go back), [i'll fire an arrow at you]!"

v, s n

[asserted robin].

int, v, s pr, v, that, s pr, v, adj, ar

"hah! [do you think] (that i'm afraid)?" [the

s pr, v

other mocked].

Capitalization	***If***; ***Hah*** first word of the quoted sentence ***I'll***; ***I'm*** personal pronoun I ***Robin*** proper noun ***Do*** first word that follows interjection with exclamation mark
End Marks	Use an exclamation mark when a quote expresses strong emotion. **PATTERN "Quote!" attribution.** Use a period at the end of a statement. Use an exclamation mark after an interjection that expresses strong emotion. Use a question mark when a quote asks a question. **PATTERN "Quote?" attribution.** Use a period at the end of a statement.
Adjective	What kind of I (man)? ***afraid*** The adjective follows the linking verb and describes the subject.
Adverb	***n't*** the contraction for *not* functions as an adverb Go where? ***back***
S V Pairs AC	*If* ***you do go*** The contraction *don't* includes both a verb (do) and an adverb (n't).
MC	***I'll fire*** The contraction *I'll* includes both a subject (I) and a helping verb (will).
MC	***Robin asserted***
MC	***you Do think***
that	*that* ***I'm*** The contraction *I'm* includes both a subject (I) and a verb (am).
MC	***other mocked***
Commas	Use a comma after an adverb clause. **PATTERN AC, MC**
Apostrophes	*Don't*, *I'll*, and *I'm* are contractions. Use apostrophes to show where letters have been removed.

Rewrite It!

"If you don't go back, I'll fire an arrow at you!" asserted Robin.

"Hah! Do you think that I'm afraid?" the other mocked.

Learn It!

Quotation Marks—Capitalization and End Marks

For more information about quotation marks, see pages G-27 and G-32.

Quotation marks indicate words are spoken. The quote is the sentence in quotation marks. The attribution is the person speaking and the speaking verb.

The stranger cried, "Obviously, I am not afraid."

The attribution may come before the quoted sentence.
Attribution, "Quote."

"Obviously, I am not afraid," the stranger cried.

The attribution may come after the quoted sentence.
"Quote," attribution.

"Obviously," the stranger cried, "I am not afraid."

The attribution may come in the middle of the quoted sentence.
"Quote," attribution, "rest of quoted sentence."

"You can cross the stream after I do."

Sometimes a quoted sentence will not have an attribution.

Regardless of where the attribution comes in relation to the quoted sentence, capitalization and punctuation rules remain the same.

Place quotation marks around the words that are spoken.

Capitalize the first word of the quoted sentence.

Capitalize the first word of the attribution when it begins the sentence.

If the quoted sentence makes a statement, place a period inside the closing quotation mark unless the attribution follows.

If the quoted sentence asks a question, place a question mark inside the closing quotation mark.

If the quoted sentence expresses strong emotion, place an exclamation mark inside the closing quotation mark.

Comma

A **comma** is used to separate items in a sentence.

, Use a comma to separate an attribution from a direct quote.

Fix It! Place quotation marks around the words that are spoken.
Place three short lines below letters that should be capitalized.
Place the correct end mark at the end of each sentence.
Place a comma between an attribution and a quote.

robin demanded, "get off the log."

"you don't scare me," the stranger replied.

Indentation

For more information about indentation, see page G-31.

An **indentation** is a blank space between the margin and the beginning of a line of text. It shows the start of a new paragraph.

In fiction (stories), there are four reasons to start a new paragraph.

New Speaker: Start a new paragraph when a new character speaks. Include the attribution with the quotation. Sentences before or after the quotation that point directly to the quotation can remain in the same paragraph.

New Topic: Start a new paragraph when the narrator or a character switches the topic.

New Place: Start a new paragraph when the story switches to a new location. If several switches are made in quick succession, such as a character's journey to find something, it may be less choppy to keep in one paragraph.

New Time: Start a new paragraph when the time changes.

The paragraph mark (¶) is called a pilcrow.

Fix It! Add the ¶ symbol or an arrow ➔ in front of each sentence that should start a new paragraph.

Robin approached the log.

¶ "Stand back!" cried the stranger.

When you rewrite the passage, indent. Start the sentence on the next line and write ½ inch from the left margin.

Read It!	Mark It!	Fix It! Day 1
you joke like a fool **bellowed** robin. i could fire this arrow through you're heart	1 article (ar)	1 indent
	4 nouns (n)	3 capitals
	2 pronouns (pr)	4 quotation marks
	2 adjectives (adj)	2 end marks
bellowed shouted with a deep roar	2 prepositional phrases	1 homophone
	3 [main clauses]	
	3 subject-verb pairs (s v)	

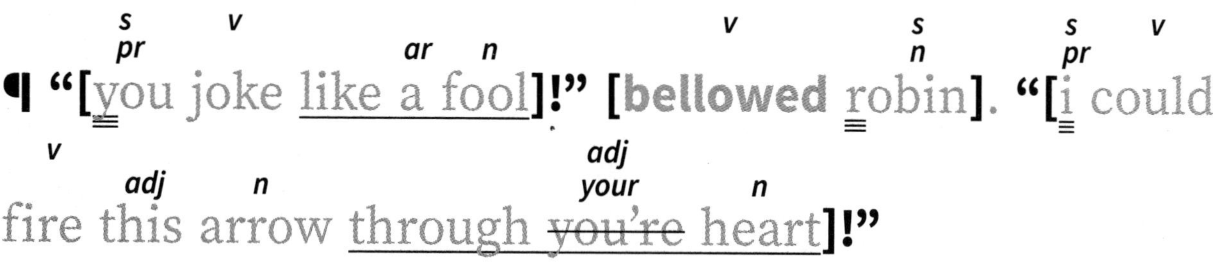
¶ "[you joke like a fool]!" [bellowed robin]. "[i could fire this arrow through ~~you're~~ your heart]!"

Indentation		new speaker
Capitalization		***You*** first word of the quoted sentence ***Robin*** proper noun ***I*** personal pronoun I; first word of the quoted sentence
End Marks		Use an exclamation mark when a quote expresses strong emotion. PATTERN **"Quote!" attribution.** Place the exclamation mark inside the closing quotation mark.
Adjective		Which arrow? ***this*** Whose heart? ***your*** The possessive pronoun *your* functions as an adjective.
S V Pairs	MC	***You joke***
	MC	***Robin bellowed***
	MC	***I could fire***
Homophones		Use ***your***, the possessive pronoun.

Rewrite It! "You joke like a fool!" bellowed Robin. "I could fire this arrow through your heart!"

Read It!	Mark It!	Fix It! Day 2
the tall stranger chuckled you stand there with a **lethal** bow i only carry a staff, are you a coward	4 articles (ar)	1 indent
	4 nouns (n)	4 capitals
	3 pronouns (pr)	2 commas
	2 adjectives (adj)	2 quotation marks
lethal deadly	2 adverbs (adv)	3 end marks
	1 prepositional phrase	
	4 [main clauses]	
	4 subject-verb pairs (s v)	
	1 opener	

① subject

¶ [the tall stranger chuckled], "[you stand there with a **lethal** bow]. [i only carry a staff],. [are you a coward]?"

Indentation	new speaker
Capitalization	***The*** first word of the sentence ***You***; ***Are*** first word of the quoted sentence ***I*** personal pronoun I; first word of the quoted sentence
End Marks	This passage contains 3 end marks. There are 4 main clauses. The attribution and the first sentence of the quotation belong together. Use a period when a quote makes a statement. Use a question mark when a quote asks a question. Place it inside the closing quotation mark.
Adjective	What kind of stranger? ***tall*** What kind of bow? ***lethal***
Adverb	Stand where? ***there*** Carry to what extent? ***only***
S V Pairs	MC ***stranger chuckled*** MC ***You stand*** MC ***I carry*** MC ***you Are***
Commas	Use a comma to separate an attribution from a direct quote. PATTERN Attribution, "Quote." Do not use a comma to connect two main clauses. MC, MC (comma splice) is always wrong.

Rewrite It! The tall stranger chuckled, "You stand there with a lethal bow. I only carry a staff. Are you a coward?"

Read It!	Mark It!	Fix It! Day 3
i have never been called a coward cried robin, who's face became **crimson**. ill teach you a lesson that you wont forget	2 articles (ar)	1 indent
	4 nouns (n)	3 capitals
	4 pronouns (pr)	3 quotation marks
	1 adjective (adj)	2 end marks
crimson deep purplish-red	2 adverbs (adv)	1 homophone
	1 *who/which* clause (w/w)	2 apostrophes
	1 *that* clause (that)	
	3 [main clauses]	
	5 subject-verb pairs (s v)	

¶ "[i have never been called a coward]!" [cried robin], (who's whose face became **crimson**). "[i'll teach you a lesson] (that you won't forget).

No closing quotation mark because quote continues.

Indentation	new speaker
Capitalization	***I***; ***I'll*** personal pronoun I; first word of the quoted sentence ***Robin*** proper noun
End Marks	This passage contains 3 end marks. There are 3 main clauses. The first quotation and the attribution are separated with an exclamation mark. Use an exclamation mark when a quote expresses strong emotion. **PATTERN "Quote!" attribution.** Use a period when a quote makes a statement.
Adjective	What kind of face? ***crimson*** The adjective follows the linking verb and describes the subject.
Adverb	Been called when? ***never*** ***n't*** the contraction for *not* functions as an adverb
S V Pairs MC	***I have been called***
MC	***Robin cried***
w/w	*whose* ***face became*** The *whose* clause describes *Robin*, the noun it follows.
MC	***I'll teach*** The contraction *I'll* includes both a subject (I) and a helping verb (will).
that	*that* ***you will forget*** The contraction *won't* includes both a verb (will) and an adverb (not).
Homophones	Use ***whose***, the possessive pronoun.
Apostrophes	*I'll* and *won't* are contractions. Use apostrophes to show where letters have been removed.

Rewrite It!

"I have never been called a coward!" cried Robin, whose face became crimson. "I'll teach you a lesson that you won't forget.

Read It!	Mark It!	Fix It! Day 4
stay where you are! after i make a staff i will test you're **sparring** skills	1 article (ar) 2 nouns (n) 3 pronouns (pr) 2 adjectives (adj) 2 adverb clauses (AC) 2 [main clauses] 4 subject-verb pairs (s v)	4 capitals 1 comma 1 quotation mark 1 end mark 1 homophone

sparring
making moves of attack and defense

No opening quotation mark because quote continues.

[(you) stay] (where you are)! (after i make a staff),
[i will test ~~you're~~ your **sparring** skills]."

Capitalization	***Stay***; ***After*** first word of the quoted sentence ***I***; ***I*** personal pronoun I
End Marks	This passage contains 2 end marks. There are 2 main clauses. Use a period when a quote makes a statement. Place it inside the closing quotation mark.
Adjective	What kind of skills? ***sparring*** Whose sparring skills? ***your*** The possessive pronoun *your* functions as an adjective.
S V Pairs	MC ***(you) Stay*** The subject of an imperative sentence is always *you*. AC *where* ***you are*** AC *after* ***I make*** MC ***I will test***
Commas	Do not put a comma in front of an adverb clause. PATTERN MC AC Use a comma after an adverb clause. PATTERN AC, MC
Homophones	Use ***your***, the possessive pronoun.

Rewrite It! Stay where you are! After I make a staff, I will test your sparring skills."

Learn It!

Coordinating Conjunction

For more information about commas with conjunctions, see pages G-12 and G-24.

A **coordinating conjunction** connects the same type of words, phrases, or clauses.

Week 2 you learned two comma rules to use when a sentence has a coordinating conjunction (for, and, nor, but, or, yet, so).

Robin was kind, funny, and brave.

a, b, and c

In this sentence the coordinating conjunction *and* connects three adjectives: *kind, funny,* and *brave.* Two comma are used.

Robin was kind and funny.

a and b

In this sentence the coordinating conjunction *and* connects two adjectives: *kind* and *funny.* No comma is used.

Today you will learn two more comma rules. Compare these sentences:

The stranger waited and whistled a tune.

MC cc 2nd verb

In this sentence the coordinating conjunction *and* connects two verbs: *waited* and *whistled.* No comma is used. This is the same pattern as **a and b** when *a* and *b* are verbs.

The stranger waited, and Robin whistled a tune.

MC, cc MC

In this sentence the coordinating conjunction *and* connects two main clauses: *stranger waited,* and *Robin whistled.* One comma is used.

Comma

A **comma** is used to separate items in a sentence.

Do not use a comma before a coordinating conjunction when it connects two verbs.
PATTERN MC cc 2nd verb

Use a comma before a coordinating conjunction when it connects two main clauses.
PATTERN MC, cc MC

Mark It! Write *cc* above each coordinating conjunction.

Fix It! Remove a comma before a *cc* that connects two verbs.
Add a comma before a *cc* that connects two main clauses.

Ask students to identify the coordinating conjunction and explain what it connects.

S V cc V
[Robin agreed to spar, and made a staff].

And connects two verbs: *agreed* and *made.* Do not use a comma. MC cc 2nd verb

S V cc S V
[Robin agreed to spar], and [he made a staff].

And connects two main clauses: *Robin agreed,* and *he made.* Use a comma. MC, cc MC

MC cc 2nd verb or MC, cc MC

Read each sentence and decide if the coordinating conjunction connects verbs or clauses.

If the coordinating conjunction connects main clauses, insert a comma.

Circle the correct comma rule pattern.

Comparing these comma patterns teaches students to look for a verb or a second subject and verb after the conjunction.

If there is just a verb, do not add a comma. MC cc 2nd verb

If there is a subject and verb, add a comma before the coordinating conjunction. MC, cc MC

Robin accepted the challenge and collected his arrows.

(MC cc 2nd verb) MC, cc MC

And connects two verbs: *accepted* and *collected.* Do not use a comma. MC cc 2nd verb.

Robin accepted the challenge, and he collected his arrows.

MC cc 2nd verb (MC, cc MC)

And connects two main clauses: *Robin accepted*, and *he collected*. Use a comma. MC, cc MC

The waterfall spilled over the cliff, and it created a whirlpool.

MC cc 2nd verb (MC, cc MC)

And connects two main clauses: *waterfall spilled*, and *it created*. Use a comma. MC, cc MC

The waterfall spilled over the cliff and created a whirlpool.

(MC cc 2nd verb) MC, cc MC

And connects two verbs: *spilled* and *created*. Do not use a comma. MC cc 2nd verb

Little John released the arrow but surprisingly missed the target.

(MC cc 2nd verb) MC, cc MC

But connects two verbs: *released* but *missed*. Do not use a comma. MC cc 2nd verb

Little John released the arrow, but he missed the target.

MC cc 2nd verb (MC, cc MC)

But connects two main clauses: *Little John released*, but *he missed*. Use a comma. MC, cc MC

Robin was an outlaw, so he could not return home.

MC cc 2nd verb (MC, cc MC)

So connects two main clauses: *Robin was*, so *he could (not) return*. Use a comma. MC, cc MC

Robin was an outlaw and could not return home.

(MC cc 2nd verb) MC, cc MC

And connects two verbs: *was* and *could (not) return*. Do not use a comma. MC cc 2nd verb

Read It!	Mark It!	Fix It! Day 1
i welcome you to try **countered** the stranger with a twinkle in his eye. im happy too wait	2 articles (ar)	1 indent
	3 nouns (n)	2 capitals
	3 pronouns (pr)	1 comma
	2 adjectives (adj)	4 quotation marks
countered	2 prepositional phrases	1 end mark
spoke in response or opposition	3 [main clauses]	1 homophone
	3 subject-verb pairs (s v)	1 apostrophe

¶ "[i welcome you to try]," [**countered** the stranger with a twinkle in his eye]. "[i'm happy ~~too~~ wait]."

(Markings: i — s, pr; welcome — v; you — pr; countered — v; the — ar; stranger — s, n; a — ar; twinkle — n; his — adj; eye — n; i'm — s v, pr; happy — adj; too → to)

Indentation	new speaker
Capitalization	***I***; ***I'm*** personal pronoun I; first word of the quoted sentence.
End Marks	This passage contains 2 end marks. There are 3 main clauses. The first quotation and the attribution belong in the same sentence. Use a period when a quote makes a statement. Place it inside the closing quotation mark.
Adjective	Whose eye? ***his*** The possessive pronoun *his* functions as an adjective. What kind of I? ***happy*** The adjective follows the linking verb and describes the subject.
S V Pairs	MC ***I welcome*** MC ***stranger countered*** MC ***I'm*** The contraction *I'm* includes both a subject (I) and a verb (am).
Note	*To try* and *to wait* are infinitives. They do not function as verbs.
Commas	Use a comma to separate a direct quote from an attribution. PATTERN **"Quote," attribution.**
Homophones	Use ***to***, the infinitive marker
Apostrophes	*I'm* is a contraction. Use an apostrophe to show where letters have been removed.

Rewrite It! "I welcome you to try," countered the stranger with a twinkle in his eye. "I'm happy to wait."

Read It! | **Mark It!** | **Fix It!** Day 2

patiently the calm giant leaned on his staff, and waited their for robin. he whistled, as he **gazed** about

1 article (ar)	2 prepositional phrases	3 capitals
3 nouns (n)	1 adverb clause (AC)	2 commas
2 pronouns (pr)	2 [main clauses]	1 end mark
2 adjectives (adj)	3 subject-verb pairs (s v)	1 homophone
3 adverbs (adv)	2 openers	
1 coordinating conjunction (cc)		

gazed
looked steadily and intently

③ -ly adverb

patiently [the calm giant leaned on his staff, and waited their there for robin]. [he whistled], (as he **gazed** about).

① subject

Capitalization	***Patiently***; ***He*** first word of the sentence ***Robin*** proper noun
End Marks	This passage contains 2 end marks. There are 2 main clauses. Use a period at the end of a statement.
Adjective	What kind of giant? ***calm*** Whose staff? ***his*** The possessive pronoun *his* functions as an adjective.
Adverb	Leaned and waited how? ***Patiently*** Waited where? ***there*** Gazed where? ***about***
S V Pairs MC	***giant leaned***, ***waited***
MC	***He whistled***
AC	*as* ***he gazed***
Commas	Do not use a comma to separate two verbs connected with a coordinating conjunction because the verbs have the same subject. PATTERN **MC cc 2nd verb** *giant leaned* and *waited* Do not put a comma in front of an adverb clause. PATTERN **MC AC**
Note	The comma PATTERNS **a and b** and **MC cc 2nd verb** are the same when *a* and *b* are verbs. However, the emphasis differs. The comma PATTERN **a and b** emphasizes that a cc connects two items (leaned and waited). The comma PATTERN **MC cc 2nd** verb emphasizes that a subject and verb (giant leaned) come before the cc, but only a verb (waited) comes after the cc. A comma is not used in either pattern.
Homophones	Use ***there***, the adverb pointing to a place.

Rewrite It! Patiently the calm giant leaned on his staff and waited there for Robin. He whistled as he gazed about.

Read It! **Mark It!** **Fix It!** Day 3

robin hood stepped into the forest found a tall oak and cut a **sturdy** staff, which measured 6 feet in length

sturdy
strong in substance or construction

3 articles (ar)	1 [main clause]	1 indent
6 nouns (n)	2 subject-verb pairs (s v)	2 capitals
3 adjectives (adj)	1 opener	2 commas
1 coordinating conjunction (cc)		1 end mark
2 prepositional phrases		1 number
1 *who/which* clause (w/w)		

(1) subject

¶ [robin hood stepped into the forest, found a tall oak, and cut a **sturdy** staff], (which measured ~~6~~ six feet in length).

Indentation	new topic
Capitalization	***Robin Hood*** proper noun; first word of the sentence
End Marks	This passage contains 1 end mark. There is 1 main clause. Use a period at the end of a statement.
Adjective	What kind of oak? ***tall*** What kind of staff? ***sturdy*** How many feet? ***six***
S V Pairs MC	***Robin Hood stepped, found, cut***
w/w	***which measured*** The *which* clause describes *staff*, the noun it follows.
Commas	Use commas to separate three or more items in a series connected with a coordinating conjunction. **PATTERN a, b, and c** *stepped*, *found*, and *cut*
Note	In this sentence a cc connects three verbs (stepped, found, and cut). Although the subject (Robin Hood) is only found before the first verb, commas are required whenever any three items in a series are connected with a cc.

Rewrite It!

Robin Hood stepped into the forest, found a tall oak, and cut a sturdy staff, which measured six feet in length.

Read It!	Mark It!	Fix It!
robin **fashioned** his weapon he secretly studied the giant and he confidently planned his 1st move	1 article (ar)	2 capitals
	4 nouns (n)	1 comma
	2 pronouns (pr)	2 end marks
	3 adjectives (adj)	1 number
fashioned gave a particular shape to; made	2 adverbs (adv)	
	1 coordinating conjunction (cc)	
	3 [main clauses]	
	3 subject-verb pairs (s v)	
	2 openers	

⑥ vss; ① subject

[robin **fashioned** his weapon]. [he secretly studied the giant], and [he confidently planned his ~~1st~~ first move].

(Marks: robin = s, n; fashioned = v; his = adj; weapon = n; he = s, pr; secretly = adv; studied = v; the = ar; giant = n; and = cc; he = s, pr; confidently = adv; planned = v; his = adj; first = adj; move = n)

Capitalization		***Robin*** proper noun; first word of the sentence ***He*** first word of the sentence
End Marks		This passage contains 2 end marks. There are 3 main clauses. A comma and coordinating conjunction connect the second and third main clauses. Use a period at the end of a statement.
Adjective		Whose weapon? ***his*** The possessive pronoun *his* functions as an adjective. Which move? ***first*** Whose first move? ***his***
Adverb		Studied how? ***secretly*** Planned how? ***confidently***
S V Pairs	MC MC MC	***Robin fashioned*** ***He studied*** ***he planned***
Commas		Use a comma to separate two main clauses connected with a coordinating conjunction. **PATTERN MC, cc MC** *he studied*, and *he planned*
Note		In this sentence a subject verb pair (he studied) comes before the coordinating conjunction, and a subject verb pair (he planned) comes after the coordinating conjunction. A comma is required.

Rewrite It! Robin fashioned his weapon. He secretly studied the giant, and he confidently planned his first move.

Learn It!

Phrase versus Clause

A **phrase** is a group of related words that contains either a noun or a verb, never both.

The most common phrase is the prepositional phrase, which never has a verb.

A **clause** is a group of related words that contains both a subject and a verb.

A **main clause** stands alone as a sentence. It expresses a complete thought.

A **dependent clause** cannot stand alone as a sentence. It must be added to a sentence that is already complete.

You have learned three types of dependent clauses: *who/which* clauses, *that* clauses, and adverb clauses.

For more information about phrases and clauses, see pages G-18 and G-20.

Decide if the following is a phrase or a clause. Circle the correct answer.

he approached the log	phrase	(clause)
near the tall oak tree	(phrase)	clause
that was a hundred years old	phrase	(clause)
where a stranger stood	phrase	(clause)
beneath a full moon	(phrase)	clause
which shone brightly	phrase	(clause)

clause: he approached the log (subject verb *he approached*)

phrase: near the tall oak tree (no verb)

clause: that was a hundred years old (subject verb *that was*)

clause: where a stranger stood (subject verb *stranger stood*)

phrase: beneath a full moon (no verb)

clause: which shone brightly (subject verb *which shone*)

Dependent clauses begin with a word that causes them to be an incomplete thought. Draw lines to connect the type of clause to the word that would begin the clause.

who/which clause   *that* clause   adverb clause   none

who   ***since***   ***that***   ***then***   ***it***

when   ***while***   ***as***   ***if***   ***at***   ***which***

who/which clause
lines to who, which

that clause
line to that

adverb clause
lines to when, while, as, since, if

none
lines to then, it, at

Every clause contains a ___subject___ and a ___verb___.

Read It!	Mark It!	Fix It! Day 1
until that day robin had never met a larger man usually, robin **towered** over others	1 article (ar) 4 nouns (n) 1 pronoun (pr) 2 adjectives (adj) 2 adverbs (adv) 2 prepositional phrases 2 [main clauses] 2 subject-verb pairs (s v) 2 openers	4 capitals 2 end marks

towered
rose above others

(2) prepositional

until that day [robin had never met a larger man].

(3) -ly adverb

usually, [robin **towered** over others].

Capitalization	***Until***; ***Usually*** first word of the sentence ***Robin***; ***Robin*** proper noun
End Marks	This passage contains 2 end marks. There are 2 main clauses. Use a period at the end of a statement.
Adjective	Which day? ***that*** What kind of man? ***larger***
Adverb	Had met when? ***never*** Robin towered over others when? ***usually*** *Usually* is a sentence adverb. It modifies the entire sentence: It was usual that Robin towered over others. For this reason, it doesn't answer a question about the verb but about the entire sentence. It requires a comma.
S V Pairs MC	***Robin had met***
MC	***Robin towered***

Rewrite It! Until that day Robin had never met a larger man. Usually, Robin towered over others.

Read It!	Mark It!	Fix It!
this **rival** was a 7-foot man! although robin's shoulders were broad the stranger's shoulders were 2 times the size	3 articles (ar) 6 nouns (n) 6 adjectives (adj) 1 adverb clause (AC) 2 [main clauses] 3 subject-verb pairs (s v) 2 openers	3 capitals 1 comma 1 end mark 2 numbers

rival
competitor; someone who tries to outdo another

① subject ⑤ clausal

[this **rival** was a seven-foot man]! (although robin's shoulders were broad), [the stranger's shoulders were two times the size].

Capitalization	***This***; ***Although*** first word of the sentence ***Robin's*** proper adjective
End Marks	This passage contains 2 end marks. There are 2 main clauses. Use a period at the end of a statement.
Adjective	Which rival? ***this*** What kind of man? ***seven-foot*** Whose shoulders? ***Robin's*** What kind of shoulders? ***broad*** The adjective follows the linking verb and describes the subject. Whose shoulders? ***stranger's*** How many times? ***two***
S V Pairs	MC ***rival was*** AC *Although* ***shoulders were*** MC ***shoulders were***
Commas	Use a comma after an adverb clause. **PATTERN** AC, MC

Rewrite It! This rival was a seven-foot man! Although Robin's shoulders were broad, the stranger's shoulders were two times the size.

Read It!	Mark It!	Fix It!
carefully robin **crafted** his weapon, which must be strong straight and sturdy. he was determined that he would win	2 nouns (n) 2 pronouns (pr) 4 adjectives (adj) 1 adverb (adv) 1 coordinating conjunction (cc) 1 *who/which* clause (w/w) 1 *that* clause (that) 2 [main clauses] 4 subject-verb pairs (s v) 2 openers	3 capitals 2 commas 1 end mark

crafted
made with skill and attention to detail

(3) -ly adverb

carefully (adv) [robin (s, n) **crafted** (v) his (adj) weapon (n)], (which (w/w, s) must (v) be (v) strong (adj), straight (adj), and (cc) sturdy (adj)). [he ((1) subject; s, pr) was (v) determined (v)] (that (that) he (s, pr) would (v) win (v)).

Capitalization		***Carefully***; ***He*** first word of the sentence ***Robin*** proper noun
End Marks		This passage contains 2 end marks. There are 2 main clauses. Use a period at the end of a statement.
Adjective		Whose weapon? ***his*** The possessive pronoun *his* functions as an adjective. What kind of which (weapon)? ***strong***, ***straight***, and ***sturdy*** The adjectives follow the linking verb and describe the subject.
Adverb		Crafted how? ***Carefully***
S V Pairs	MC	***Robin crafted***
	w/w	***which must be*** The *which* clause describes *weapon*, the noun it follows.
	MC	***He was determined***
	that	*that* ***he would win***
Commas		Use commas to separate three or more items in a series connected with a coordinating conjunction. PATTERN **a, b, and c** *strong*, *straight*, and *sturdy*

Rewrite It! Carefully Robin crafted his weapon, which must be strong, straight, and sturdy. He was determined that he would win.

Read It!	Mark It!	Fix It! Day 4
as robin worked he smiled for he had found his adventure. despite it's **risk** robin welcomed a challenge	1 article (ar)	4 capitals
	5 nouns (n)	2 commas
	2 pronouns (pr)	1 end mark
	2 adjectives (adj)	1 homophone
risk possibility of suffering injury	1 coordinating conjunction (cc)	
	1 prepositional phrase	
	1 adverb clause (AC)	
	3 [main clauses]	
	4 subject-verb pairs (s v)	
	2 openers	

(5) clausal

(as robin worked), [he smiled], for [he had found his adventure]. (2) prepositional despite ~~it's~~ its **risk** [robin welcomed a challenge].

Capitalization		***As***; ***Despite*** first word of the sentence ***Robin***; ***Robin*** proper noun
End Marks		This passage contains 2 end marks. There are 3 main clauses. A comma and coordinating conjunction connect the first and second main clauses. Use a period at the end of a statement.
Adjective		Whose adventure? ***his*** The possessive pronoun *his* functions as an adjective. Whose risk? ***its*** The possessive pronoun *its* functions as an adjective.
S V Pairs	AC	*As **Robin worked***
	MC	***he smiled***
	MC	***he had found***
	MC	***Robin welcomed***
Commas		Use a comma after an adverb clause. **PATTERN AC, MC** Use a comma to separate two main clauses connected with a coordinating conjunction. **PATTERN MC, cc MC** *he smiled,* for *he had found*
Homophones		Use ***its***, the possessive pronoun.

Rewrite It! As Robin worked, he smiled, for he had found his adventure. Despite its risk Robin welcomed a challenge.

Learn It!

Usage

Some words are close in spelling but have different meanings and uses. Correctly use the words *then* and *than*.

For more information about usage, see page G-35.

Then is an adverb meaning next or immediately after.

Then Robin approached the log. It was then Robin's turn.

Than is a word used to show a comparison.

The stranger was taller than Robin.

Fix It! Place a line through the incorrect word and write the correct word above it.

Then ***than***

~~Than~~ Robin, who was smaller ~~then~~ the stranger, taunted him.

Read It!	Mark It!	Fix It!
robin hood then **goaded** the giant man. im ready stranger. fight me, if you dare	1 article (ar)	1 indent
	3 nouns (n)	4 capitals
	3 pronouns (pr)	2 commas
goaded provoked or annoyed	2 adjectives (adj)	1 quotation
	1 adverb (adv)	1 end mark
	1 adverb clause (AC)	1 apostrophe
	3 [main clauses]	
	4 subject-verb pairs (s v)	
	1 opener	

(1) subject

¶ [robin hood then **goaded** the giant man]. "[i'm ready], stranger. [(you) fight me], (if you dare).

No closing quotation mark because quote continues.

Indentation	new speaker
Capitalization	***Robin Hood*** proper noun; first word of the sentence ***I'm*** personal pronoun I; first word of a quoted sentence ***Fight*** first word of a quoted sentence
End Marks	This passage contains 3 end marks. There are 3 main clauses. *Robin Hood ... man* is a complete thought. It is not an attribution. For this reason, it requires a period. Use a period when a quote makes a statement.
Adjective	What kind of man? ***giant*** What kind of I (Robin)? ***ready*** The adjective follows the linking verb and describes the subject.
Adverb	Goaded when? ***then***
S V Pairs	MC ***Robin Hood goaded*** MC ***I'm*** The contraction *I'm* includes both a subject (I) and a verb (am). MC ***(you) Fight*** The subject of an imperative sentence is always *you*. AC ***if you dare***
Commas	Place commas around a noun of direct address (NDA). ***, stranger*** Do not put a comma in front of an adverb clause. **PATTERN MC AC**
Apostrophes	*I'm* is a contraction. Use an apostrophe to show where letters have been removed.

Rewrite It! Robin Hood then goaded the giant man. "I'm ready, stranger. Fight me if you dare.

Read It!	Mark It!	Fix It! Day 2
when one of us falls into the stream than the **victor** will be the better man	3 articles (ar)	1 capital
	3 nouns (n)	1 comma
	2 pronouns (pr)	1 quotation
	1 adjective (adj)	1 end mark
victor	1 adverb (adv)	1 usage
winner; person who defeats an opponent	2 prepositional phrases	
	1 adverb clause (AC)	
	1 [main clause]	
	2 subject-verb pairs (s v)	

No opening quotation mark because quote continues.

(when one of us falls into the stream), [~~than~~ then the **victor** will be the better man]."

AC: when one falls; s pr: one; pr: us; v: falls; ar: the; n: stream; adv: then; ar: the; s n: victor; v: will be; ar: the; adj: better; n: man

Capitalization	***When*** first word of the quoted sentence
End Marks	This passage contains 1 end mark. There is 1 main clause. Use a period when a quote makes a statement. Place it inside the closing quotation mark.
Adjective	What kind of man? ***better***
Adverb	Will be when? ***then***
S V Pairs AC	*When **one falls***
MC	***victor will be***
Commas	Use a comma after an adverb clause. **PATTERN AC, MC**
Usage	Use ***then***, the adverb meaning *next* or *immediately after*.

Rewrite It! When one of us falls into the stream, then the victor will be the better man."

Read It! | **Mark It!** | **Fix It!** Day 3

ah its a fair test agreed the stranger. he who is more **adept** with the staff is most certainly the better man

adept
skilled

4 articles (ar)	1 prepositional phrase	1 indent
4 nouns (n)	1 *who/which* clause (w/w)	2 capitals
2 pronouns (pr)	3 [main clauses]	2 commas
3 adjectives (adj)	4 subject-verb pairs (s v)	4 quotations
3 adverbs (adv)		1 end mark
1 interjection		1 apostrophe

¶ "ah, [it's a fair test]," [agreed the stranger]. "[he (who is more **adept** with the staff) is most certainly the better man]."

Indentation	new speaker
Capitalization	***Ah***; ***He*** first word of the quoted sentence
End Marks	This passage contains 2 end marks. There are 3 main clauses. The first quotation and the attribution belong in the same sentence. Use a period when a quote makes a statement. Place it inside the closing quotation mark.
Adjective	What kind of test? ***fair*** What kind of who (he)? ***adept*** The adjective follows the linking verb and describes the subject. What kind of man? ***better***
Adverb	An adverb modifies a verb, an adjective, or another adverb. This sentence has one of each: *certainly* modifies the verb *is*; *more* modifies the adjective *adept*; *most* modifies the adverb *certainly*. Adept to what extent? ***more*** Is how? ***certainly*** Certainly to what extent? ***most***
S V Pairs	MC ***it's*** The contraction *it's* includes both a subject (it) and a verb (is). MC ***stranger agreed*** MC ***He is*** w/w ***who is*** The *who* clause describes *He*, the pronoun it follows.
Commas	Use a comma after an interjection that does not express strong emotion. Use a comma to separate an attribution from a direct quote. **PATTERN "Quote," attribution.**
Apostrophes	*It's* is a contraction. Use an apostrophe to show where letters have been removed.

Rewrite It!

"Ah, it's a fair test," agreed the stranger. "He who is more adept with the staff is most certainly the better man."

Read It!	Mark It!	Fix It! Day 4
the giant **nimbly** twirled his staff above his head, it whistled through the air, as robin stepped onto the log	3 articles (ar)	1 indent
	6 nouns (n)	3 capitals
	1 pronoun (pr)	2 commas
	2 adjectives (adj)	2 end marks
nimbly easily and rapidly	1 adverb (adv)	
	3 prepositional phrases	
	1 adverb clause (AC)	
	2 [main clauses]	
	3 subject-verb pairs (s v)	
	2 openers	

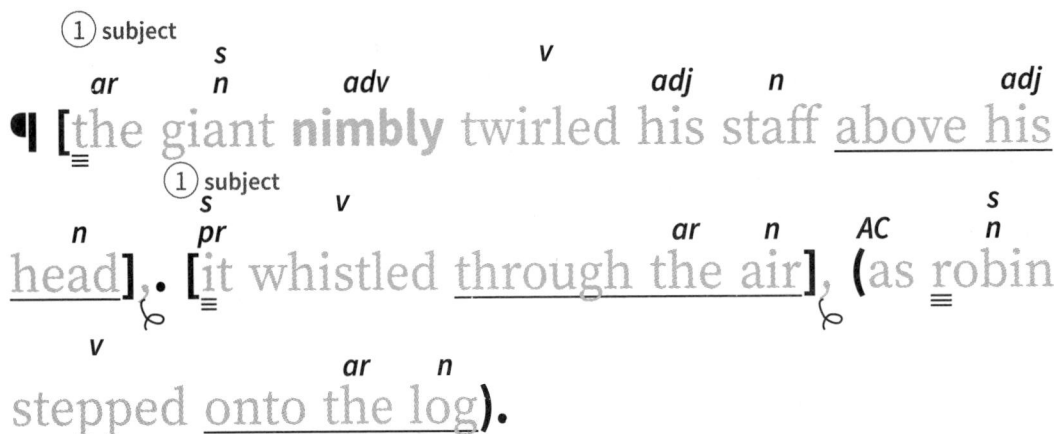

¶ [the giant **nimbly** twirled his staff above his head],. [it whistled through the air], (as robin stepped onto the log).

Indentation		new topic
Capitalization		***The***; ***It*** first word of the sentence ***Robin*** proper noun
End Marks		This passage contains 2 end marks. There are 2 main clauses. Use a period at the end of a statement.
Adjective		Whose staff? ***his*** The possessive pronoun *his* functions as an adjective. Whose head? ***his***
Adverb		Twirled how? ***nimbly***
S V Pairs	MC	***giant twirled***
	MC	***It whistled***
	AC	*as* ***Robin stepped***
Commas		Do not use a comma to connect two main clauses. MC, MC (comma splice) is always wrong. Do not put a comma in front of an adverb clause. **PATTERN MC AC**

Rewrite It! The giant nimbly twirled his staff above his head. It whistled through the air as Robin stepped onto the log.

Learn It!

Possessive Adjective

An **adjective** describes a noun or pronoun.

An adjective tells which one, what kind, how many, or whose.

When a noun is followed by an apostrophe + s, it functions as a possessive adjective and shows ownership. It answers the question *whose.*

Robin marveled at the stranger's skill.

The noun *stranger* is followed by an apostrophe + s. Because *stranger's* functions as a possessive adjective, we call it an adjective, not a noun.
Whose skill? *stranger's*

Without the apostrophe, the noun would be plural.
There are not several *strangers* (plural).

Find It! Look for nouns that show ownership or possession. They will end in *s* and answer the question *whose.*

Fix It! Place an apostrophe before the *s* to show that the noun is functioning as a possessive adjective.

Mark It! Write ***adj*** above each adjective.

adj
The stranger dodged Robin**'**s blow.

Think About It!

Many words can be used as different parts of speech. However, a word can perform only one part of speech at a time.

Plural Noun: The foresters mocked Robin.

In this sentence *foresters* ends with an *s*. The *s* indicates that *foresters* is a plural noun. There is more than one forester.

Possessive Adjective: The forester's mockery angered Robin.

In this sentence *forester's* ends with an apostrophe + *s*. The apostrophe + s indicates that *forester's* is a possessive adjective. Whose mockery? *forester's*

For more information about possessive adjectives, see page G-28.

Ask students to identify the possessive adjective.

Whose blow? ***Robin's***

The apostrophe + s indicates that *Robin's* is a possessive adjective, not a plural noun.

forester's = 1 forester

foresters' = 2+ foresters

In this book, the possessive adjectives are singular and require an apostrophe *s*.

Read It!	Mark It!	Fix It!
quickly robin approached his **adversary** on the bridge he dodged the stranger's staff, and than returned a blow to the strangers head	4 articles (ar) 6 nouns (n) 1 pronoun (pr) 3 adjectives (adj) 2 adverbs (adv) 1 coordinating conjunction (cc) 2 prepositional phrases 2 [main clauses] 2 subject-verb pairs (s v) 2 openers	3 capitals 1 comma 2 end marks 1 usage 1 apostrophe

Day 1

adversary
opponent; someone who opposes or attacks

③ -ly adverb

quickly [robin approached his **adversary** on the bridge]. [he dodged the stranger's staff, and ~~than~~ then returned a blow to the stranger's head].

① subject

Capitalization	***Quickly***; ***He*** first word of the sentence ***Robin*** proper noun
End Marks	This passage contains 2 end marks. There are 2 main clauses. Use a period at the end of a statement.
Adjective	Whose adversary? ***his*** The possessive pronoun *his* functions as an adjective. Whose staff? ***stranger's*** Whose head? ***stranger's*** Change *strangers* to *stranger's*.
Adverb	Approached how? ***quickly*** Returned when? ***then***
S V Pairs MC MC	***Robin approached*** ***He dodged***, ***returned***
Commas	Do not use a comma to separate two verbs connected with a coordinating conjunction if the verbs have the same subject. **PATTERN MC cc 2nd verb** *he dodged* and *returned*
Usage	Use ***then***, the adverb meaning *next* or *immediately after*.
Apostrophes	*Stranger's* is a possessive adjective, not a plural noun. Use an apostrophe to show ownership.

Rewrite It! Quickly Robin approached his adversary on the bridge. He dodged the stranger's staff and then returned a blow to the stranger's head.

Read It!	Mark It!	Fix It!
most would have tumbled into the water but the stranger **parried** robins blow to the right. both men began to sweat	3 articles (ar)	3 capitals
	5 nouns (n)	1 comma
	1 pronoun (pr)	1 end mark
	2 adjectives (adj)	1 apostrophe
parried blocked; warded off	1 coordinating conjunction (cc)	
	2 prepositional phrases	
	3 [main clauses]	
	3 subject-verb pairs (s v)	
	2 openers	

① subject

[most would have tumbled into the water], but [the stranger **parried** robin's blow to the right].

⑥ vss

[both men began to sweat].

Capitalization		***Most***; ***Both*** first word of the sentence ***Robin's*** proper adjective
End Marks		This passage contains 2 end marks. There are 3 main clauses. A comma and coordinating conjunction connect the first and second main clauses. Use a period at the end of a statement.
Adjective		Whose blow? ***Robin's*** Change *Robins* to *Robin's*. Which men? ***both***
S V Pairs	MC	***Most would have tumbled***
	MC	***stranger parried***
	MC	***men began***
Note		*To sweat* is an infinitive. It does not function as a verb.
Commas		Use a comma to separate two main clauses connected with a coordinating conjunction. PATTERN **MC, cc MC** *most would have tumbled,* but *stranger parried*
Apostrophes		*Robin's* is a possessive adjective, not a plural noun. Use an apostrophe to show ownership.

Rewrite It! Most would have tumbled into the water, but the stranger parried Robin's blow to the right. Both men began to sweat.

Read It!	Mark It!	Fix It!
in response the 7-foot man fiercely returned another blow. it would have easily **leveled** a weaker opponent	2 articles (ar)	2 capitals
	4 nouns (n)	1 end mark
	1 pronoun (pr)	1 number
	3 adjectives (adj)	
leveled knocked down	2 adverbs (adv)	
	1 prepositional phrase	
	2 [main clauses]	
	2 subject-verb pairs (s v)	
	2 openers	

(2) prepositional

in response [the ~~7~~ seven-foot man fiercely returned another blow]. [it would have easily **leveled** a weaker opponent].

(1) subject

Capitalization	***In***; ***It*** first word of the sentence
End Marks	This passage contains 2 end marks. There are 2 main clauses. Use a period at the end of a statement.
Adjective	What kind of man? ***seven-foot*** Which blow? ***another*** What kind of opponent? ***weaker***
Adverb	Returned how? ***fiercely*** Would have leveled how? ***easily***
S V Pairs MC	***man returned***
MC	***It would have leveled***

Rewrite It! In response the seven-foot man fiercely returned another blow. It would have easily leveled a weaker opponent.

Read It!	Mark It!	Fix It! Day 4
when robin hood **deftly** pushed the opponents staff to the side he showed him that this was no easy fight	2 articles (ar)	3 capitals
	4 nouns (n)	1 comma
	3 pronouns (pr)	1 end mark
	2 adjectives (adj)	1 apostrophe
deftly skillfully	2 adverbs (adv)	
	1 prepositional phrase	
	1 *that* clause (that)	
	1 adverb clause (AC)	
	1 [main clause]	
	3 subject-verb pairs (s v)	
	1 opener	

(5) clausal

(when robin hood **deftly** pushed the opponent's staff to the side), [he showed him] (that this was no easy fight).

Capitalization	***When*** first word of the sentence ***Robin Hood*** proper noun
End Marks	This passage contains 1 end mark. There is 1 main clause. Use a period at the end of a statement.
Adjective	Whose staff? ***opponent's*** Change *opponents* to *opponent's*. What kind of fight? ***easy***
Adverb	Pushed how? ***deftly*** ***no*** functions as an adverb
S V Pairs AC MC that	*When* ***Robin Hood pushed*** ***he showed*** *that* ***this was***
Commas	Use a comma after an adverb clause. **PATTERN AC, MC**
Apostrophes	*Opponent's* is a possessive adjective, not a plural noun. Use an apostrophe to show ownership.

Rewrite It! When Robin Hood deftly pushed the opponent's staff to the side, he showed him that this was no easy fight.

Learn It!

Adverb Clause

An **adverb clause** is a group of words that begins with a www word and contains a subject and a verb. An adverb clause is a dependent clause, which means it must be added to a sentence that is already complete.

For more information about www words, see page G-13.

Week 8 you learned that an adverb clause begins with a www word. A www word is called a subordinating conjunction. The acronym *www.asia.b* reminds us of the eight most common subordinating conjunctions.

Memorize It! **when while where as since if although because**

These are not the only words that begin an adverb clause. Other words can function as www words too.

Memorize It! **after before until unless whenever whereas than**

A www word must have a subject and verb after it to begin an adverb clause.

Mark It! Place parentheses around the adverb clause and write ***AC*** above the www word. Write ***v*** above each verb and ***s*** above each subject.

AC ***s*** ***v***

The stranger would cross **(**unless Robin stopped him**)**.

Ask students to identify the subject and verb in the adverb clause.

What is the verb?
stopped

Who stopped?
Robin

Adverb Clause or Prepositional Phrase

These words usually begin adverb clauses.

when	while	where	**as**	**since**	if	although	**because**
after	**before**	**until**	unless	whenever	whereas	than	

These words usually begin prepositional phrases.

aboard	around	between	in	opposite	toward
about	**as**	beyond	inside	out	under
above	at	by	instead of	outside	underneath
according to	**because of**	concerning	into	over	unlike
across	**before**	despite	like	past	**until**
after	behind	down	minus	regarding	unto
against	below	during	near	**since**	up, upon
along	beneath	except	of	through	with
amid	beside	for	off	throughout	within
among	besides	from	on, onto	to	without

The words *after, as, because, before, since* and *until* appear on both lists. When you mark the sentences, consider the patterns.

Adverb Clause: (Before they met), Robin won every fight.

Before they met is an adverb clause.
PATTERN www word (Before) + subject (they) + verb (met)

Prepositional Phrase: <u>Before the fight</u> Robin was undefeated.

Before the fight is a prepositional phrase.
PATTERN preposition (Before) + noun (fight) (no verb)

Read It!	Mark It!	Fix It!
after an hour neither had **budged** an inch, both stood where they had begun	2 articles (ar)	1 indent
	2 nouns (n)	1 comma
	3 pronouns (pr)	2 capitals
	1 prepositional phrase	2 end marks
budged moved even slightly	1 adverb clause (AC)	
	2 [main clauses]	
	3 subject-verb pairs (s v)	
	2 openers	

Day 1

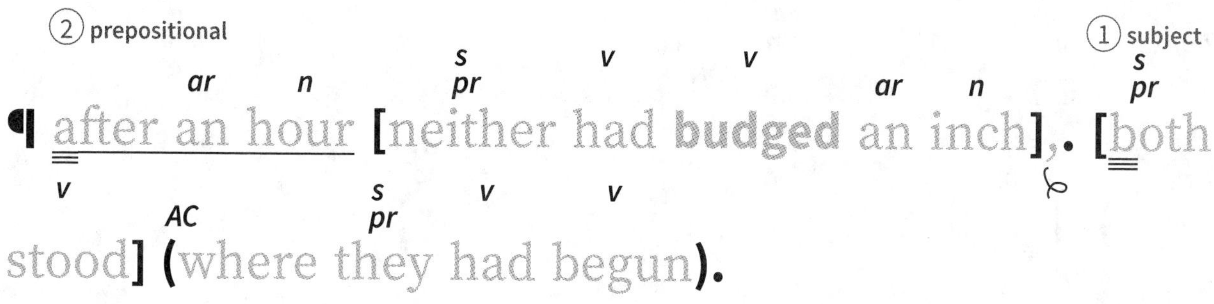

Indentation	new time
Capitalization	***After***; ***Both*** first word of the sentence
End Marks	This passage contains 2 end marks. There are 2 main clauses. Use a period at the end of a statement.
S V Pairs MC	***neither had budged***
MC	***Both stood***
AC	*where* ***they had begun***
Commas	Do not use a comma to connect two main clauses. MC, MC (comma splice) is always wrong.

Rewrite It! After an hour neither had budged an inch. Both stood where they had begun.

Read It! | **Mark It!** | **Fix It!** | Day 2

as they **battled** both men gave, and received many blows until cuts and bruises covered there bodies. each had aching muscles to

battled
fought

6 nouns (n)
2 pronouns (pr)
4 adjectives (adj)
1 adverb (adv)
2 coordinating conjunctions (cc)
2 adverb clauses (AC)
2 [main clauses]
4 subject-verb pairs (s v)
2 openers

2 capitals
2 commas
1 end mark
2 homophones

(5) clausal

(as they **battled**), [both men gave, and received many blows] (until cuts and bruises covered ~~there~~ their bodies). (6) vss [each had aching muscles ~~to~~ too].

Capitalization	***As***; ***Each*** first word of the sentence
End Marks	This passage contains 2 end marks. There are 2 main clauses. Use a period at the end of a statement.
Adjective	Which men? ***both*** How many blows? ***many*** Whose bodies? ***their*** The possessive pronoun *their* functions as an adjective. What kind of muscles? ***aching***
Adverb	***too*** functions as an adverb
S V Pairs	AC *As* ***they battled*** MC ***men gave***, ***received*** AC *until* ***cuts***, ***bruises covered*** MC ***Each had***
Commas	Use a comma after an adverb clause. PATTERN AC, MC Do not use a comma to separate two verbs connected with a coordinating conjunction if the verbs have the same subject. PATTERN MC cc 2nd verb *men gave* and *received* Do not put a comma in front of an adverb clause. PATTERN MC AC Do not use a comma to separate two items connected with a coordinating conjunction. PATTERN a and b *cuts* and *bruises*
Homophones	Use ***their***, the possessive pronoun Use ***too***, which means also in this sentence.

Rewrite It! As they battled, both men gave and received many blows until cuts and bruises covered their bodies. Each had aching muscles too.

Read It!	Mark It!	Fix It!
despite **fatigue** neither considered quitting, or seemed likely to tumble off the bridge	1 article (ar) 3 nouns (n) 1 pronoun (pr) 1 adverb (adv) 1 coordinating conjunction (cc) 2 prepositional phrases 1 [main clause] 1 subject-verb pair (s v) 1 opener	1 capital 1 comma 1 end mark

fatigue
weariness from bodily or mental effort

② prepositional

despite **fatigue** [neither considered quitting, or seemed likely to tumble off the bridge].

Capitalization	***Despite*** first word of the sentence
End Marks	This passage contains 1 end mark. There is 1 main clause. Use a period at the end of a statement.
Noun	*Quitting* functions as a noun. *Quitting* is the thing that neither considered. A word that ends in -ing functions as a verb only if it follows a helping verb. (See Week 13 Day 3.)
Adverb	Seemed to tumble how? ***likely***
S V Pairs MC	***neither considered*, *seemed***
Note	*To tumble* is an infinitive. It does not function as a verb.
Commas	Do not use a comma to separate two verbs connected with a coordinating conjunction if the verbs have the same subject. **PATTERN MC cc 2nd verb** *neither considered* or *seemed*
Note	Because *neither* is a subject, the conjunction *or* is correct. If *neither* were used as a conjunction (neither Robin nor the stranger), then *nor* would be required.

Rewrite It! Despite fatigue neither considered quitting or seemed likely to tumble off the bridge.

Read It!	Mark It!	Fix It!
as the 2 men rested each man **privately** believed that he had never met a more skillful opponent	2 articles (ar)	1 capital
	3 nouns (n)	1 comma
	1 pronoun (pr)	1 end mark
	3 adjectives (adj)	1 number
privately secretly	3 adverbs (adv)	
	1 *that* clause (that)	
	1 adverb clause (AC)	
	1 [main clause]	
	3 subject-verb pairs (s v)	
	1 opener	

⑤ clausal

(as the ~~2~~ two men rested), [each man **privately** believed] (that he had never met a more skillful opponent).

Capitalization	***As*** first word of the sentence
End Marks	This passage contains 1 end mark. There is 1 main clause. Use a period at the end of a statement.
Adjective	How many men? ***two*** Which man? ***each*** What kind of opponent? ***skillful***
Adverb	Believed how? ***privately*** Had met when? ***never*** Skillful to what extent? ***more***
S V Pairs AC	*As **men rested***
MC	***man believed***
that	*that **he had met***
Commas	Use a comma after an adverb clause. PATTERN AC, MC

Rewrite It! As the two men rested, each man privately believed that he had never met a more skillful opponent.

Review It!

Coordinating Conjunction

A **coordinating conjunction** connects the same type of words, phrases, or clauses.

Read each sentence and decide what the coordinating conjunction connects.

If the coordinating conjunction connects main clauses, insert a comma.

If the coordinating conjunction connects three items in a series, insert commas.

Circle the correct comma rule pattern.

MC cc 2nd verb is one application of *a and b*, but the emphasis is different. Use *MC cc 2nd verb* when *a and b* are verbs.

Robin lost the fight, for he was thinking about a lovely maiden.

(MC, cc MC) MC cc 2nd verb a and b a, b, and c

For connects two main clauses: *Robin lost*, for *he was thinking*. Use a comma. MC, cc MC

Maid Marian was a noblewoman and lived in a castle.

MC, cc MC (MC cc 2nd verb) a and b a, b, and c

And connects two verbs: *was* and *lived*. Do not use a comma. MC cc 2nd verb

She had bright eyes and a warm smile.

MC, cc MC MC cc 2nd verb (a and b) a, b, and c

And connects two nouns: *eyes* and *smile*. Do not use a comma. a and b

She could ride skillfully, climb trees, and shoot an arrow straight.

MC, cc MC MC cc 2nd verb a and b (a, b, and c)

And connects three verbs: *ride*, *climb*, and *shoot*. Use two commas. a, b, and c

Maid Marian was courageous and loyal to the men of Sherwood Forest.

MC, cc MC MC cc 2nd verb (a and b) a, b, and c

And connects two adjectives: *courageous* and *loyal*. Do not use a comma. a and b

Maid Marian hated thievery, but she pitied the poor.

(MC, cc MC) MC cc 2nd verb a and b a, b, and c

But connects two main clauses: *Maid Marian hated*, but *she pitied*. Use a comma. MC, cc MC

She was known for her beauty, bravery, and boldness.

MC, cc MC MC cc 2nd verb a and b (a, b, and c)

And connects three nouns: *beauty*, *bravery*, and *boldness*. Use two commas. a, b, and c

Later she married Robin Hood and joined him in Sherwood Forest.

MC, cc MC (MC cc 2nd verb) a and b a, b, and c

And connects two verbs: *married* and *joined*. Do not use a comma. MC cc 2nd verb

Read It!	Mark It!	Fix It! Day 1
although both were wounded the battle continued finally, robin **delivered** a mighty blow, which struck his opponents ribs	2 articles (ar)	1 indent
	4 nouns (n)	3 capitals
	1 pronoun (pr)	1 comma
	3 adjectives (adj)	2 end marks
delivered struck or threw	1 adverb (adv)	1 apostrophe
	1 *who/which* clause (w/w)	
	1 adverb clause (AC)	
	2 [main clauses]	
	4 subject-verb pairs (s v)	
	2 openers	

⑤ clausal

AC, s pr, v, v; ar, s n, v

¶ (although both were wounded), [the battle continued].

③ -ly adverb

adv, s n, v, ar, adj, n, w/w, s, v

finally, [robin **delivered** a mighty blow], (which struck

adj, adj, n

his opponent's ribs).

Indentation	new topic
Capitalization	***Although***; ***Finally*** first word of the sentence ***Robin*** proper noun
End Marks	This passage contains 2 end marks. There are 2 main clauses. Use a period at the end of a statement.
Adjective	What kind of blow? ***mighty*** Whose ribs? ***opponent's*** Change *opponents* to *opponent's*. Whose opponent's ribs? ***his*** The possessive pronoun *his* functions as an adjective.
Adverb	Robin delivered a mighty blow when? ***Finally*** *Finally* is a sentence adverb. It modifies the entire sentence: It was final that Robin delivered a mighty blow. For this reason, it doesn't answer a question about the verb but about the entire sentence. It requires a comma.
S V Pairs AC	*Although* ***both were wounded***
MC	***battle continued***
MC	***Robin delivered***
w/w	***which struck*** The *which* clause describes *blow*, the noun it follows.
Commas	Use a comma after an adverb clause. **PATTERN AC, MC**
Apostrophes	*Opponent's* is a possessive adjective, not a plural noun. Use an apostrophe to show ownership.

Rewrite It! Although both were wounded, the battle continued. Finally, Robin delivered a mighty blow, which struck his opponent's ribs.

Read It!	Mark It!	Fix It! Day 2
instantly the stranger **recovered** raised his arms and brought his staff down on robins head. this caused blood to flow	1 article (ar) 5 nouns (n) 1 pronoun (pr) 3 adjectives (adj) 2 adverbs (adv) 1 coordinating conjunction (cc) 1 prepositional phrase 2 [main clauses] 2 subject-verb pairs (s v) 2 openers	3 capitals 2 commas 1 end mark 1 apostrophe

recovered
regained one's balance or strength

③ -ly adverb

instantly [the stranger **recovered**, raised his arms, and brought his staff down on robin's head]. [this caused blood to flow].

⑥ vss

Capitalization	***Instantly***; ***This*** first word of the sentence ***Robin's*** proper adjective
End Marks	This passage contains 2 end marks. There are 2 main clauses. Use a period at the end of a statement.
Adjective	Whose arms? ***his*** The possessive pronoun *his* functions as an adjective. Whose staff? ***his*** Whose head? ***Robin's*** Change *robins* to *Robin's*.
Adverb	Recovered when? ***instantly*** Brought staff where? ***down***
S V Pairs	MC ***stranger recovered***, ***raised***, ***brought*** MC ***This caused***
Note	*To flow* is an infinitive. It does not function as a verb.
Commas	Use commas to separate three or more items in a series connected with a coordinating conjunction. PATTERN **a, b, and c** *recovered*, *raised*, and *brought*
Apostrophes	*Robin's* is a possessive adjective, not a plural noun. Use an apostrophe to show ownership.

Rewrite It! Instantly the stranger recovered, raised his arms, and brought his staff down on Robin's head. This caused blood to flow.

Read It!	Mark It!	Fix It!
the jolt **inflamed** robin so he swung at the other man. the stranger ducked and avoided robins staff	3 articles (ar)	4 capitals
	5 nouns (n)	1 comma
	1 pronoun (pr)	1 end mark
	2 adjectives (adj)	1 apostrophe
inflamed made angry; incited to violence	2 coordinating conjunctions (cc)	
	1 prepositional phrase	
	3 [main clauses]	
	3 subject-verb pairs (s v)	
	2 openers	

Day 3

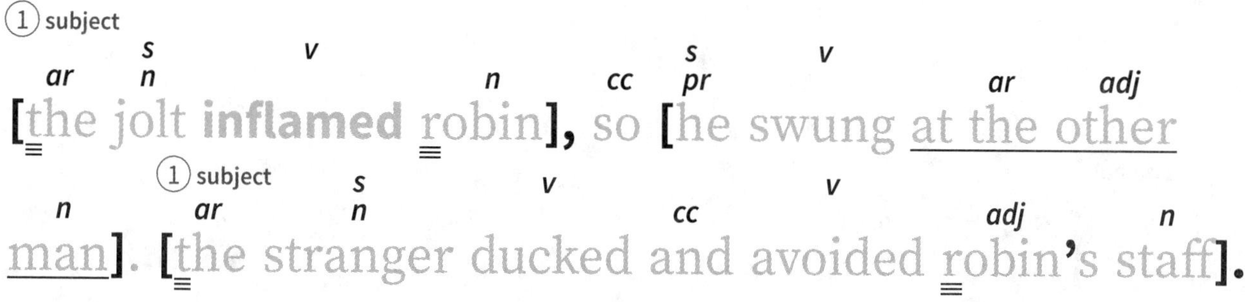

Capitalization		***The***; ***The*** first word of the sentence ***Robin*** proper noun ***Robin's*** proper adjective
End Marks		This passage contains 2 end marks. There are 3 main clauses. A comma and coordinating conjunction connect the first and second main clauses. Use a period at the end of a statement.
Adjective		Which man? ***other*** Whose staff? ***Robin's*** Change *robins* to *Robin's*.
S V Pairs	MC	***jolt inflamed***
	MC	***he swung***
	MC	***stranger ducked***, ***avoided***
Commas		Use a comma to separate two main clauses connected with a coordinating conjunction. **PATTERN MC, cc MC** *jolt inflamed*, so *he swung* Do not use a comma to separate two verbs connected with a coordinating conjunction if the verbs have the same subject. **PATTERN MC cc 2nd verb** *stranger ducked* and *avoided*
Apostrophes		*Robin's* is a possessive adjective, not a plural noun. Use an apostrophe to show ownership.

Rewrite It! The jolt inflamed Robin, so he swung at the other man. The stranger ducked and avoided Robin's staff.

Read It!	Mark It!	Fix It!
at once the stranger **counterattacked**. as robin lost his footing he tumbled into the chilly water	2 articles (ar)	3 capitals
	5 nouns (n)	1 comma
	1 pronoun (pr)	1 end mark
	2 adjectives (adj)	
counterattacked made an attack in reply	2 prepositional phrases	
	1 adverb clause (AC)	
	2 [main clauses]	
	3 subject-verb pairs (s v)	
	2 openers	

② prepositional ⑤ clausal

at once (n) [the (ar) stranger (s n) **counterattacked** (v)]. (as (AC) robin (s n) lost (v) his (adj) footing (n)), [he (s pr) tumbled (v) into the (ar) chilly (adj) water (n)].

Capitalization		***At***; ***As*** first word of the sentence ***Robin*** proper noun
End Marks		This passage contains 2 end marks. There are 2 main clauses. Use a period at the end of a statement.
Noun		*Footing* functions as a noun. *Footing* is the thing that Robin lost. A word that ends in -ing functions as a verb only if it follows a helping verb. (See Week 13 Day 3.)
Adjective		Whose footing? ***his*** The possessive pronoun *his* functions as an adjective. What kind of water? ***chilly***
S V Pairs	MC	***stranger counterattacked***
	AC	*As* ***Robin lost***
	MC	***he tumbled***
Commas		Use a comma after an adverb clause. **PATTERN AC, MC**

Rewrite It! At once the stranger counterattacked. As Robin lost his footing, he tumbled into the chilly water.

Learn It!

Pronoun

A **pronoun** replaces a noun in order to avoid repetition. It refers back to some person or thing recently mentioned and takes the place of that person or thing.

There are many types of pronouns. Week 1 you reviewed **personal pronouns**, which take the place of common and proper nouns. Week 9 you learned **indefinite pronouns**, which do not refer to any particular person or thing. Week 9 you also learned **demonstrative pronouns**, which point to a particular person or thing.

Review the pronoun lists in Appendix III.

A **reflexive pronoun** ends in *-self* (singular) or *-selves* (plural) and refers to the subject of the same sentence.

For more information about reflexive pronouns, see page G-6.

Mark It! Write *pr* above each pronoun.

The men hid themselves (*pr*) in the forest.

Robin stood up for himself (*pr*).

In both sentences the subject and the pronoun following the verb refer to the same person, so the reflexive pronoun is used.

Read It!	Mark It!	Fix It! Day 1
robin was drenched, he heartily laughed at himself, because he knew that he looked **ridiculous**	1 noun (n) 4 pronouns (pr) 2 adjectives (adj) 1 adverb (adv) 1 prepositional phrase 1 *that* clause (that) 1 adverb clause (AC) 2 [main clauses] 4 subject-verb pairs (s v) 2 openers	2 capitals 2 commas 2 end marks

ridiculous
laughable; worthy of mockery

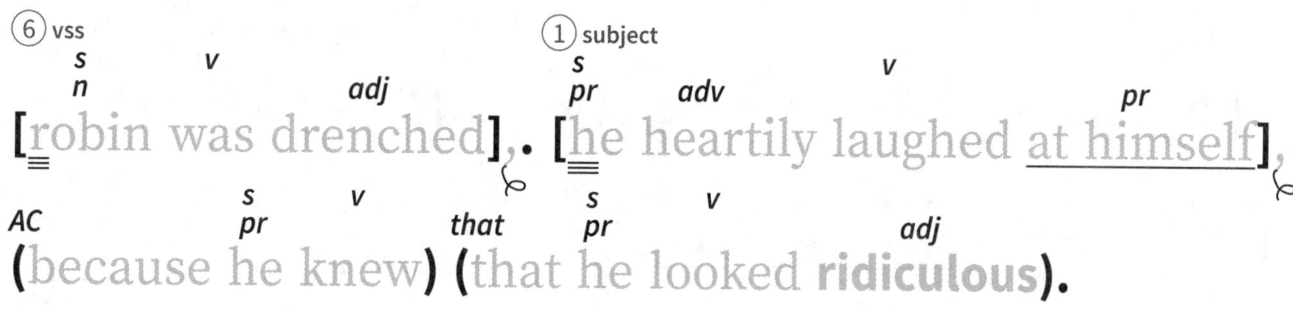

Capitalization		***Robin*** proper noun; first word of the sentence ***He*** first word of the sentence
End Marks		This passage contains 2 end marks. There are 2 main clauses. Use a period at the end of a statement.
Adjective		What kind of Robin? ***drenched*** The adjective follows the linking verb and describes the subject. What kind of he (Robin)? ***ridiculous*** The adjective follows the linking verb and describes the subject.
Adverb		Laughed how? ***heartily***
S V Pairs	MC	***Robin was***
	MC	***He laughed***
	AC	*because* ***he knew***
	that	*that* ***he looked***
Commas		Do not use a comma to connect two main clauses. MC, MC (comma splice) is always wrong. Do not put a comma in front of an adverb clause. **PATTERN MC AC**

Rewrite It! Robin was drenched. He heartily laughed at himself because he knew that he looked ridiculous.

Read It!	Mark It!	Fix It!
the giant **strutted** across the log, and jokingly called ive proven myself the better man with a laugh robin waded too the bank **strutted** walked with a proud attitude	5 articles (ar) 6 nouns (n) 2 pronouns (pr) 1 adjective (adj) 1 adverb (adv) 1 coordinating conjunction (cc) 3 prepositional phrases 3 [main clauses] 3 subject-verb pairs (s v) 2 openers	2 indents 4 capitals 2 commas 2 quotations 2 end marks 1 homophone 1 apostrophe

① subject

¶ [the giant **strutted** across the log, and jokingly called],
"[i've proven myself the better man]." ¶ ② prepositional with a laugh
[robin waded ~~too~~ to the bank].

Indentation	new speaker; new topic
Capitalization	***The***; ***With*** first word of the sentence ***I've*** personal pronoun I; first word of the quoted sentence ***Robin*** proper noun
End Marks	This passage contains 2 end marks. There are 3 main clauses. The attribution and the quotation belong in the same sentence. Use a period when a quote makes a statement. Place it inside the closing quotation mark. Use a period at the end of a statement.
Adjective	What kind of man? ***better***
Adverb	Called how? ***jokingly***
S V Pairs	MC ***giant strutted, called*** MC ***I've proven*** The contraction *I've* includes both a subject (I) and a helping verb (have). MC ***Robin waded***
Commas	Do not use a comma to separate two verbs connected with a coordinating conjunction if the verbs have the same subject. PATTERN **MC cc 2nd verb** *giant strutted* and *called* Use a comma to separate an attribution from a direct quote. PATTERN **Attribution, "Quote."**
Homophones	Use **to**, the preposition.
Apostrophes	*I've* is a contraction. Use an apostrophe to show where letters have been removed.

Rewrite It!

The giant strutted across the log and jokingly called, "I've proven myself the better man."

With a laugh Robin waded to the bank.

Read It!

give me your hand roared the stranger.
i must admit that you **wield** you're staff with great skill

wield
use effectively

Mark It!

1 article (ar)
4 nouns (n)
3 pronouns (pr)
3 adjectives (adj)
1 prepositional phrase
1 *that* clause (that)
3 [main clauses]
4 subject-verb pairs (s v)

Fix It!

1 indent
2 capitals
4 quotations
2 end marks
1 homophone

¶ [(you) "give me your hand]!" [roared the stranger].
"[i must admit] (that you **wield** ~~you're~~ your staff with great skill)."

Indentation	new speaker
Capitalization	***Give*** first word of the quoted sentence ***I*** personal pronoun I; first word of the quoted sentence
End Marks	This passage contains 3 end marks. There are 3 main clauses. The quotation and attribution are separated with an exclamation mark. Use an exclamation mark when a quote expresses strong emotion. **PATTERN "Quote!" attribution.** Use a period when a quote makes a statement. Place it inside the closing quotation mark.
Adjective	Whose hand? ***your*** The possessive pronoun *your* functions as an adjective. Whose staff? ***your*** What kind of skill? ***great***
S V Pairs MC	***(you) Give*** The subject of an imperative sentence is always *you*.
MC	***stranger roared***
MC	***I must admit***
that	*that* ***you wield***
Homophones	Use ***your***, the possessive pronoun.

Rewrite It!

"Give me your hand!" roared the stranger. "I must admit that you wield your staff with great skill."

Read It!	Mark It!	Fix It! Day 4
robin hood then lifted his horn to his lips, and blew 3 short blasts, which **echoed** through the forest	1 article (ar) 5 nouns (n) 4 adjectives (adj) 1 adverb (adv) 1 coordinating conjunction (cc) 2 prepositional phrases 1 *who/which* clause (w/w) 1 [main clause] 2 subject-verb pairs (s v) 1 opener	1 indent 2 capitals 1 comma 1 end mark 1 number

echoed
produced a repetition of a sound

(1) subject

¶ [robin hood then lifted his horn to his lips, and blew ~~3~~ three short blasts], (which **echoed** through the forest).

Indentation	new topic
Capitalization	***Robin Hood*** proper noun; first word of the sentence
End Marks	This passage contains 1 end mark. There is 1 main clause. Use a period at the end of a statement.
Adjective	Whose horn? ***his*** The possessive pronoun *his* functions as an adjective. Whose lips? ***his*** What kind of blasts? ***short*** How many short blasts? ***three***
Adverb	Lifted when? ***then***
S V Pairs MC	***Robin Hood lifted***, ***blew***
w/w	***which echoed*** The *which* clause describes *blasts*, the noun it follows.
Commas	Do not use a comma to separate two verbs connected with a coordinating conjunction if the verbs have the same subject. **PATTERN MC cc 2nd verb** *Robin Hood lifted* and *blew*

Rewrite It! Robin Hood then lifted his horn to his lips and blew three short blasts, which echoed through the forest.

Review It!

Who/Which Clause

A *who/which* clause adds detail to a sentence. It is a dependent clause, which means if you remove the *who/which* clause, you will still have a sentence.

Combine the two sentences by changing one into a *who/which* clause.

The outlaws distrusted the stranger. The outlaws rushed to help Robin.

The outlaws, who distrusted the stranger, rushed to help Robin.

The outlaws, who rushed to help Robin, distrusted the stranger.

If you remove the *who* clause, you still have a sentence: The outlaws rushed to help Robin. The outlaws distrusted the stranger.

The water flowed under the bridge. The water moved swiftly.

The water, which flowed under the bridge, moved swiftly.

The water, which moved swiftly, flowed under the bridge.

If you remove the *which* clause, you still have a sentence: The water moved swiftly. The water flowed under the bridge.

Complete the *who/which* clauses. Remember to include commas. There are multiple right answers.

Robin , who ... , was drenched.

The bridge , which ... , was just a log.

Students should insert a *who* clause after the word Robin and a *which* clause after the word bridge.

The possibilities are endless.

Robin, *who fell into the water*; *who was knocked off the bridge*; *who was laughing*; *who lost the fight*; *who met his match,* was drenched.

The bridge, *which spanned the stream*; *which was sturdy*; *which the men wanted to cross*; *which was wobbly*; *which didn't break,* was just a log.

Read It!	Mark It!	Fix It!
suddenly shouts were heard in the distance. branches **rustled** and 20 strong outlaws burst from there hiding places	1 article (ar)	2 capitals
	5 nouns (n)	1 comma
	4 adjectives (adj)	1 end mark
	1 adverb (adv)	1 homophone
rustled made sounds from being moved or stirred	1 coordinating conjunction (cc)	1 number
	2 prepositional phrases	
	3 [main clauses]	
	3 subject-verb pairs (s v)	
	2 openers	

Day 1

(3) -ly adverb

adv s/n v v ar n

suddenly [shouts were heard in the distance].

(1) subject s/n v cc adj twenty adj s/n v

[branches **rustled**], and [~~20~~ strong outlaws burst

adj their adj n

from ~~there~~ hiding places].

Capitalization	***Suddenly***; ***Branches*** first word of the sentence
End Marks	This passage contains 2 end marks. There are 3 main clauses. A comma and coordinating conjunction connect the second and third main clauses. Use a period at the end of a statement.
Adjective	What kind of outlaws? ***strong*** How many strong outlaws? ***twenty*** What kind of places? ***hiding*** Whose hiding places? ***their*** The possessive pronoun *their* functions as an adjective.
Adverb	Were heard when? ***Suddenly***
S V Pairs	MC ***shouts were heard*** MC ***Branches rustled*** MC ***outlaws burst***
Commas	Use a comma to separate two main clauses connected with a coordinating conjunction. **PATTERN MC, cc MC** *Branches rustled*, and *outlaws burst*
Homophones	Use ***their***, the possessive pronoun.

Rewrite It! Suddenly shouts were heard in the distance. Branches rustled, and twenty strong outlaws burst from their hiding places.

Read It!	Mark It!	Fix It!
will stutely, who was robins **steadfast** friend, immediately cried robin youre drenched from head two foot	5 nouns (n)	1 indent
	1 pronoun (pr)	4 capitals
	3 adjectives (adj)	2 commas
	1 adverb (adv)	2 quotations
steadfast	2 prepositional phrases	1 end mark
unwavering; loyal	1 *who/which* clause (w/w)	1 homophone
	2 [main clauses]	2 apostrophes
	3 subject-verb pairs (s v)	
	1 opener	

Day 2

(1) subject

¶ [will stutely, (who was robin's **steadfast** friend), immediately cried], "robin, [you're drenched from head ~~two~~ to foot]!"

Indentation	new speaker
Capitalization	***Will Stutely*** proper noun; first word of the sentence ***Robin's*** proper adjective ***Robin*** proper noun; first word of the quoted sentence
End Marks	This passage contains 1 end mark. There are 2 main clauses. The attribution and the quotation belong in the same sentence. Use a period when a quote makes a statement. Place it inside the closing quotation mark.
Adjective	What kind of friend? ***steadfast*** Whose steadfast friend? ***Robin's*** Change *robins* to *Robin's*. What kind of you (Robin)? ***drenched*** The adjective follows the linking verb and describes the subject.
Adverb	Cried when? ***immediately***
S V Pairs MC	***Will Stutely cried***
w/w	***who was*** The *who* clause describes *Will Stutely*, the noun it follows.
MC	***you're*** The contraction *you're* includes both a subject (you) and a verb (are).
Commas	Use a comma to separate an attribution from a direct quote. PATTERN **Attribution, "Quote."** Place commas around a noun of direct address (NDA). ***Robin,***
Homophones	Use ***to***, the preposition.
Apostrophes	*Robin's* is a possessive adjective, not a plural noun. Use an apostrophe to show ownership. *You're* is a contraction. Use an apostrophe to show where letters have been removed.

Rewrite It!

Will Stutely, who was Robin's steadfast friend, immediately cried, "Robin, you're drenched from head to foot!"

Read It!	Mark It!	Fix It!
with a twinkle in his eye, robin answered i certainly am this **rugged** fellow knocked me into the water, after he gave me a beating	3 articles (ar) 6 nouns (n) 4 pronouns (pr) 3 adjectives (adj) 1 adverb (adv) 3 prepositional phrases 1 adverb clause (AC) 3 [main clauses] 4 subject-verb pairs (s v) 1 opener	1 indent 4 capitals 2 commas 2 quotations 2 end marks

rugged
rough, harsh, or stern

(2) prepositional

¶ with a twinkle in his eye, [robin answered], "[i certainly am]. [this **rugged** fellow knocked me into the water], (after he gave me a beating)."

Indentation	new speaker
Capitalization	***With*** first word of the sentence ***Robin*** proper noun ***I*** personal pronoun I; first word of the quoted sentence ***This*** first word of the quoted sentence
End Marks	This passage contains 2 end marks. There are 3 main clauses. The attribution and the first sentence of the quotation belong together. Use a period when a quote makes a statement. Place it inside the closing quotation mark.
Noun	*Beating* follows the article *a*, so it functions as a noun. *Beating* is the thing that the fellow gave Robin.
Adjective	Whose eye? ***his*** The possessive pronoun *his* functions as an adjective. What kind of fellow? ***rugged*** Which rugged fellow? ***This***
Adverb	Am to what extent? ***certainly***
S V Pairs	MC ***Robin answered*** MC ***I am*** MC ***fellow knocked*** AC *after* ***he gave***
Commas	Use a comma to separate an attribution from a direct quote. PATTERN Attribution, "Quote." Do not put a comma in front of an adverb clause. PATTERN MC AC

Rewrite It!

With a twinkle in his eye, Robin answered, "I certainly am. This rugged fellow knocked me into the water after he gave me a beating."

Read It!	Mark It!	Fix It! Day 4
he needs a beating himself cried will. before robin could stop them his men **pounced** on the stranger, who's strength was not a match for 20 men	3 articles (ar)	2 indents
	8 nouns (n)	4 capitals
	4 pronouns (pr)	1 comma
pounced	2 adjectives (adj)	2 quotations
seized suddenly	1 adverb (adv)	2 end marks
	2 prepositional phrases	1 homophone
	1 *who/which* clause (w/w)	1 number
	1 adverb clause (AC)	
	3 [main clauses]	
	5 subject-verb pairs (s v)	
	1 opener	

(1) subject

s v v s
pr ar n pr n AC

¶ "[he needs a beating himself]!" [cried will]. ¶ (before

s v v s v
n pr adj n ar

robin could stop them), [his men **pounced** on the

pr s v adj
n w/w whose n adv ar n twenty n

stranger], (~~who's~~ strength was not a match for ~~20~~ men).

Indentation	new speaker; new topic
Capitalization	***He***; ***Before*** first word of the quoted sentence ***Will***; ***Robin*** proper noun
End Marks	This passage contains 3 end marks. There are 3 main clauses. The quotation and the attribution are separated with an exclamation mark. Use an exclamation mark when a quote expresses strong emotion. PATTERN **"Quote!" attribution.** Use a period at the end of a statement.
Noun	In this sentence *beating* follows the article *a*, so it functions as a noun.
Adjective	Whose twenty men? ***his*** The possessive pronoun *his* functions as an adjective. How many men? ***twenty***
Adverb	***not*** functions as an adverb
S V Pairs MC	***He needs***
MC	***Will cried***
AC	*Before* ***Robin could stop***
MC	***men pounced***
w/w	*whose* ***strength was*** The *whose* clause describes *stranger*, the noun it follows.
Commas	Use a comma after an adverb clause. PATTERN **AC, MC**
Homophones	Use ***whose***, the possessive pronoun.

Rewrite It!

"He needs a beating himself!" cried Will.

Before Robin could stop them, his men pounced on the stranger, whose strength was not a match for twenty men.

Review It!

Strong Verb, Quality Adjective, and -ly Adverb

A strong verb, a quality adjective, and an -ly adverb are three different ways to dress up writing. These stylistic devices add a strong image and feeling.

A **strong verb** is an action verb, never a linking or helping verb.

A **quality adjective** is more specific than a weak adjective. A weak adjective is overused, boring, or vague.

An **-ly adverb** is used to enhance the meaning of the verb, adjective, or adverb that it modifies.

Answers will vary.

Discuss with your students how the strong word changes the meaning. For example, *traveled* implies they are on a journey, while *rushed* and *hurried* suggest quick action.

Underline the weak word in the sentence and circle a stronger word in the list below. Think about the meaning of the words in the context of the sentence.

One word in each list is a weak substitute.

The outlaws ran to Robin's aid.

fled traveled hopped hurried rushed

The outlaws would not *hop* (move in bouncing leaps) to Robin's aid.

The hungry men ate a hearty stew.

slurped devoured consumed nibbled feasted on

Hungry men do not *nibble* (eat in small pieces) their food.

The stranger was big.

broad gigantic towering roomy huge

A place can be *roomy*, but not a person (the stranger).

Robin was a good man.

noble delicious admirable impressive hardworking

Food, not a person (Robin), is *delicious*.

He was awfully wet.

very noticeably surprisingly thoroughly uncommonly

Very is not an -ly adverb, and it does not add a strong image or feeling.

Continue to look for strong verbs, quality adjectives, and -ly adverbs in this book and write them on the collection pages found in Appendix II.

Read It!	Mark It!	Fix It!
although the giant moved quickly robins men dragged him to the water, he **struggled** furiously	2 articles (ar)	3 capitals
	3 nouns (n)	2 commas
	2 pronouns (pr)	2 end marks
	1 adjective (adj)	1 apostrophe
struggled fought with an opponent or adversary	2 adverbs (adv)	
	1 prepositional phrase	
	1 adverb clause (AC)	
	2 [main clauses]	
	3 subject-verb pairs (s v)	
	2 openers	

Day 1

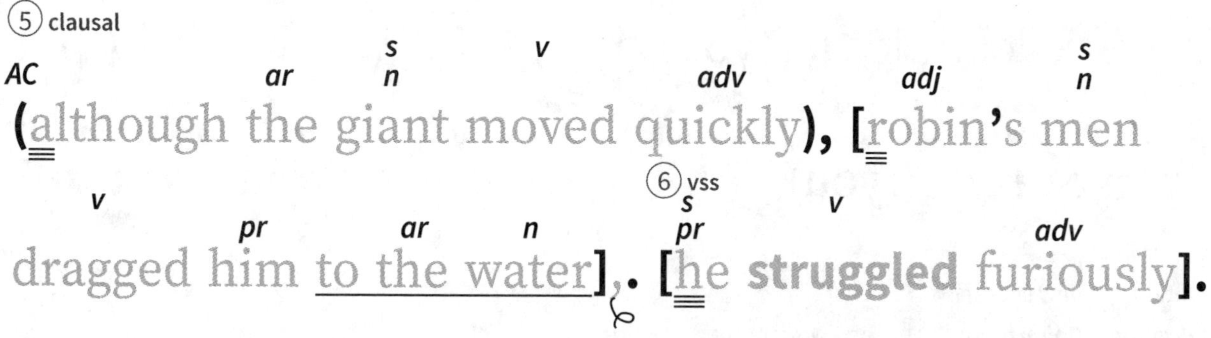

Capitalization	***Although***; ***He*** first word of the sentence ***Robin's*** proper adjective
End Marks	This passage contains 2 end marks. There are 2 main clauses. Use a period at the end of a statement.
Adjective	Whose men? ***Robin's*** Change *robins* to *Robin's*.
Adverb	Moved how? ***quickly*** Struggled how? ***furiously***
S V Pairs AC	*Although* ***giant moved***
MC	***men dragged***
MC	***He struggled***
Commas	Use a comma after an adverb clause. **PATTERN AC, MC** Do not use a comma to connect two main clauses. MC, MC (comma splice) is always wrong.
Apostrophes	***Robin's*** is a possessive adjective, not a plural noun. Use an apostrophe to show ownership.

Rewrite It! Although the giant moved quickly, Robin's men dragged him to the water. He struggled furiously.

Read It!	Mark It!	Fix It! Day 2
robin exclaimed stop! it was a fight that he won fairly. dont harm this **blameless** man	1 article (ar)	1 indent
	3 nouns (n)	4 capitals
	2 pronouns (pr)	1 comma
	2 adjectives (adj)	2 quotations
blameless guiltless or faultless	2 adverbs (adv)	1 end mark
	1 *that* clause (that)	1 apostrophe
	4 [main clauses]	
	5 subject-verb pairs (s v)	
	1 opener	

(1) subject

¶ [robin exclaimed], [(you) "stop]! [it was a fight] (that he won fairly). [(you) don't harm this **blameless** man]!"

Indentation	new speaker
Capitalization	***Robin*** proper noun; first word of the sentence ***Stop***; ***It***; ***Don't*** first word of the quoted sentence
End Marks	This passage contains 3 end marks. There are 4 main clauses. The attribution and the first sentence of the quotation belong together. Use an exclamation mark when a quote expresses strong emotion.
Adjective	What kind of man? ***blameless*** Which blameless man? ***this***
Adverb	Won how? ***fairly*** ***n't*** the contraction for *not* functions as an adverb
S V Pairs MC	***Robin exclaimed***
MC	***(you) Stop*** The subject of an imperative sentence is always *you*.
MC	***It was***
that	*that* ***he won***
MC	***(you) Do harm*** The subject of an imperative sentence is always *you*.
Commas	Use a comma to separate an attribution from a direct quote. **PATTERN Attribution, "Quote!"**
Apostrophes	*Don't* is a contraction. Use an apostrophe to show where letters have been removed.

Rewrite It! Robin exclaimed, "Stop! It was a fight that he won fairly. Don't harm this blameless man!"

Read It!	Mark It!	Fix It!
robin than bowed to the stranger, and **introduced** himself. i am the outlaw robin hood and this is my band of merry men	2 articles (ar)	1 indent
	6 nouns (n)	4 capitals
	3 pronouns (pr)	2 commas
	2 adjectives (adj)	1 quotation
introduced presented a person to another person	1 adverb (adv)	1 end mark
	2 coordinating conjunctions (cc)	1 usage
	2 prepositional phrases	
	3 [main clauses]	
	3 subject-verb pairs (s v)	
	1 opener	

① subject

¶ [robin ~~than~~ then bowed to the stranger, and **introduced** himself.] "[i am the outlaw robin hood], and [this is my band of merry men].

No closing quotation mark because quote continues.

Indentation	new topic
Capitalization	***Robin*** proper noun; first word of the sentence ***I*** personal pronoun I; first word of the quoted sentence ***Robin Hood*** proper noun
End Marks	This passage contains 2 end marks. There are 3 main clauses. *Robin then bowed ... himself* is a complete thought. It is not an attribution. For this reason, it requires a period. Use a period at the end of a statement. Use a period when a quote makes a statement.
Adjective	Whose band? ***my*** The possessive pronoun *my* functions as an adjective. What kind of men? ***merry***
Adverb	Bowed when? ***then***
S V Pairs	MC ***Robin bowed**, **introduced*** MC ***I am*** MC ***this is***
Commas	Do not use a comma to separate two verbs connected with a coordinating conjunction if the verbs have the same subject. **PATTERN MC cc 2nd verb** *Robin bowed* and *introduced* Use a comma to separate two main clauses connected with a coordinating conjunction. **PATTERN MC, cc MC** *I am*, and *this is*
Usage	Use ***then***, the adverb meaning *next* or *immediately after*.

Rewrite It!

Robin then bowed to the stranger and introduced himself. "I am the outlaw Robin Hood, and this is my band of merry men.

Read It! | **Mark It!** | **Fix It!** Day 4

stranger will you stay with me and be one of us? if youll join me i will **appoint** you my right-hand man

appoint
name or assign to a position

2 nouns (n)
8 pronouns (pr)
2 adjectives (adj)
1 coordinating conjunction (cc)
2 prepositional phrases
1 adverb clause (AC)
2 [main clauses]
3 subject-verb pairs (s v)

3 capitals
2 commas
1 quotation
1 end mark
1 apostrophe

No opening quotation mark because quote continues.

stranger, [will you stay with me and be one of us]? (if you'll join me), [i will **appoint** you my right-hand man]."

Capitalization	***Stranger***; ***If*** first word of the quoted sentence ***I*** personal pronoun I
End Marks	This passage contains 2 end marks. There are 2 main clauses. Use a period when a quotation makes a statement. Place it inside the closing quotation mark.
Adjective	What kind of man? ***right-hand*** Whose right-hand man? ***my*** The possessive pronoun *my* functions as an adjective.
S V Pairs MC	***you will stay, be***
AC	*If* ***you'll join*** The contraction *you'll* includes both a subject (you) and a helping verb (will).
MC	***I will appoint***
Commas	Place commas around a noun of direct address (NDA). ***Stranger,*** Do not use a comma to separate two verbs connected with a coordinating conjunction if the verbs have the same subject. PATTERN **MC cc 2nd verb** *you stay* and *be* Use a comma after an adverb clause. PATTERN **AC, MC**
Apostrophes	*You'll* is a contraction. Use an apostrophe to show where letters have been removed.

Rewrite It! Stranger, will you stay with me and be one of us? If you'll join me, I will appoint you my right-hand man."

Learn It!

Adjective

Week 3 you learned that an adjective describes a noun or pronoun.

Often, two or more adjectives come before a noun. The adjectives are **coordinate** if each adjective independently describes the noun that follows.

For more information about coordinate adjectives, see page G-14.

Comma

A **comma** is used to separate items in a sentence. Use a comma to separate coordinate adjectives. Because the order of coordinate adjectives is not important, the adjectives are separated with a comma.

Use a comma to separate coordinate adjectives.

Two tests help determine whether the adjectives before a noun are coordinate.

Can you reverse their order?

Can you add *and* between them?

If you answer yes, the adjectives are coordinate. Use a comma.

Coordinate adjectives independently describe the noun.

adj *adj* *n*

They entered the untouched thick forest.

The two adjectives *untouched* and *thick* describe the noun *forest*.

Are they coordinate adjectives? Do they need a comma?

Reverse the order.

... the thick untouched forest. Yes, you can reverse the order.

Add *and* between the adjectives.

... the untouched and thick forest. Yes, you can add *and*.

They entered a forest that was both an untouched forest and a thick forest.

adj *adj* *n*

They entered the untouched**,** thick forest.

Thick and *untouched* are coordinate adjectives and separated with a comma.

When two adjectives come before a noun, have students test the adjectives by reversing their order and by adding *and* between them. If yes to the tests, then yes to a comma.

Fix It! Add a comma between coordinate adjectives.

adj *adj*

Marian was a courageous**,** thoughtful maiden.

Reverse order: a thoughtful courageous maiden. Yes, you can reverse the order.

Add *and*: a courageous and thoughtful maiden. Yes, you can add *and*.

These are coordinate adjectives. A comma is needed.

Read It!	Mark It!	Fix It!
the stranger, who was still annoyed because of his unjust harsh **thrashing**, did not readily agree	1 article (ar)	1 indent
	2 nouns (n)	1 capital
	4 adjectives (adj)	1 comma
	3 adverbs (adv)	1 end mark
thrashing whipping	1 prepositional phrase	
	1 *who/which* clause (w/w)	
	1 [main clause]	
	2 subject-verb pairs (s v)	
	1 opener	

(1) subject

¶ [the stranger, (who was still annoyed because of his unjust, harsh **thrashing**), did not readily agree].

Indentation	new topic
Capitalization	***The*** first word of the sentence
End Marks	This passage contains 1 end mark. There is 1 main clause. Use a period at the end of a statement.
Noun	*Thrashing* functions as a noun. *Thrashing* is the thing that annoyed him. A word that ends in -ing functions as a verb only if it follows a helping verb. (See Week 13 Day 3.)
Adjective	What kind of who (stranger)? ***annoyed*** The adjective follows the linking verb and describes the subject. What kind of thrashing? ***unjust***, ***harsh*** Whose unjust, harsh thrashing? ***his***
Adverb	Annoyed when? ***still*** ***not*** functions as an adverb Did not agree how? ***readily***
S V Pairs MC	***stranger did agree***
w/w	***who was*** The *who* clause describes *stranger*, the noun it follows.
Commas	Use a comma to separate coordinate adjectives (unjust, harsh thrashing).

Rewrite It! The stranger, who was still annoyed because of his unjust, harsh thrashing, did not readily agree.

Read It! | **Mark It!** | **Fix It!** Day 2

can you handle your bow and arrows better then you handle your long thick staff? if you cant i wont join your **motley** band he retorted

motley
made up of varying elements or members

4 nouns (n)	2 adverb clauses (AC)	3 capitals
5 pronouns (pr)	3 [main clauses]	3 commas
6 adjectives (adj)	5 subject-verb pairs (s v)	2 quotations
3 adverbs (adv)		1 end mark
1 coordinating conjunction (cc)		1 usage
		2 apostrophes

"[Can you handle your bow and arrows better] (~~then~~ than you handle your long, thick staff)? (If you can't), [I won't join your **motley** band]," [he retorted].

Capitalization	***Can***; ***If*** first word of the quoted sentence ***I*** personal pronoun I
End Marks	This passage contains 2 end marks. There are 3 main clauses. The second sentence of the quotation and the attribution belong in the same sentence. Use a period at the end of a statement.
Adjective	Whose bow and arrows? ***your*** The possessive pronoun *your* functions as an adjective. What kind of staff? ***long***, ***thick*** Whose long, thick staff? ***your*** What kind of band? ***motley*** Whose motley band? ***your***
Adverb	Can handle how? ***better*** ***n't***; ***n't*** the contraction for *not* functions as an adverb
S V Pairs	MC ***you Can handle*** — AC ***If you can*** — MC ***he retorted*** AC *than* ***you handle*** — MC ***I will join*** The contraction *won't* includes both a helping verb (will) and an adverb (not).
Commas	Do not use a comma to separate two items connected with a coordinating conjunction. **PATTERN a and b** *bow* and *arrows* Do not put a comma in front of an adverb clause. **PATTERN MC AC** Use a comma to separate coordinate adjectives (long, thick staff). Use a comma after an adverb clause. **PATTERN AC, MC** Use a comma to separate a direct quote from an attribution. **PATTERN "Quote," attribution.**
Usage	Use ***than***, a word to show comparison. In this sentence *than* functions as a www word because a subject and verb follow it.
Apostrophes	*Can't* and *won't* are contractions. Use apostrophes to show where letters have been removed.

Rewrite It! "Can you handle your bow and arrows better than you handle your long, thick staff? If you can't, I won't join your motley band," he retorted.

Read It!	Mark It!		Fix It! Day 3
robin laughed to himself, with encouragement from his faithful **devoted** men, robin accepted the challenge	1 article (ar)	2 [main clauses]	1 indent
	5 nouns (n)	2 subject-verb pairs (s v)	3 capitals
devoted	1 pronoun (pr)	2 openers	2 commas
loyal, deeply attached	3 adjectives (adj)		2 end marks
	3 prepositional phrases		

(6) vss (2) prepositional

¶ [robin laughed to himself], . with encouragement from his faithful, **devoted** men, [robin accepted the challenge].

Indentation	new topic
Capitalization	***Robin*** proper noun; first word of the sentence ***With*** first word of the sentence ***Robin*** proper noun
End Marks	This passage contains 2 end marks. There are 2 main clauses. Use a period at the end of a statement.
Adjective	What kind of men? ***faithful***, ***devoted*** Whose faithful, devoted men? ***his*** The possessive pronoun *his* functions as an adjective.
S V Pairs	MC ***Robin laughed*** MC ***Robin accepted***
Commas	Do not use a comma to separate two main clauses. Use a period. MC, MC is always wrong. Use a comma to separate coordinate adjectives (faithful, devoted men).

Rewrite It!

Robin laughed to himself. With encouragement from his faithful, devoted men, Robin accepted the challenge.

Read It!	Mark It!	Fix It! Day 4
he may have lost the lengthy painful **bout** with his staff but he knew that he could win a contest with his bow and arrows	2 articles (ar)	1 capital
	5 nouns (n)	2 commas
	3 pronouns (pr)	1 end mark
	4 adjectives (adj)	
bout contest of strength	2 coordinating conjunctions (cc)	
	2 prepositional phrases	
	1 *that* clause (that)	
	2 [main clauses]	
	3 subject-verb pairs (s v)	
	1 opener	

① subject

s v v v / pr ar adj adj n

[he may have lost the lengthy, painful **bout**

adj n cc s pr v that s pr v

with his staff], but [he knew] (that he could

v ar n adj n cc n

win a contest with his bow and arrows).

Capitalization	***He*** first word of the sentence
End Marks	This passage contains 1 end mark. There are 2 main clauses. A comma and coordinating conjunction connect the main clauses. Use a period at the end of a statement.
Adjective	What kind of bout? ***lengthy***, ***painful*** Whose staff? ***his*** The possessive pronoun *his* functions as an adjective. Whose bow and arrows? ***his***
S V Pairs MC	***He may have lost***
MC	***he knew***
that	*that* ***he could win***
Commas	Use a comma to separate coordinate adjectives (lengthy, painful bout). Use a comma to separate two main clauses connected with a coordinating conjunction. **PATTERN MC, cc MC** *He may have lost*, but *he knew* Do not use a comma to separate two items connected with a coordinating conjunction. **PATTERN a and b** *bow* and *arrows*

Rewrite It! He may have lost the lengthy, painful bout with his staff, but he knew that he could win a contest with his bow and arrows.

Learn It!

Adjective

Week 3 you learned that an adjective describes a noun or pronoun.

Often, two or more adjectives come before a noun. Week 25 you learned that adjectives are **coordinate** if each adjective independently describes the noun that follows. Because the order of the coordinate adjectives is not important, the adjectives are separated with a comma.

Adjectives are **cumulative** if the first adjective describes the second adjective and the noun that follows. Cumulative adjectives follow this specific order: quantity, opinion, size, age, shape, color, origin, material, purpose.

For more information about cumulative adjectives, see page G-14.

Comma

Because cumulative adjectives must be arranged in a specific order, the adjectives are not separated with a comma.

Do not use a comma to separate cumulative adjectives.

Cumulative adjectives build on each other.

Two tests help determine whether the adjectives before a noun are coordinate or cumulative.

Can you reverse their order?

Can you add *and* between them?

If you answer yes, the adjectives are coordinate. Use a comma.
If you answer no, the adjectives are cumulative. Do not use a comma.

adj *adj* *n*
They entered the immense green forest.

The two adjectives *immense* and *green* describe the noun *forest.*

Are they coordinate adjectives? Do they need a comma?

Reverse the order.

... the green immense forest.

No, you cannot reverse the order: size comes before color.

Add *and* between the adjectives.

... immense and green forest.

No, you cannot add *and.*

adj *adj* *n*
They entered the immense green forest.

Immense and *green* are cumulative adjectives and are not separated with a comma.

The first adjective (immense) describes the second adjective and the noun together (green forest).

They entered a green forest that was immense, not an immense forest that was also a green forest.

When two adjectives come before a noun, have students test the adjectives by reversing their order and by adding *and* between them. If no to the tests, then no to a comma.

Fix It! Remove the comma between cumulative adjectives.

adj *adj*
Marian was a brave, young maiden.

Reverse order: a young brave maiden. No, you cannot reverse the order: opinion comes before age.

Add *and*: a brave and young maiden. No, you cannot add *and.*

These are cumulative adjectives. A comma is not needed.

Think About It!

Adjectives can be grouped into categories. Cumulative adjectives follow this specific order: quantity, opinion, size, age, shape, color, origin, material, purpose.

Categories	***Some Examples***		
quantity	three	several	few
opinion	proficient	funny	smart
size	long	small	huge
age	old	young	ancient
shape	circular	curvy	square
color	red	blue	green
origin	English	African	Catholic
material	wooden	plastic	cotton
purpose	bullseye (target)	frying (pan)	baseball (glove)

Cumulative adjectives build on each other. Robin was a *skilled English* archer. He practiced with *several proficient young* men. If someone said he practiced with *young proficient several* men, your ear would tell you that was wrong. That is why the tests work. We have been trained to hear and say adjectives in a certain order, and if you try to rearrange the order of the adjectives, it sounds awkward.

Robin was a skilled English archer.

Skilled comes before *English* because *opinion* comes before *origin.*

He practiced with *several proficient young* men.

Quantity comes before *opinion,* and *opinion* comes before *age.*

They shot *long wooden* arrows.

Size comes before *material.*

They aimed at a *circular bullseye* target.

Shape comes before *purpose.*

Read It!	Mark It!	Fix It! Day 1
robin **instructed** will stutely to make a target from smooth, white bark, which measured 4 fingers in height and 5 fingers in width	1 article (ar)	1 indent
	8 nouns (n)	3 capitals
	4 adjectives (adj)	1 comma
	1 coordinating conjunction (cc)	1 end mark
instructed gave orders or directions	3 prepositional phrases	2 numbers
	1 *who/which* clause (which)	
	1 [main clause]	
	2 subject-verb pairs (s v)	
	1 opener	

① subject

¶ [robin **instructed** will stutely to make a target from smooth, white bark], (which measured 4 fingers in height and 5 fingers in width).

Indentation	new topic
Capitalization	***Robin*** proper noun; first word of the sentence ***Will Stutely*** proper noun
End Marks	This passage contains 1 end mark. There is 1 main clause. Use a period at the end of a statement.
Adjective	What kind of bark? ***white*** What kind of white bark? ***smooth*** How many fingers? ***four*** How many fingers? ***five***
S V Pairs MC	***Robin instructed***
w/w	***which measured*** The *which* clause describes *bark*, the noun it follows.
Note	*To make* is an infinitive. It does not function as a verb.
Commas	Do not use a comma to separate cumulative adjectives (smooth white bark). Do not use a comma to separate two items connected with a coordinating conjunction. **PATTERN a and b** *four fingers* and *five fingers*

Rewrite It!

Robin instructed Will Stutely to make a target from smooth white bark, which measured four fingers in height and five fingers in width.

Read It!	Mark It!	Fix It! Day 2
carefully will positioned robin and the stranger for the contest he than **paced** the distance to a large, old, oak tree	4 articles (ar)	4 capitals
	6 nouns (n)	2 commas
	1 pronoun (pr)	2 end marks
	3 adjectives (adj)	1 usage
paced measured a distance by walking and counting the number of steps taken	2 adverbs (adv)	
	1 coordinating conjunction (cc)	
	2 prepositional phrases	
	2 [main clauses]	
	2 subject-verb pairs (s v)	
	2 openers	

③ -ly adverb

adv s n v n cc ar n

carefully [will positioned robin and the stranger

① subject

ar n s pr adv then v ar n

for the contest]. [he ~~than~~ **paced** the distance

ar adj adj adj n

to a large, old, oak tree].

Capitalization		***Carefully***; ***He*** first word of the sentence ***Will***; ***Robin*** proper noun
End Marks		This passage contains 2 end marks. There are 2 main clauses. Use a period at the end of a statement.
Adjective		What kind of tree? ***oak*** What kind of oak tree? ***old*** What kind of old oak tree? ***large***
Adverb		Positioned how? ***Carefully*** Paced when? ***then***
S V Pairs	MC MC	***Will positioned*** ***He paced***
Commas		Do not use a comma to separate two items connected with a coordinating conjunction. **PATTERN a and b** *Robin* and *stranger* Do not use a comma to separate cumulative adjectives (large old oak tree).
Usage		Use ***then***, the adverb meaning *next* or *immediately after*.

Rewrite It! Carefully Will positioned Robin and the stranger for the contest. He then paced the distance to a large old oak tree.

Read It!	Mark It!	Fix It! Day 3
while will nailed the target to the tree the stranger chose a straight, wooden arrow from robins **quiver**	4 articles (ar)	3 capitals
	6 nouns (n)	2 commas
	3 adjectives (adj)	1 end mark
	2 prepositional phrases	1 apostrophe
quiver a container for holding arrows	1 adverb clause (AC)	
	1 [main clause]	
	2 subject-verb pairs (s v)	
	1 opener	

⑤ clausal

AC (while will nailed the target to the tree), [the stranger chose a straight, wooden arrow from robin's **quiver**].

Capitalization	***While*** first word of the sentence ***Will*** proper noun ***Robin's*** proper adjective
End Marks	This passage contains 1 end mark. There is 1 main clause. Use a period at the end of a statement.
Adjective	What kind of arrow? ***wooden*** What kind of wooden arrow? ***straight*** Whose quiver? ***Robin's*** Change *robins* to *Robin's*.
S V Pairs AC	*While* ***Will nailed***
MC	***stranger chose***
Commas	Use a comma after an adverb clause. **PATTERN AC, MC** Do not use a comma to separate cumulative adjectives (straight wooden arrow).
Apostrophes	*Robin's* is a possessive adjective, not a plural noun. Use an apostrophe to show ownership.

Rewrite It! While Will nailed the target to the tree, the stranger chose a straight wooden arrow from Robin's quiver.

Read It!	Mark It!	Fix It! Day 4
robins, merry men watched **attentively** as the stranger prepared to shoot at the small, white target, which will had hung 80 yards away	2 articles (ar)	2 capitals
	5 nouns (n)	2 commas
	5 adjectives (adj)	1 end mark
	2 adverbs (adv)	1 apostrophe
attentively observantly; while giving attention	1 prepositional phrase	1 number
	1 *who/which* clause (w/w)	
	1 adverb clause (AC)	
	1 [main clause]	
	3 subject-verb pairs (s v)	
	1 opener	

(1) subject

[robin's, merry men watched **attentively**] (as the stranger prepared to shoot at the small, white target), (which will had hung ~~80~~ eighty yards away).

Capitalization	***Robin's*** proper adjective; first word of the sentence ***Will*** proper noun
End Marks	This passage contains 1 end mark. There is 1 main clause. Use a period at the end of a statement.
Adjective	What kind of men? ***merry*** Whose merry men? ***Robin's*** Change *robins* to *Robin's*. What kind of target? ***white*** What kind of white target? ***small*** How many yards? ***eighty***
Adverb	Watched how? ***attentively*** Hung where? ***away***
S V Pairs MC	***men watched***
AC	*as* ***stranger prepared***
w/w	*which* **Will had hung** The *which* clause describes *target*, the noun it follows.
Note	*To shoot* is an infinitive. It does not function as a verb.
Commas	Do not use a comma to separate cumulative adjectives (small white target). Do not put a comma in front of an adverb clause. PATTERN MC AC
Apostrophes	*Robin's* is a possessive adjective, not a plural noun. Use an apostrophe to show ownership.

Rewrite It! Robin's merry men watched attentively as the stranger prepared to shoot at the small white target, which Will had hung eighty yards away.

Review It!

#2 Prepositional and #5 Clausal Openers

A **#2 prepositional opener** is a sentence that begins with a prepositional phrase.

Write the pattern for a #2 prepositional opener.

preposition + noun (no verb)

A **#5 clausal opener** is a sentence that begins with a www word (when, while, where, as, since, if, although, because) and contains a subject and a verb.

Write the pattern for a #5 clausal opener.

www word + subject + verb

Some words can begin either a #2 prepositional opener or a #5 clausal opener. Always check for a verb. If there is a verb, it is a clause. If there is not a verb, it is a prepositional phrase.

Complete the following sentences using the verbs and nouns in the list or words of your choice. Include a subject noun and verb to complete #5 clausal openers. Include a noun or article + noun to complete #2 prepositional openers. You may add other words to complete the thought.

[2] Beneath T ______ Robin laughed.

[5] Because ______ he was pleased.

[2] Without ______ he seemed troubled.

[5] As ______ Robin lost his balance.

[2] Past ______ a fawn stood quietly.

[5] When ______ it was safe.

[2] Because of ______ Robin was tired.

[5] After ______ he knew it was a mistake.

Edit the above sentences by making sure the commas are inserted correctly.

There are multiple right answers for completing the sentences. These are some possibilities.

[2] Beneath the tall cliff; the rising moon
No verb

[5] Because Robin sprinted across the finish line; Robin trusted his merry men
s v = Robin sprinted; Robin trusted

[2] Without his bow and arrows; aid from his merry men
No verb

[5] As Robin slipped on the bridge; Robin rushed across the bridge
s v = Robin slipped; Robin rushed

[2] Past the wide bushes; the budding apple tree
No verb

[5] When the deer charged its attacker; the deer fled from the hunter
s v = deer charged; deer fled

[2] Because of the three-day competition; the grueling hike
No verb

[5] After Robin mocked the foresters; Robin leaped
s v = Robin mocked; Robin leaped

Read It!	Mark It!	Fix It!
confidently the stranger pulled the bowstring aimed at the target and **released** the arrow, which flew straight	4 articles (ar)	1 capital
	4 nouns (n)	2 commas
	2 adverbs (adv)	1 end mark
	1 coordinating conjunction (cc)	
released	1 prepositional phrase	
freed from something that fastened or restrained	1 *who/which* clause (w/w)	
	1 [main clause]	
	2 subject-verb pairs (s v)	
	1 opener	

③ -ly adverb

adv ar s n v ar n

confidently [the stranger pulled the bowstring,

v ar n cc v ar n

aimed at the target, and **released** the arrow],

w/w s v adv

(which flew straight).

Capitalization	***Confidently*** first word of the sentence
End Marks	This passage contains 1 end mark. There is 1 main clause. Use a period at the end of a statement.
Adverb	Pulled, aimed, and released how? ***Confidently*** Flew how? ***straight***
S V Pairs MC	***stranger pulled, aimed, released***
w/w	***which flew*** The *which* clause describes *arrow*, the noun it follows.
Commas	Use commas to separate three or more items in a series connected with a coordinating conjunction. **PATTERN a, b, and c** *pulled*, *aimed*, and *released*

Rewrite It! Confidently the stranger pulled the bowstring, aimed at the target, and released the arrow, which flew straight.

Read It!	Mark It!	Fix It!
as it hit the center of the target robins men clapped there hands at the unexpected **impressive** shot	3 articles (ar) 5 nouns (n) 1 pronoun (pr) 4 adjectives (adj) 2 prepositional phrases 1 adverb clause (AC) 1 [main clause] 2 subject-verb pairs (s v) 1 opener	2 capitals 2 commas 1 end mark 1 homophone 1 apostrophe

impressive
admirable; remarkable

(5) clausal

AC (as *s pr* it *v* hit the *ar* center *n* of the *ar* target *n*), [Robin's *adj* men *s n* clapped *v* ~~there~~ their *adj* hands *n* at the *ar* unexpected *adj*, impressive *adj* shot *n*].

Capitalization	***As*** first word of the sentence ***Robin's*** proper adjective
End Marks	This passage contains 1 end mark. There is 1 main clause. Use a period at the end of a statement.
Adjective	Whose men? ***Robin's*** Change *robins* to *Robin's*. Whose hands? ***their*** The possessive pronoun *their* functions as an adjective. What kind of shot? ***unexpected***, ***impressive***
S V Pairs AC	*As* ***it hit***
MC	***men clapped***
Commas	Use a comma after an adverb clause. PATTERN AC, MC Use a comma to separate coordinate adjectives (unexpected, impressive shot).
Homophones	Use ***their***, the possessive pronoun.
Apostrophes	***Robin's*** is a possessive adjective, not a plural noun. Use an apostrophe to show ownership.

Rewrite It! As it hit the center of the target, Robin's men clapped their hands at the unexpected, impressive shot.

Read It!	Mark It!	Fix It! Day 3
with care robin hood stepped to the mark, he **notched** an arrow. playfully he winked at his men, and boldly took his shot	2 articles (ar)	1 indent
	6 nouns (n)	5 capitals
notched fit the arrow to the bow	2 pronouns (pr)	2 commas
	2 adjectives (adj)	2 end marks
	2 adverbs (adv)	
	1 coordinating conjunction (cc)	
	3 prepositional phrases	
	3 [main clauses]	
	3 subject-verb pairs (s v)	
	3 openers	

(2) prepositional

¶ with care [robin hood stepped to the mark],.

(6) vss (3) -ly adverb

[he **notched** an arrow]. playfully [he winked at his men, and boldly took his shot].

Indentation	new topic
Capitalization	***With***; ***He***; ***Playfully*** first word of the sentence ***Robin Hood*** proper noun
End Marks	This passage contains 3 end marks. There are 3 main clauses. Use a period at the end of a statement.
Adjective	Whose men? ***his*** The possessive pronoun *his* functions as an adjective. Whose shot? ***his***
Adverb	Winked how? ***playfully*** Took how? ***boldly***
S V Pairs	MC ***Robin Hood stepped*** MC ***He notched*** MC ***he winked, took***
Commas	Do not use a comma to connect two main clauses. MC, MC (comma splice) is always wrong. Do not use a comma to separate two verbs connected with a coordinating conjunction if the verbs have the same subject. **PATTERN MC cc 2nd verb** *he winked* and *took*

Rewrite It! With care Robin Hood stepped to the mark. He notched an arrow. Playfully he winked at his men and boldly took his shot.

Read It! | **Mark It!** | **Fix It!** | Day 4

robins arrow split the strangers arrow and than everyone shouted for joy, because robin had shot **flawlessly**

flawlessly
perfectly; faultlessly

1 article (ar)
4 nouns (n)
1 pronoun (pr)
2 adjectives (adj)
2 adverbs (adv)
1 coordinating conjunction (cc)
1 prepositional phrase
1 adverb clause (AC)
2 [main clauses]
3 subject-verb pairs (s v)
1 opener

2 capitals
2 commas
1 end mark
1 usage
2 apostrophes

(1) subject

[robin's arrow split the stranger's arrow], and [~~than~~ then everyone shouted for joy], (because robin had shot **flawlessly**).

Capitalization	***Robin's*** proper adjective; first word of the sentence ***Robin*** proper noun
End Marks	This passage contains 1 end mark. There are 2 main clauses. A comma and coordinating conjunction connect the main clauses. Use a period at the end of a statement.
Adjective	Whose arrow? ***Robin's*** Change *robins* to *Robin's*. Whose arrow? ***stranger's*** Change *strangers* to *stranger's*.
Adverb	Everyone shouted when? ***then*** Had shot how? ***flawlessly***
S V Pairs MC	***arrow split***
MC	***everyone shouted***
AC	*because* ***Robin had shot***
Commas	Use a comma to separate two main clauses connected with a coordinating conjunction. PATTERN MC, cc MC *arrow split* and *everyone shouted* Do not put a comma in front of an adverb clause. PATTERN MC AC
Usage	Use ***then***, the adverb meaning *next* or *immediately after*.
Apostrophes	*Robin's* and *stranger's* are possessive adjectives, not plural nouns. Use apostrophes to show ownership.

Rewrite It! Robin's arrow split the stranger's arrow, and then everyone shouted for joy because Robin had shot flawlessly.

Review It!

Quotations

Quotation marks indicate words are spoken. The quote is the sentence in quotation marks. The attribution is the person speaking and the speaking verb.

Read the story below. Place quotation marks around the words that are spoken. Insert attributions. Use ideas listed in the margin or words of your choice.

"Watch those two silly men," the mama bird told her baby ______________________________. "They are fighting over who crosses first!"

"Will the tall man win?" the baby bird asked ______________________________.

"He looks stronger," Mama answered ______________________________, "but the other is quick on his feet."

"Oh!" the little bird cried ______________________________. "The smaller one has fallen in!"

"Well, pride goes before a fall!" Mama wisely concluded ______________________________.

Read It!	Mark It!	Fix It! Day 1
robin i can't believe my eyes cried the stranger. that shot was a **magnificent** shot! i will gladly join you're band	2 articles (ar)	1 indent
	6 nouns (n)	4 capitals
	2 pronouns (pr)	1 comma
magnificent	4 adjectives (adj)	4 quotations
extraordinary; superb	2 adverbs (adv)	2 end marks
	4 [main clauses]	1 homophone
	4 subject-verb pairs (s v)	

¶ "robin, [i can't believe my eyes]!" [cried the stranger]. "[that shot was a **magnificent** shot]! [i will gladly join ~~you're~~ your band]."

(Markings: robin n; i s pr; can't v, adv; believe v; my adj; eyes n; cried v; the ar; stranger s n; that adj; shot s n; was v; a ar; magnificent adj; shot n; i s pr; will v; gladly adv; join v; your adj; band n)

Indentation	new speaker
Capitalization	***Robin*** proper noun; first word of the quoted sentence ***I*** personal pronoun I ***That*** first word of the quoted sentence ***I*** personal pronoun I; first word of the quoted sentence
End Marks	This passage contains 4 end marks. There are 4 main clauses. The quotation and the attribution are separated with an exclamation mark. Use an exclamation mark when a quote expresses strong emotion. **PATTERN "Quote!" attribution.** Use a period when a quote makes a statement. Place it inside the closing quotation mark.
Adjective	Whose eyes? ***my*** The possessive pronoun *my* functions as an adjective. Which shot? ***That*** In this passage *that* functions as an adjective. What kind of shot? ***magnificent*** Whose band? ***your*** The possessive pronoun *your* functions as an adjective.
Adverb	***n't*** the contraction for *not* functions as an adverb Join how? ***gladly***
S V Pairs	MC ***I can believe*** MC ***stranger cried*** MC ***shot was*** Although this group of words begins with the word *that*, it is not a dependent clause because *that* functions as an adjective and the words express a complete thought. MC ***I will join***
Commas	Place commas around a noun of direct address (NDA). ***Robin,***
Homophones	Use ***your***, the possessive pronoun.

Rewrite It!

"Robin, I can't believe my eyes!" cried the stranger. "That shot was a magnificent shot! I will gladly join your band."

Read It! | **Mark It!** | **Fix It!** Day 2

than i have gained a useful strong man and we are honored that you would join us. tell me your name robin **urged**

urged
pleaded; tried to persuade

Mark It!		Fix It!
1 article (ar)	1 *that* clause (that)	1 indent
3 nouns (n)	4 [main clauses]	4 capitals
5 pronouns (pr)	5 subject-verb pairs (s v)	3 commas
4 adjectives (adj)		2 quotations
1 adverb (adv)		1 end mark
1 coordinating conjunction (cc)		1 usage

¶ "[~~than~~ Then i have gained a useful, strong man], and [we are honored] (that you would join us). [(you) tell me your name]," [robin **urged**].

Indentation	new speaker
Capitalization	***Then***; ***Tell*** first word of the quoted sentence ***I*** personal pronoun I ***Robin*** proper noun
End Marks	This passage contains 2 end marks. There are 4 main clauses. A comma and coordinating conjunction connect the first and second main clauses. The second sentence of the quotation and the attribution belong in the same sentence. Use a period at the end of a statement.
Adjective	What kind of man? ***useful***, ***strong*** What kind of we (Robin and merry men)? ***honored*** The adjective follows the linking verb and describes the subject. Whose name? ***your*** The possessive pronoun *your* functions as an adjective.
Adverb	Gained when? ***Then***
S V Pairs	MC ***I have gained*** MC ***we are*** that *that* ***you would join*** MC ***(you) Tell*** The subject of an imperative sentence is always *you*. MC ***Robin urged***
Commas	Use a comma to separate coordinate adjectives (useful, strong man). Use a comma to separate two main clauses connected with a coordinating conjunction. **PATTERN MC, cc MC** *I have gained*, and *we are* Use a comma to separate a direct quote from an attribution. **PATTERN "Quote," attribution.**
Usage	Use ***then***, the adverb meaning *next* or *immediately after*.

Rewrite It! "Then I have gained a useful, strong man, and we are honored that you would join us. Tell me your name," Robin urged.

Read It!

men call me john little i promise that i will serve you faithfully he proudly responded, as he **extended** his hand in friendship

extended
stretched out

Mark It!

4 nouns (n)
6 pronouns (pr)
1 adjective (adj)
2 adverbs (adv)
1 prepositional phrase
1 *that* clause (that)
1 adverb clause (AC)
3 [main clauses]
5 subject-verb pairs (s v)

Fix It! Day 3

1 indent
5 capitals
2 commas
2 quotations
2 end marks

¶ "[men call me john little]. [i promise] (that i will serve you faithfully)," [he proudly responded], (as he **extended** his hand in friendship).

Indentation	new speaker
Capitalization	***Men*** first word of the quoted sentence ***John Little*** proper noun ***I*** personal pronoun I; first word of the quoted sentence ***I*** personal pronoun I
End Marks	This passage contains 2 end marks. There are 3 main clauses. The second sentence of the quotation and the attribution belong in the same sentence. Use a period when a quote makes a statement. Use a period at the end of a statement.
Adjective	Whose hand? ***his*** The possessive pronoun *his* functions as an adjective.
Adverb	Will serve how? ***faithfully*** Responded how? ***proudly***
S V Pairs	MC ***Men call*** MC ***I promise*** that *that **I will serve*** MC ***he responded*** AC *as **he extended***
Commas	Use a comma to separate a direct quote from an attribution. PATTERN **"Quote," attribution.** Do not put a comma in front of an adverb clause. PATTERN **MC AC**

Rewrite It!

"Men call me John Little. I promise that I will serve you faithfully," he proudly responded as he extended his hand in friendship.

Read It!	Mark It!	Fix It!
john little is a funny name for a man whose your size **snickered** will stutely. he laughed, until tears ran down his face	2 articles (ar)	1 indent
	7 nouns (n)	5 capitals
	1 pronoun (pr)	1 comma
	3 adjectives (adj)	2 quotations
snickered	2 prepositional phrases	2 end marks
giggled; laughed disrespectfully	1 *who/which* clause (w/w)	1 homophone
	1 adverb clause (AC)	
	3 [main clauses]	
	5 subject-verb pairs (s v)	
	1 opener	

Day 4

¶ "[john little is a funny name for a man] (~~whose~~ who's your size)!" [snickered will stutely]. [he laughed], (until tears ran down his face).

① subject

Indentation	new speaker
Capitalization	***John Little*** proper noun; first word of the quoted sentence ***Will Stutely*** proper noun ***He*** first word of the sentence
End Marks	This passage contains 3 end marks. There are 3 main clauses. The quotation and the attribution are separated with an exclamation mark. Use an exclamation mark when a quote expresses strong emotion. **PATTERN "Quote!" attribution.** Use a period at the end of a statement.
Adjective	What kind of name? ***funny*** Whose size? ***your*** The possessive pronoun *your* functions as an adjective. Whose face? ***his*** The possessive pronoun *his* functions as an adjective.
S V Pairs MC	***John Little is***
w/w	***who's*** The contraction *who's* includes both a subject (who) and a verb (is). The *who* clause describes *man*, the noun it follows.
MC	***Will Stutely snickered***
MC	***He laughed***
AC	*until* ***tears ran***
Commas	Do not put a comma in front of an adverb clause. **PATTERN MC AC**
Homophones	Use **who's**, the contraction for *who is*.

Rewrite It! "John Little is a funny name for a man who's your size!" snickered Will Stutely. He laughed until tears ran down his face.

Review It!

Verb

An **action verb** shows action or ownership.

A **linking verb** links the subject to a noun or adjective.

A **helping verb** helps an action verb or a linking verb.

Circle the correct answers. Each statement has two correct answers.

An action verb

(a.) can be a strong verb
b. is always followed by another verb
c. always follows a helping verb
(d.) always expresses ownership or action

A linking verb can be followed by

a. an action verb
b. a linking verb
(c.) a noun
(d.) an adjective

A helping verb can be followed by

(a.) an action verb
(b.) a linking verb
c. a noun
d. an adjective

Circle **H** for helping or **L** for linking to identify the underlined verbs in the following sentences.

H (L) That <u>is</u> a fine shot!

Is is followed by a noun (shot) so is a linking verb.

(H) L That's the finest I <u>have</u> ever beheld!

Have is followed by an action verb (beheld) so is a helping verb.

(H) L Both archers <u>would</u> gladly compete at the next tournament.

Would is followed by an action verb (compete) so is a helping verb.

H (L) Both <u>are</u> skillful.

Are is followed by an adjective (skillful) so is a linking verb.

Read It!	Mark It!	Fix It! Day 1
than robin hood, and his entire band **howled** with delight, after a moment the stranger, who silently watched them, slowly smiled	2 articles (ar) 5 nouns (n) 1 pronoun (pr) 2 adjectives (adj) 3 adverbs (adv) 1 coordinating conjunction (cc) 2 prepositional phrases 1 *who/which* clause (w/w) 2 [main clauses] 3 subject-verb pairs (s v) 2 openers	1 indent 4 capitals 2 commas 2 end marks 1 usage

howled
made a loud cry; shouted or laughed

① subject
adv Then, s n, cc, adj, adj, s n, v

¶ [~~than~~ robin hood, and his entire band **howled**

② prepositional
n, ar, n, ar, s n

with delight],. after a moment [the stranger,

w/w s, adv, v, pr, adv v

(who silently watched them), slowly smiled].

Indentation	new topic
Capitalization	***Then***; ***After*** first word of the sentence ***Robin Hood*** proper noun
End Marks	This passage contains 2 end marks. There are 2 main clauses. Use a period at the end of a statement.
Adjective	Which band? ***entire*** Whose entire band? ***his*** The possessive pronoun *his* functions as an adjective.
Adverb	Howled when? ***Then*** Watched how? ***silently*** Smiled how? ***slowly***
S V Pairs MC	***Robin Hood***, ***band howled***
MC	***stranger smiled***
w/w	***who watched*** The *who* clause describes *stranger*, the noun it follows.
Commas	Do not use a comma to separate two items connected with a coordinating conjunction. PATTERN **a and b** *Robin Hood* and *band* Do not use a comma to connect two main clauses. MC, MC (comma splice) is always wrong.
Usage	Use ***then***, the adverb meaning *next* or *immediately after*.

Rewrite It! Then Robin Hood and his entire band howled with delight. After a moment the stranger, who silently watched them, slowly smiled.

Read It!	Mark It!	Fix It! Day 2
robin laughed his men laughed and soon the stranger laughed to. merrily the forest rang with the **jubilant** noise of the men	4 articles (ar)	2 capitals
	6 nouns (n)	2 commas
	2 adjectives (adj)	1 end mark
	3 adverbs (adv)	1 homophone
jubilant	1 coordinating conjunction (cc)	
joyous; triumphant	2 prepositional phrases	
	4 [main clauses]	
	4 subject-verb pairs (s v)	
	2 openers	

(1) subject
[robin laughed], [his men laughed], and [soon the stranger laughed ~~to~~]. merrily [the forest rang with the **jubilant** noise of the men].

(3) -ly adverb

s n robin; v laughed; adj his; s n men; v laughed; cc and; adv soon; ar the; s n stranger; v laughed; adv too; adv merrily; ar the; s n forest; v rang; ar the; adj jubilant; n noise; ar the; n men

Capitalization		***Robin*** proper noun; first word of the sentence ***Merrily*** first word of the sentence
End Marks		This passage contains 2 end marks. There are 4 main clauses. A coordinating conjunction connects the first, second, and third main clauses. Use a period at the end of a statement.
Adjective		Whose men? ***his*** The possessive pronoun *his* functions as an adjective. What kind of noise? ***jubilant***
Adverb		Laughed when? ***soon*** ***too*** functions as an adverb Rang how? ***Merrily***
S V Pairs	MC	***Robin laughed***
	MC	***men laughed***
	MC	***stranger laughed***
	MC	***forest rang***
Commas		In this sentence a conjunction connects three main clauses. Use commas to separate three or more items in a series connected with a coordinating conjunction. PATTERN **a, b, and c** *Robin laughed*, *men laughed*, and *stranger laughed*
Homophones		Use ***too***, which means also in this sentence.

Rewrite It! Robin laughed, his men laughed, and soon the stranger laughed too. Merrily the forest rang with the jubilant noise of the men.

Read It!	Mark It!	Fix It! Day 3
little john is an ideal name for him **quipped** will stutely. little john is the perfect name shouted the merry men	3 articles 6 nouns (n) 1 pronoun (pr) 3 adjectives (adj) 1 prepositional phrase 4 [main clauses] 4 subject-verb pairs (s v)	2 indents 6 capitals 4 quotations 3 end marks

quipped
spoke a clever or witty remark

¶ "[little john is an ideal name for him]!" [quipped will stutely]. ¶ "[little john is the perfect name]!" [shouted the merry men].

Indentation		new speaker; new speaker
Capitalization		***Little John***; ***Little John*** proper noun; first word of the quoted sentence ***Will Stutely*** proper noun
End Marks		This passage contains 4 end marks. There are 4 main clauses. In both cases, the quotation and the attribution are separated with an exclamation mark. Use an exclamation mark when a quote expresses strong emotion. PATTERN **"Quote!" attribution.** Use a period at the end of a statement.
Adjective		What kind of name? ***ideal*** What kind of name? ***perfect*** What kind of men? ***merry***
S V Pairs	MC	***Little John is***
	MC	***Will Stutely quipped***
	MC	***Little John is***
	MC	***men shouted***

Rewrite It!

"Little John is an ideal name for him!" quipped Will Stutely.

"Little John is the perfect name!" shouted the merry men.

Read It! | **Mark It!** | **Fix It!** Day 4

at last robin said men, we can **guffaw**, until the sun sets but laughter will not feed us. join us little john. you must be hungry too

guffaw
laugh loudly and vigorously

Mark It!		Fix It!
1 article (ar)	1 prepositional phrase	1 indent
6 nouns (n)	1 adverb clause (AC)	7 capitals
4 pronouns (pr)	5 [main clauses]	4 commas
1 adjective (adj)	6 subject-verb pairs (s v)	2 quotations
2 adverbs (adv)	1 opener	1 end mark
1 coordinating conjunction (cc)		

② prepositional

¶ at last [robin said], "[men, we can **guffaw**], (until the sun sets), but [laughter will not feed us]. [(you) join us], little john. [you must be hungry too]."

Indentation	new speaker
Capitalization	***At*** first word of the sentence ***Robin***; ***Little John*** proper noun ***Men***; ***Join***; ***You*** first word of the quoted sentence
End Marks	This passage contains 3 end marks. There are 5 main clauses. The attribution and the first sentence of the quotation belong together. A comma and coordinating conjunction connect the second and third main clauses. Use a period at the end of a statement. Place it inside the closing quotation mark.
Adjective	What kind of you (Little John)? ***hungry*** The adjective follows the linking verb and describes the subject.
Adverb	***not*** functions as an adverb ***too*** functions as an adverb
S V Pairs	MC ***Robin said*** MC ***we can guffaw*** AC *until* ***sun sets*** MC ***laughter will feed*** MC ***(you) Join*** The subject of an imperative sentence is always *you*. MC ***You must be***
Commas	Use a comma to separate an attribution from a direct quote. PATTERN **Attribution, "Quote."** Do not put a comma in front of an adverb clause. PATTERN **MC AC** Use a comma to separate two main clauses connected with a coordinating conjunction. **PATTERN MC, cc MC** *we can guffaw*, but *laughter will feed* Place commas around a noun of direct address (NDA). **, *Little John***

Rewrite It! At last Robin said, "Men, we can guffaw until the sun sets, but laughter will not feed us. Join us, Little John. You must be hungry too."

Review It!

Fill in the blanks below with different parts of speech in order to create a silly version of "Robin Hood."

After you have completed the list on this page, transfer your words to the blanks in the story on page 181.

1 adjective ____________________

1 noun (place) ____________________

1 action verb ____________________

1 adjective ____________________

1 action verb (past tense) ____________________

1 -ly adverb ____________________

1 adjective ____________________

1 noun ____________________

1 noun (time period) ____________________

1 noun (place) ____________________

1 -ly adverb ____________________

2 nouns ____________________ ____________________

1 noun (animal) ____________________

1 -ly adverb ____________________

1 speaking verb ____________________

2 adjectives ____________________ ____________________

1 adjective ____________________

1 -ly adverb ____________________

1 action verb (past tense) ____________________

1 -ly adverb ____________________

1 noun (food) ____________________

1 adjective ____________________

Read It! | **Mark It!** | **Fix It!** Day 1

robin and his men **retraced** their steps through the ancient, green woodland, until they reached there camp, which provided safety from the kings men

retraced
went back over; traced backward

2 articles (ar)	1 adverb clause (AC)	1 indent
7 nouns (n)	1 [main clause]	1 capital
1 pronoun (pr)	3 subject-verb pairs (s v)	2 commas
6 adjectives (adj)	1 opener	1 end mark
1 coordinating conjunction (cc)		1 homophone
2 prepositional phrases		1 apostrophe
1 *who/which* clause (w/w)		

① subject

s n | cc | adj | s n | v | adj | n

¶ [robin and his men **retraced** their steps through

ar | adj | adj | n | AC | s pr | v | adj their

the ancient, green woodland], (until they reached ~~there~~

n | w/w | s | v | n | ar | adj | n

camp), (which provided safety from the king's men).

Indentation	new topic or new place
Capitalization	***Robin*** proper noun; first word of the sentence
End Marks	This passage contains 1 end mark. There is 1 main clause. Use a period at the end of a statement.
Adjective	Whose men? ***his*** The possessive pronoun *his* functions as an adjective. Whose steps? ***their*** The possessive pronoun *their* functions as an adjective. What kind of woodland? ***green*** What kind of green woodland? ***ancient*** Whose camp? ***their*** Whose men? ***king's*** Change *kings* to *king's*.
S V Pairs MC	***Robin, men retraced***
AC	*until* ***they reached***
w/w	***which provided*** The *which* clause describes *camp*, the noun it follows.
Commas	Do not use a comma to separate two items connected with a coordinating conjunction. **PATTERN a and b** *Robin* and *men* Do not use a comma to separate cumulative adjectives (ancient green woodland). Do not put a comma in front of an adverb clause. **PATTERN MC AC**
Homophones	Use ***their***, the possessive pronoun.
Apostrophes	*King's* is a possessive adjective, not a plural noun. Use an apostrophe to show ownership.

Rewrite It!

Robin and his men retraced their steps through the ancient green woodland until they reached their camp, which provided safety from the king's men.

Read It!	Mark It!	Fix It! Day 2
after the men returned they feasted sang and danced into the evening during there **festivity** little john was the honored guest	3 articles (ar) 5 nouns (n) 1 pronoun (pr) 2 adjectives (adj) 1 coordinating conjunction (cc) 2 prepositional phrases 1 adverb clause (AC) 2 [main clauses] 3 subject-verb pairs (s v) 2 openers	4 capitals 3 commas 2 end marks 1 homophone

festivity
a merry or joyous celebration

(5) clausal

(after the men returned), [they feasted, sang, and danced into the evening]. (2) prepositional during ~~there~~ their **festivity** [little john was the honored guest].

Capitalization	***After***; ***During*** first word of the sentence ***Little John*** proper noun
End Marks	This passage contains 2 end marks. There are 2 main clauses. Use a period at the end of a statement.
Adjective	Whose festivity? ***their*** The possessive pronoun *their* functions as an adjective. What kind of guest? ***honored***
S V Pairs	AC *After* ***men returned*** MC ***they feasted***, ***sang***, ***danced*** MC ***Little John was***
Commas	Use a comma after an adverb clause. **PATTERN AC, MC** Use commas to separate three or more items in a series connected with a coordinating conjunction. **PATTERN a, b, and c** *feasted*, *sang*, and *danced*
Homophones	Use ***their***, the possessive pronoun.

Rewrite It! After the men returned, they feasted, sang, and danced into the evening. During their festivity Little John was the honored guest.

Read It!	Mark It!	Fix It! Day 3
each family **warmly** welcomed him and soon he was one of them. eventually, the sun set, and the moon rose above the treetops	3 articles (ar) 4 nouns (n) 4 pronouns (pr) 1 adjective (adj) 3 adverbs (adv) 2 coordinating conjunctions (cc) 2 prepositional phrases 4 [main clauses] 4 subject-verb pairs (s v) 2 openers	2 capitals 1 comma 1 end mark

warmly
in a way that shows friendliness toward a person

① subject

[each family **warmly** welcomed him], and [soon he was one of them]. ③ -ly adverb eventually, [the sun set], and [the moon rose above the treetops].

Capitalization		***Each***; ***Eventually*** first word of the sentence
End Marks		This passage contains 2 end marks. There are 4 main clauses. A comma and coordinating conjunction connect the first and second main clauses and the third and fourth main clauses. Use a period at the end of a statement.
Adjective		Which family? ***Each***
Adverb		Welcomed how? ***warmly*** Was when? ***soon*** The sun set and moon rose when? ***Eventually*** *Eventually* is a sentence adverb. It modifies the entire sentence: It was eventual that the sun set and the moon rose. For this reason, it doesn't answer a question about the verb but about the entire sentence. It requires a comma.
S V Pairs	MC	***family welcomed***
	MC	***he was***
	MC	***sun set***
	MC	***moon rose***
Commas		Use a comma to separate two main clauses connected with a coordinating conjunction. **PATTERN MC, cc MC** *family welcomed*, and *he was* Use a comma to separate two main clauses connected with a coordinating conjunction. **PATTERN MC, cc MC** *sun set*, and *moon rose*

Rewrite It! Each family warmly welcomed him, and soon he was one of them. Eventually, the sun set, and the moon rose above the treetops.

Read It!	Mark It!	Fix It! Day 4
for many years little john lived with the merry men served as there second-in-command and proved a jolly **trustworthy** companion too robin hood	2 articles (ar) 6 nouns (n) 5 adjectives (adj) 1 coordinating conjunction (cc) 4 prepositional phrases 1 [main clause] 1 subject-verb pair (s v) 1 opener	1 indent 5 capitals 3 commas 1 end mark 2 homophones

trustworthy
able to be relied on as honest or truthful

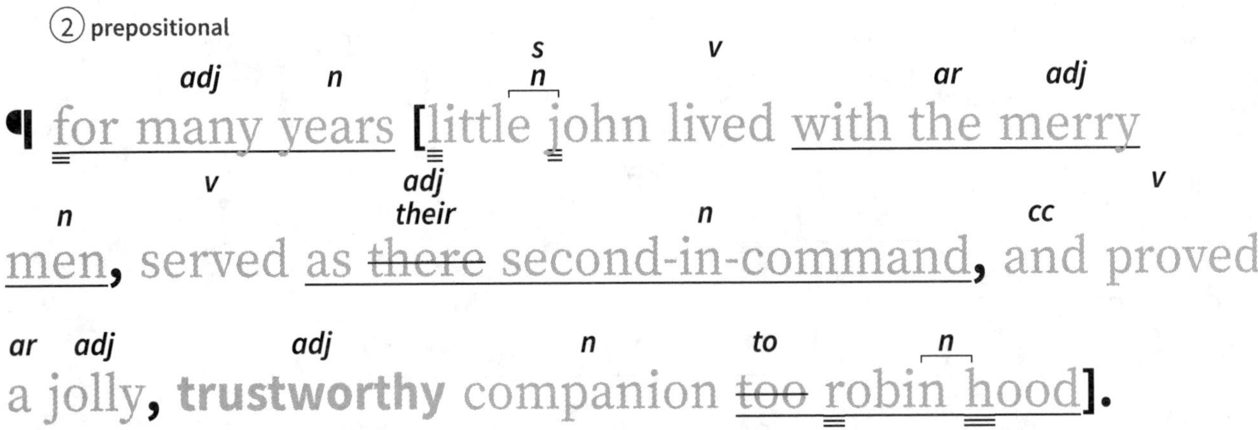

② prepositional
¶ for many years [little john lived with the merry men, served as there their second-in-command, and proved a jolly, trustworthy companion too to robin hood].

Indentation	new time
Capitalization	***For*** first word of the sentence ***Little John***; ***Robin Hood*** proper noun
End Marks	This passage contains 1 end mark. There is 1 main clause. Use a period at the end of a statement.
Adjective	How many years? ***many*** What kind of men? ***merry*** Whose second-in-command? ***their*** The possessive pronoun *their* functions as an adjective. What kind of companion? ***jolly, trustworthy***
S V Pairs MC	***Little John lived, served, proved***
Commas	Use commas to separate three or more items in a series connected with a coordinating conjunction. **PATTERN a, b, and c** *lived*, *served*, and *proved* Use a comma to separate coordinate adjectives (jolly, trustworthy companion).
Homophones	Use ***their***, the possessive pronoun. Use ***to***, the preposition.

Rewrite It! For many years Little John lived with the merry men, served as their second-in-command, and proved a jolly, trustworthy companion to Robin Hood.

Word Game!

Use the words you chose on page 175 to complete the story.

Maid Marian

by ____________
your name

Maid Marian, who was very ____________ (adjective), lived in a ____________ (noun (place)) under the protection of King Richard. He had left the country to ____________ (action verb) in battle. While the king was away, John, his ____________ (adjective) brother, ____________ (action verb (past tense)) the land. Because John ____________ (-ly adverb) taxed the peasants, Maid Marian was ____________ (adjective). She wanted Robin Hood's ____________ (noun).

One ____________ (noun (time period)) Maid Marian ventured into the ____________ (noun (place)), looking for Robin Hood.

She said to him, "John's sheriff has become ____________ (-ly adverb) rich by taxing the peasants. He has taken their ____________ (noun) and ____________ (noun). Tuesday he will ride through the forest on a ____________ (noun (animal)) to protect a wagonload of stolen goods. ____________ (-ly adverb) make him return them to the poor."

Robin Hood ____________ (speaking verb), "You are as ____________ (adjective) as you are ____________ (adjective). I will follow your plan."

In this way Maid Marian helped Robin and his men return to the ____________ (adjective) poor what was ____________ (-ly adverb) taken from them.

When King Richard later returned from the wars, he ____________ (action verb (past tense)) peace. Because Robin Hood was no longer an outlaw, he and Maid Marian ____________ (-ly adverb) were married. They served ____________ (noun (food)) at the ____________ (adjective) wedding feast, and all had a merry time!

Appendices

Robin Hood

In the olden days of England, King Richard reigned over the land. A legendary outlaw lived in Sherwood Forest in central England. His name was Robin Hood. Robin and the loyal men with him rambled through the countryside. They hunted in the deep forests. Robin was skilled with the bow. In truth, he was the most experienced archer in England.

Why was Robin Hood an outlaw under the wrath of the law? It's an interesting story for children and adults. The sheriff of Nottingham had challenged the local archers to a shooting match and even offered a prize. Robin was just eighteen. He readily accepted the challenge, grabbed his bow, and left his hometown. Robin strolled merrily. The trip shouldn't take him more than two or three days. Robin whistled and thought about the contest, which would be entertaining. He wasn't worried about the other archers. The day seemed pleasant and carefree. However, Robin's mood would soon change.

Robin met fifteen foresters who worked for the king. They were sitting beneath a huge oak and were feasting sociably. A man who had a scar on his face confronted Robin. He called Robin's bow and arrows cheap and shoddy. Then Robin grew angry. No young man likes other men to taunt him about his prize possessions. He boasted that he was as skillful with a bow and arrow as any man. He was headed to Nottingham to prove his skill in a champion match. He planned to shoot with other archers for the grand prize, which was a barrel of exceptional ale and a new bow. One forester laughed at him and retorted that he had big words for a little boy! He said that he should drink his ale with milk.

Robin immediately took offense and challenged the forester. "Sir, do you see the deer at the edge of the wood? I bet you twenty pounds that I can hit it."

Composedly Robin took his bow in his hand, grabbed an arrow from its pouch, and drew the feather to his ear. The arrow hit the buck. The foresters seethed with rage, especially the man who lost the bet.

The loser heatedly responded, "Fool, you killed the king's deer. It's a capital offense. By law you're going to die."

In anger the forester impulsively sprang to his feet, grabbed his bow, and shot an arrow at Robin. Robin Hood was fortunate that the arrow barely missed him. Without delay the furious forester reached for a second arrow. In self-defense young Robin shot an arrow, which struck the man. He toppled forward with a cry.

Robin Hood was very upset. It tortured his conscience that he'd killed a man. Fearfully Robin Hood escaped to Sherwood Forest. He was an outlaw on two accounts and could not return home. In a single day he had shot a deer that the king reserved for his own table and had slain a man too.

The sheriff of Nottingham was related to the dead forester. Firmly he vowed that Robin must be punished. Within a few days Robin heard that a lavish reward of two hundred pounds would be given to the man who captured him.

For an entire year Robin sheltered in Sherwood Forest while he met other outlaws and gained valuable hunting skills. Eventually, he gathered a band of loyal men. These good men had been displaced for many reasons. Some men, who were famished, shot deer because they had too little food. They'd narrowly escaped from the foresters when they were hunting the king's deer. Others, who were strong and goodhearted, had lost their farms because the greedy king wanted their lands. Tragically, some had been devastated by unreasonable taxes that they couldn't pay. Throughout England poor families fled from their homes and secretly hid in Sherwood Forest. A band of forty-five brave peasants, who greatly admired Robin Hood, chose him to be their leader.

Robin's followers declared that they would rob everyone who had robbed them. Especially if powerful men plundered the poor, Robin and his men would recapture their goods and would return them. To those in need, these men would offer aid and protection. They earnestly swore that they would never harm a maid, wife, or widow. Because of the desperate times, these men, whose families were hungry, stole money from corrupt noblemen. They gave it to the peasants.

The peasants loved Robin and his merry men. They often told tales of their courageous deeds. Repeatedly Robin and his men moved their camp because they were always in peril. For entertainment the men enjoyed competitions, target practice, and fishing in the cold, gurgling brook. The children of the merry men romped along the bank. They laughed and joked together.

Although everyone seemed happy, Robin was restless. "For fourteen days we've enjoyed very little sport, my friends," he complained. "While I journey to Nottingham to seek adventures, you can wait for me here," Robin directed. He told his men that they should come quickly when they heard his signal, which would be three short blasts on his bugle.

Robin Hood roamed through the forest. He searched for adventure. At a sharp curve in a path, Robin neared a log, which spanned a broad pebbly stream and acted as a narrow bridge. As he approached the log, he noticed a large, stout stranger, who was approaching the log from the other side. Robin quickened his pace. The stranger did too. Both wanted to cross.

"Go back, sir," demanded Robin rudely. "The one who's the better man should cross first."

The confident stranger responded, "You go back. I am the better man."

Naturally, this riled Robin since his merry men always respected him and obeyed him immediately. "If you don't go back, I'll fire an arrow at you!" asserted Robin.

"Hah! Do you think that I'm afraid?" the other mocked.

"You joke like a fool!" bellowed Robin. "I could fire this arrow through your heart!"

The tall stranger chuckled, "You stand there with a lethal bow. I only carry a staff. Are you a coward?"

"I have never been called a coward!" cried Robin, whose face became crimson. "I'll teach you a lesson that you won't forget. Stay where you are! After I make a staff, I will test your sparring skills."

"I welcome you to try," countered the stranger with a twinkle in his eye. "I'm happy to wait." Patiently the calm giant leaned on his staff and waited there for Robin. He whistled as he gazed about.

Robin Hood stepped into the forest, found a tall oak, and cut a sturdy staff, which measured six feet in length. Robin fashioned his weapon. He secretly studied the giant, and he confidently planned his first move. Until that day Robin had never met a larger man. Usually, Robin towered over others. This rival was a seven-foot man! Although Robin's shoulders were broad, the stranger's shoulders were two times the size. Carefully Robin crafted his weapon, which must be strong, straight, and sturdy. He was determined that he would win. As Robin worked, he smiled, for he had found his adventure. Despite its risk Robin welcomed a challenge.

Robin Hood then goaded the giant man. "I'm ready, stranger. Fight me if you dare. When one of us falls into the stream, then the victor will be the better man."

"Ah, it's a fair test," agreed the stranger. "He who is more adept with the staff is most certainly the better man."

The giant nimbly twirled his staff above his head. It whistled through the air as Robin stepped onto the log. Quickly Robin approached his adversary on the bridge. He dodged the stranger's staff and then returned a blow to the stranger's head. Most would have tumbled into the water, but the stranger parried Robin's blow to the right. Both men began to sweat. In response the seven-foot man fiercely returned another blow. It would have easily leveled a weaker opponent. When Robin Hood deftly pushed the opponent's staff to the side, he showed him that this was no easy fight.

After an hour neither had budged an inch. Both stood where they had begun. As they battled, both men gave and received many blows until cuts and bruises covered their bodies. Each had aching muscles too. Despite fatigue neither considered quitting or seemed likely to tumble off the bridge. As the two men rested, each man privately believed that he had never met a more skillful opponent.

Although both were wounded, the battle continued. Finally, Robin delivered a mighty blow, which struck his opponent's ribs. Instantly the stranger recovered, raised his arms, and brought his staff down on Robin's head. This caused blood to flow. The jolt inflamed Robin, so he swung at the other man. The stranger ducked and avoided Robin's staff. At once the stranger counterattacked. As Robin lost his footing, he tumbled into the chilly water. Robin was drenched. He heartily laughed at himself because he knew that he looked ridiculous.

The giant strutted across the log and jokingly called, "I've proven myself the better man."

With a laugh Robin waded to the bank.

"Give me your hand!" roared the stranger. "I must admit that you wield your staff with great skill."

Robin Hood then lifted his horn to his lips and blew three short blasts, which echoed through the forest. Suddenly shouts were heard in the distance. Branches rustled, and twenty strong outlaws burst from their hiding places.

Will Stutely, who was Robin's steadfast friend, immediately cried, "Robin, you're drenched from head to foot!"

With a twinkle in his eye, Robin answered, "I certainly am. This rugged fellow knocked me into the water after he gave me a beating."

"He needs a beating himself!" cried Will.

Before Robin could stop them, his men pounced on the stranger, whose strength was not a match for twenty men. Although the giant moved quickly, Robin's men dragged him to the water. He struggled furiously.

Robin exclaimed, "Stop! It was a fight that he won fairly. Don't harm this blameless man!"

Robin then bowed to the stranger and introduced himself. "I am the outlaw Robin Hood, and this is my band of merry men. Stranger, will you stay with me and be one of us? If you'll join me, I will appoint you my right-hand man."

The stranger, who was still annoyed because of his unjust, harsh thrashing, did not readily agree. "Can you handle your bow and arrows better than you handle your long, thick staff? If you can't, I won't join your motley band," he retorted.

Robin laughed to himself. With encouragement from his faithful, devoted men, Robin accepted the challenge. He may have lost the lengthy, painful bout with his staff, but he knew that he could win a contest with his bow and arrows.

Robin instructed Will Stutely to make a target from smooth white bark, which measured four fingers in height and five fingers in width. Carefully Will positioned Robin and the stranger for the contest. He then paced the distance to a large old oak tree. While Will nailed the target to the tree, the stranger chose a straight wooden arrow from Robin's quiver. Robin's merry men watched attentively as the stranger prepared to shoot at the small white target, which Will had hung eighty yards away. Confidently the stranger pulled the bowstring, aimed at the target, and released the arrow, which flew straight. As it hit the center of the target, Robin's men clapped their hands at the unexpected, impressive shot.

With care Robin Hood stepped to the mark. He notched an arrow. Playfully he winked at his men and boldly took his shot. Robin's arrow split the stranger's arrow, and then everyone shouted for joy because Robin had shot flawlessly.

"Robin, I can't believe my eyes!" cried the stranger. "That shot was a magnificent shot! I will gladly join your band."

"Then I have gained a useful, strong man, and we are honored that you would join us. Tell me your name," Robin urged.

"Men call me John Little. I promise that I will serve you faithfully," he proudly responded as he extended his hand in friendship.

"John Little is a funny name for a man who's your size!" snickered Will Stutely. He laughed until tears ran down his face.

Then Robin Hood and his entire band howled with delight. After a moment the stranger, who silently watched them, slowly smiled. Robin laughed, his men laughed, and soon the stranger laughed too. Merrily the forest rang with the jubilant noise of the men.

"Little John is an ideal name for him!" quipped Will Stutely.

"Little John is the perfect name!" shouted the merry men.

At last Robin said, "Men, we can guffaw until the sun sets, but laughter will not feed us. Join us, Little John. You must be hungry too."

Robin and his men retraced their steps through the ancient green woodland until they reached their camp, which provided safety from the king's men. After the men returned, they feasted, sang, and danced into the evening. During their festivity Little John was the honored guest. Each family warmly welcomed him, and soon he was one of them. Eventually, the sun set, and the moon rose above the treetops.

For many years Little John lived with the merry men, served as their second-in-command, and proved a jolly, trustworthy companion to Robin Hood.

-ly Adverb

An **-ly adverb** dresses up writing because it creates a strong image or feeling.

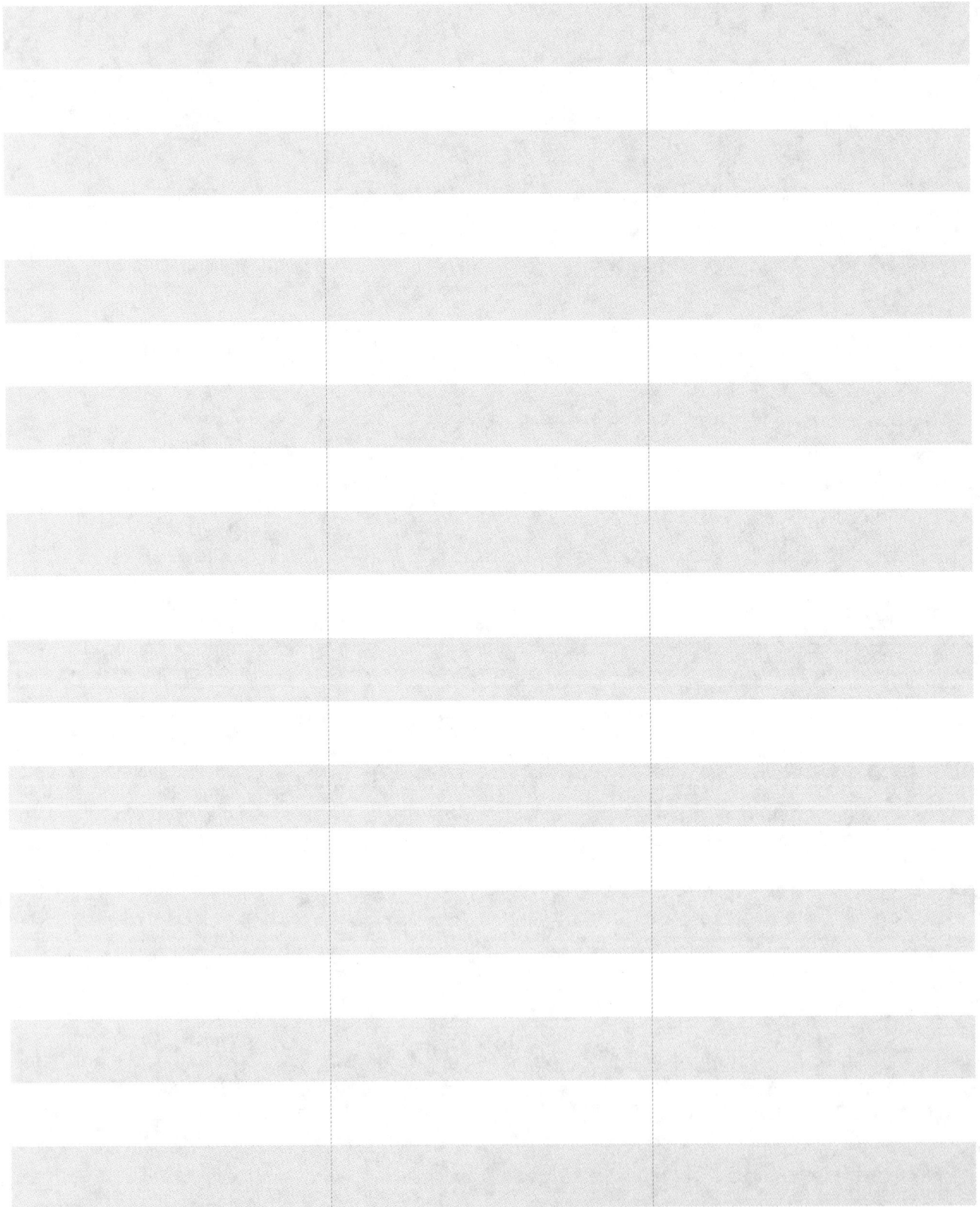

Strong Verb

A **strong verb** dresses up writing because it creates a strong image or feeling. A strong verb is an action verb, never a linking or helping verb.

Quality Adjective

A **quality adjective** dresses up writing because it creates a strong image or feeling. A quality adjective is more specific than a weak adjective, which is overused, boring, or vague.

Pronoun

A **pronoun** replaces a noun in order to avoid repetition.

A **personal pronoun** takes the place of common and proper nouns. It should agree with its antecedent in number, person, and case.

A **reflexive pronoun** ends in -self or -selves and refers to the subject of the same sentence.

	3 cases	**Subjective** function as	**Objective** function as	**Possessive** function as		**Reflexive** refers to
2 numbers	3 persons	subject subject complement	object of a preposition direct object indirect object	adjective	pronoun	subject of same sentence
singular	*1st*	I	me	my	mine	myself
	2nd	you	you	your	yours	yourself
	3rd	he, she, it	him, her, it	his, her, its	his, hers, its	himself, herself, itself
plural	*1st*	we	us	our	ours	ourselves
	2nd	you	you	your	yours	yourselves
	3rd	they	them	their	theirs	themselves

A **relative pronoun** begins a dependent *who/which* clause. The pronoun *who* has three forms: *who* (subjective), *whom* (objective), *whose* (possessive).

who, whom, whose, which, that

An **interrogative pronoun** is used to ask a question.

what, whatever, which, whichever, who, whoever, whom, whose

A **demonstrative pronoun** points to a particular person or thing. When a word on the demonstrative list is placed before a noun, it functions as an adjective, not a pronoun.

this, that, these, those

An **indefinite pronoun** is not definite. It does not refer to any particular person or thing. When a word on the indefinite list is placed before a noun, it functions as an adjective, not a pronoun.

Singular and Plural	**Plural**	**Singular**			
all	both		each	much	one
any	few	another	either	neither	other
more	many	anybody	everybody	nobody	somebody
most	others	anyone	everyone	no one	someone
none	own	anything	everything	nothing	something
some	several	anywhere	everywhere	nowhere	somewhere

Preposition

A **preposition** starts a phrase that shows the relationship between a noun or pronoun and another word in the sentence. **PATTERN preposition + noun (no verb)**

This is not an exhaustive list. When in doubt, consult a dictionary.

aboard	amid	beneath	down	into	opposite	throughout	up
about	among	beside	during	like	out	to	upon
above	around	besides	except	minus	outside	toward	with
according to	as	between	for	near	over	under	within
across	at	beyond	from	of	past	underneath	without
after	because of	by	in	off	regarding	unlike	
against	before	concerning	inside	on	since	until	
along	behind	despite	instead of	onto	through	unto	

Verb

A **verb** shows action, links the subject to another word, or helps another verb.

An **action verb** shows action or ownership.

A **linking verb** links the subject to a noun or adjective.

am, is, are, was, were, be, being, been (be verbs)

seem, become, appear, grow, remain, taste, sound, smell, feel, look (verbs dealing with the senses)

A **helping verb** helps an action verb or a linking verb.

am, is, are, was, were, be, being, been (be verbs)

have, has, had, do, does, did, may, might, must, can, will, shall, could, would, should

Conjunction

A **conjunction** connects words, phrases, or clauses.

An **coordinating conjunction** (cc) connects the same type of words, phrases, or clauses.

FANBOYS for, and, nor, but, or, yet, so

A **subordinating conjunction** (www word) connects an adverb clause to a main clause.

www.asia.b when, while, where, as, since, if although, because
before, after, until, unless, whenever, whereas, than

Fix It!
Grammar

Glossary

FOURTH EDITION

Fourth Edition version 2, January 2022

Contents

Parts of Speech

Every word belongs to a word group—a **part of speech**. There are eight parts of speech. Many words can be used as different parts of speech. However, a word will only perform one part of speech at a time. (*Light* is a verb in The fireworks *light* the sky. *Light* is a noun in We need more *light*. *Light* is an adjective in It is a *light* load.)

One must look at how words are used in a sentence to determine their parts of speech. To see how these parts of speech are used as IEW dress-ups and sentence openers, see the Stylistic Techniques section beginning on page G-37.

Noun

A **noun** names a person, place, thing, or idea.

To determine if a word is a noun, ask if an article adjective (a, an, the) comes before it or if it is countable.

Noun Tests:

the ______

two ______

A **common noun** names a general person, place, or thing. It is not capitalized.

A **proper noun** names a specific person, place, or thing. It is capitalized.

The *king* is a common noun, but *King James* is a proper noun.

A *beagle* is a common noun, but the name of my pet beagle *Benji* is a proper noun.

A **compound noun** is two or more words combined to form a single noun. They can be written three different ways. To spell compound words correctly, consult a dictionary.

separate words	*fairy tale; Robin Hood; ice cream*
hyphenated words	*merry-go-round; son-in-law; seventy-two*
one word	*grandmother; railroad; moonlight*

Pronoun

A **pronoun** replaces a noun in order to avoid repetition. The noun the pronoun replaces is called an antecedent.

A **personal pronoun** refers back to an antecedent recently mentioned and takes the place of that noun. The pronoun should agree with its antecedent in number, person, and case.

2 numbers	3 persons / 3 cases	*Subjective* function as: subject, subject complement	*Objective* function as: object of a preposition, direct object, indirect object	*Possessive* function as: adjective	*Possessive* function as: pronoun
singular	*1st*	I	me	my	mine
	2nd	you	you	your	yours
	3rd	he, she, it	him, her, it	his, her, its	his, hers, its
plural	*1st*	we	us	our	ours
	2nd	you	you	your	yours
	3rd	they	them	their	theirs

Number means one (singular) or more than one (plural).

Person means who is speaking (1st), spoken to (2nd), or spoken about (3rd).

Case refers to the way a pronoun functions in a sentence.

Both a **reflexive pronoun** (used in the objective case) and an **intensive pronoun** (used as an appositive) end in *-self* or *-selves* and refer back to a noun or pronoun in the same sentence.

Dorinda fancied *herself* quite stylish. Dorinda *herself* played as others worked.

A **relative pronoun** (*who, which, that*) begins a dependent clause. Use *who* for people and *which* or *that* for things. See page G-21.

Robin lived in Sherwood Forest, *which* belonged to the king.

Robin knew the other men *who* lived in the forest.

Robin battled with Little John, *whom* he had met on the log.

Robin knew the families *whose* lands had been stolen.

Forms of *who* include *whom* and *whose.*

who subjective case
whom objective case
whose possessive case

An **interrogative pronoun** is used to ask a question. The most common include *what, whatever, which, whichever, who, whoever, whom, whose.*

Who owns that house? *Whatever* do you mean? *Whose* coat is this?

Not all question words are pronouns. Words like *why* and *how* are adverbs.

A **demonstrative pronoun** (*this, that, these, those*) points to a particular person or thing.

This is my mother and *that* is our house. *These* are mine. *Those* are yours.

An **indefinite pronoun** is not definite. It does not refer to any particular person or thing.

Everyone will attend. *All* of the cookies are gone. *Most* of the cake is gone.

Singular and Plural	**Plural**	**Singular**			
all	both		each	much	one
any	few	another	either	neither	other
more	many	anybody	everybody	nobody	somebody
most	others	anyone	everyone	no one	someone
none	own	anything	everything	nothing	something
some	several	anywhere	everywhere	nowhere	somewhere

When a word on the demonstrative or indefinite list is placed before a noun, it functions as an adjective, not a pronoun.

Both cookies are gone.
I live in *that* house.

Noun and Pronoun Functions

Both nouns and pronouns perform many jobs or functions in a sentence.

A **subject** performs a verb action. It tells who or what the clause is about.

The soldier marched in formation.
Who marched? *soldier* (subject)

Function is different from part of speech.

A noun or pronoun can perform only one function in a sentence.

A **subject complement** follows a linking verb and renames the subject (also called a predicate noun) or describes the subject (also called a predicate adjective).

The soldier is a *woman*. The king is *he*. The castle is *theirs*.

The **object of a preposition** is the last word in a prepositional phrase. See page G-18.

A **direct object** follows an action verb and answers the question *what* or *whom*.

The soldier built a fire.
Built what? *a fire* (direct object)

The soldier treated him kindly.
Treated whom? *him* (direct object)

When the sentence is a command, the subject, *you*, is implied. See imperative mood, page G-11.

An **indirect object** appears only when there is a direct object. Indirect objects come between the verb and direct object and tell who or what received the direct object.

The dwarf gave the soldier a purse.
Gave what? *purse* (direct object). Who received it? *soldier* (indirect object)

The woman knitted him a scarf.
Knitted what? *scarf* (direct object). Who received it? *him* (indirect object)

To tell the difference between an indirect object and a direct object, revise the sentence and insert *to* or *for* in front of the indirect object.

The dwarf gave a purse *to* the soldier.

The woman knitted a scarf *for* him.

A **possessive case pronoun** that functions as an adjective comes before a noun, whereas a possessive case pronoun that functions as a pronoun is used alone.

That is *my* house.

That is *mine*.

A **noun of direct address** (NDA) is a noun used to refer to someone directly. It appears in dialogue and names the person spoken to.

"Timmy, after dinner we can read books," Johnny said.

An **appositive** is a noun that renames the noun that comes before it.

Place commas around an appositive if it is nonessential to the meaning of the sentence.

Robin Hood**,** *the archer***,** led his men through the forest.
(nonessential, commas)

The appositive is an invisible *who/which* clause. See page G-39.

Do not place commas around an appositive if it is essential to the meaning of the sentence. See page G-26.

The archer *Robin Hood* led his men through the forest.
(essential, no commas) The appositive is essential because it defines which archer led his men.

Preposition

A **preposition** starts a phrase that shows the relationship between a noun or pronoun and another word in the sentence.

PATTERN

preposition + noun (no verb)

A preposition usually shows a relationship dealing with space or time.

The squirrel sat *on the branch* (space) *in the morning* (time).

A word functions as a preposition when it is part of a prepositional phrase. See page G-18.

A prepositional phrase always begins with a preposition and ends with a noun or pronoun. The phrase may have adjectives in between, but never a verb.

The noun or pronoun that ends the prepositional phrase is called the object of the preposition. When the object of the preposition is a pronoun, it will be one of the objective case pronouns: *me, you, him, her, it, us, you, them.*

Some words on the preposition list may function as another part of speech.

When a word that looks like a preposition follows a verb but does not have a noun afterward, it is not functioning as a preposition but as an adverb.

The mouse fell down. (fell where? *down*)
Down is not followed by a noun.
This is an adverb, not a prepositional phrase.

Timmy wore his vest inside (wore vest where? *inside*)
Inside is not followed by a noun.
This is an adverb, not a prepositional phrase.

When a word that looks like a preposition is followed by a subject and a verb, it is a not functioning as a preposition but as a subordinating conjunction (www word).

As Johnny gave orders, the mice listened
As Johnny gave orders contains a subject (Johnny) and a verb (gave).
This is a clause, not a prepositional phrase.

The mice hid *after the cat arrived.*
After the cat arrived contains a subject (cat) and a verb (arrived).
This is a clause, not a prepositional phrase.

If it is something a squirrel can do with a tree, it is probably a prepositional phrase.

A squirrel
climbs *up the tree,*
sits *in the tree,*
runs *around the tree.*

This is not an exhaustive list. When in doubt, consult a dictionary.

Prepositions List

aboard	around	between	in	opposite	toward
about	as	beyond	inside	out	under
above	at	by	instead of	outside	underneath
according to	because of	concerning	into	over	unlike
across	before	despite	like	past	until
after	behind	down	minus	regarding	unto
against	below	during	near	since	up, upon
along	beneath	except	of	through	with
amid	beside	for	off	throughout	within
among	besides	from	on, onto	to	without

Verb

A **verb** shows action, links the subject to another word, or helps another verb.

To determine if a word is a verb, use the verb test.

An **action verb** shows action or ownership.

She *chopped* vegetables.

The chef *prepared* lunch.

Dorinda *has* a beauty mark.

They *own* a lovely palace.

A **linking verb** links the subject to a noun or an adjective. When the subject complement is a noun, the noun after the linking verb renames the subject. When the subject complement is an adjective, the adjective after the linking verb describes the subject.

Robin Hood *was* (linking verb) an outlaw (subject complement, noun).
Outlaw is another name for Robin Hood.

The soup *smelled* (linking verb) delicious (subject complement, adjective).
Delicious describes soup.

The soup *is* (linking verb) salty (subject complement, adjective).
Salty describes soup.

A **helping verb** helps an action verb or a linking verb. It is paired with the main verb (action or linking) to indicate tense, voice, and mood.

The chef *would* prepare supper.
Would helps prepare.

The soup *had* tasted strange.
Had helps tasted.

Verb Test:

I _______.

It _______.

Some verbs function as either action or linking verbs.

He *smells* (action) gas.

The gas *smells* (linking) bad.

If you can substitute *is* for the verb, it is probably functioning as a linking verb.

Linking Verbs List

am, is, are, was, were, be, being, been (be verbs)

seem, become, appear, grow, remain

taste, sound, smell, feel, look (verbs dealing with the senses)

Helping Verbs List

am, is, are, was, were, be, being, been (be verbs)

have, has, had, do, does, did, may, might, must

can, will, shall, could, would, should

Be verbs dominate our language and perform important functions as both linking and helping verbs.

Students should memorize the *be* verbs: am, is, are, was, were, be, being, been.

Verbal

A **verbal** is a word formed from a verb that is usually not functioning as a verb. A verbal often functions as a noun, adjective, or adverb.

An **infinitive** is formed by placing *to* in front of the simple present form of a verb.

An infinitive functions as an adjective, adverb, or noun, but never as a verb.

Dorinda has some things *to learn.*

Frederick is eager *to hear* a story.

A **participle** is formed by adding the suffix *-ing* or *-ed* to the simple present form of a verb.

splash + ing = splashing; splash + ed = splashed

A participle functions as a verb if it has a helping verb.

He *was splashing,* which frightened the fish.

For years, she *had longed* to visit the city.

If a participle does not have a helping verb, it functions as an adjective. A participle-adjective may appear directly before a noun or after a linking verb.

Robin Hood was known for his *hunting* skills.

It was a *botched* case. The case was *botched.*

A participle may also form a participial phrase that describes a noun in the sentence.

Springing to his feet, Robin Hood confronted the challenger.
Springing to his feet describes Robin Hood, the subject after the comma.

Robin Hood whistled merrily, *thinking of Maid Marian.*
Thinking of Maid Marian describes Robin Hood, the subject of the sentence.

A **gerund** is formed by adding the suffix *-ing* to the simple present form of a verb.

splash + ing = splashing

A gerund functions as a noun, never as a verb.

His *splashing* frightened the fish.
Splashing is the subject of the sentence and therefore a noun.

The fish were frightened by his *splashing.*
Splashing is the object of the preposition *by* and therefore a noun.

To + verb and verbs ending in -ing should not be marked as strong verbs.

For clarity in meaning, avoid splitting infinitives when possible.

To split an infinitive is to insert one or more adverbs between *to* and the verb, as in *to foolishly insert.*

Some words do not form the past participle by adding -ed. There are many irregular verb forms.

eat/eaten
not eated

creep/crept
not creeped

draw/drew
not drawed

If in doubt, consult a dictionary.

Tense

Verb tense indicates when an action occurs. There are six tenses in English: simple past, simple present, simple future, past perfect, present perfect, and future perfect.

The **simple tense** is simply formed by using different forms of the verb.

I *biked.* I *bike.* I *will bike.*

He *ran.* He *runs.* He *will run.*

The **perfect tense** is formed by adding a form of *have* to the past participle verb form.

I *had biked.* I *have biked.* I *will have biked.*

He *had run.* He *has run.* He *will have run.*

Most writing occurs in the **past tense**, either simple or perfect. When telling about two events that occurred in the past, the more recent event is written in the simple past tense, and the earlier event is written in the past perfect tense.

The soldiers *cried* (past tense) because they *had lost* (past perfect) their gifts.

Simple past is commonly called *past*; simple present, *present*; and simple future, *future.*

Forms of *have* include *have, has,* and *had.*

Use *had* + the past participle of a verb to form the past perfect.

Voice

Verb voice indicates if the subject is doing or receiving the action. There are two voices in English: active and passive.

In **active voice**, the subject of the sentence is doing the verb action. The active voice creates a strong image and feeling because it highlights the doer of the action. Most sentences should be written in active voice.

Will climbed the tree.
The subject (Will) is doing the verb (climbed).

In **passive voice**, the subject receives the action of the verb. The subject is not doing any action. The verb is always in the form of a verb phrase (two or more words) that contains a *be* verb and a past participle. Because the passive voice is often wordy and dull, avoid overusing the passive voice.

The *tree was climbed* by Will. The *tree was climbed.*
In both sentences the subject (the tree) is not doing the verb action (was climbed). Someone or something else is doing the verb action. In the first sentence who is doing the verb is specified (Will). In the second sentence it is implied.

Action verbs, not linking verbs, can be passive or active.

To create a strong image and feeling, write sentences where the subject actively does the verb action.

Sam kicked the ball is better than *The ball was kicked by Sam.*

Advanced

PATTERN subject (person/thing being acted on) **+ be verb + past participle + by someone or something** (either in the sentence or implied). The passive sentence must have all four elements.

The tree (thing being acted on) was (be verb) climbed (past participle) by Will (by someone).
The castle (the thing being acted on) would be (be verb) demolished (past participle) by the soldiers (by someone).

Understanding passive voice helps distinguish if an -ed word is operating as a verb or an adjective.

The sandwich (the thing being acted on) was (be verb) devoured (past participle).
Someone must have devoured the sandwich, so the "by someone" is implied.
Since this sentence follows the passive voice pattern, *devoured* is a verb.

Molly (subject) was (be verb) famished (-ed word).
Since *famished* is a state of being, not something being done to Molly, there is no implied "by someone" phrase. Thus, *famished* is an adjective that follows a linking verb (was), describing Molly.

Mood

Verb mood indicates how an action is expressed, telling if it is a fact, opinion, command, or suggestion. There are three moods in English: indicative, imperative, and subjunctive.

The **indicative mood** makes statements or asks questions.

I will swim. Will you swim with me?

The **imperative mood** gives a command or makes a request. The subject of an imperative sentence is always *you.*

Swim. Swim to the other side of the pond.

The **subjunctive mood** expresses contrary-to-fact conditions with *wish* or *if* statements in the third person. It is used infrequently.

If Sam were concerned, he would take swimming lessons.
Sam is not concerned, so the subjunctive *Sam were* is correct.

Sam's mother wishes that he were a stronger swimmer.
Sam is not a stronger swimmer, so the subjunctive *he were* is correct.

Conjunction

A conjunction connects words, phrases, or clauses.

A **coordinating conjunction** connects the same type of words, phrases, or clauses. The items the coordinating conjunction connects must be grammatically the same: two or more nouns, two or more present participles, two or more dependent clauses, two or more main clauses, and so forth.

Memorize the cc's using the acronym FANBOYS: *for, and, nor, but, or, yet, so.*

There are seven coordinating conjunctions: *for, and, nor, but, or, yet, so.*

Use a comma before a coordinating conjunction when it connects three or more items in a series.
PATTERN a, b, and c

He *ran* to the window**,** *opened* it**,** and *jumped* out.

Use a comma before a coordinating conjunction when it connects two main clauses (a compound sentence).
PATTERN MC, cc MC

The *cook yelled***,** and the *mouse ran.*

Do not use a comma before a coordinating conjunction when it connects two items in a series unless they are main clauses.
PATTERN a and b

The cook saw the *vegetables* (no comma) but not the *mouse.*

Do not use a comma before a coordinating conjunction when it connects two verbs (a compound verb) with the same subject.
PATTERN MC cc 2nd verb

The cook *yelled* (no comma) and *ran.*

Starting sentences with a coordinating conjunction is discouraged in formal writing on the basis that a coordinating conjunction connects things of equal grammatical construction within a sentence.

In academic papers students should avoid beginning a sentence with a cc.

In fictional papers dialogue can mimic real speech patterns. Thoughts often begin with *and* or *but.*

Faulty parallelism occurs when a coordinating conjunction does not connect things of equal grammatical construction. This means that the items in a series are not parallel.

He *ran* to the window, *opened* it, and *jumping* out.
Ran, opened, and jumping are not the same verb form. To correct, change jumping to jumped: He *ran, opened,* and *jumped.*

A **subordinating conjunction** (also called a www word) usually connects an adverb clause to a main clause. The adverb clause is a dependent clause, which cannot stand alone as a sentence. It begins with a www word and contains a subject and a verb.

PATTERN

www word + subject + verb

There are many subordinating conjunctions. The most common are taught using the acronym ***www.asia.b***: when, while, where, as, since, if, although, because. Other words function as subordinating conjunctions: after, before, until, unless, whenever, whereas, than.

Memorize the most common www words using the acronym *www.asia.b:* when, while, where, as, since, if, although, because.

Use a comma after an adverb clause that comes before a main clause.
PATTERN AC, MC

When it rained, Timmy stayed indoors.

Do not use a comma before an adverb clause.
PATTERN MC AC

Timmy stayed indoors (no comma) *when it rained.*

A word functions as a subordinating conjunction only when it is followed by a subject and verb. This is why recognizing the pattern www word + subject + verb is important. If a verb is not present, the group of words is likely a prepositional phrase and not a clause. See pages G-18 and G-21.

A **conjunctive adverb** connects ideas or provides a transition.

Common conjunctive adverbs are *however, therefore, then, moreover, consequently, otherwise, nevertheless, thus, furthermore, instead, otherwise.*

Place commas around a conjunctive adverb if it interrupts the flow of the sentence. The exception is one-syllable conjunctive adverbs like *then.*

Moreover, Robin Hood had many followers.
Robin Hood was a talented archer and, *moreover*, a good leader.
Then (no comma) he took an arrow from his quiver.

If a conjunctive adverb is used to connect two main clauses that express similar ideas, place a semicolon before the conjunctive adverb and a comma after.
PATTERN MC; ca, MC.

The outlaws lived in the forest; *however*, the forest belonged to the king.

When you add a conjunctive adverb to a main clause, it is still a main clause, which is not the case with subordinating conjunctions or relative pronouns.

Adjective

An **adjective** describes a noun or pronoun. An adjective tells which one, what kind, how many, or whose.

An adjective comes before the noun it describes or follows a linking verb and describes the subject. See page G-9.

The scared mice jumped from the first basket and ran under the cook's feet.
What kind of mice? *scared* Which basket? *first* Whose feet? *cook's*

The mice appeared *scared.*
Scared follows *appeared* (linking verb) and describes *mice* (subject).

An **article adjective** signals a noun is coming. The article adjectives are *a, an, the.* Sometimes adjectives come between the article and its noun.

The tall stranger entered *the* room.

The boy appeared to be *a* reluctant, timid soldier.

A **comparative adjective** is formed by adding the adverb *more* or the ending *-er* to an adjective. A comparative adjective compares two nouns.

The rose was *more* beautiful than the daisy.

The boy stood *taller* than his mother.

A **superlative adjective** is formed by adding the adverb *most* or the ending *-est* to an adjective. A superlative adjective compares three or more nouns.

This is the *most* interesting book I have read.

The Little Mermaid was the *youngest* in her family.

Most one-syllable adjectives form the comparative and superlative by adding the suffix *-er* or *-est.* Three or more syllable adjectives form the comparative with *more* and the superlative with *most.* Two-syllable adjectives are formed both ways. If in doubt, consult a dictionary.

Use a comma to separate **coordinate adjectives.** Adjectives are coordinate if each adjective independently describes the noun that follows. The order is not important.

The woman had a thin face with a pointed**,** protruding nose.
It sounds right to say both *protruding, pointed nose* and *pointed and protruding nose.* The adjectives are coordinate and the comma is necessary.

Do not use a comma to separate **cumulative adjectives.** Adjectives are cumulative if the first adjective describes the second adjective and the noun that follows. Cumulative adjectives follow this specific order: quantity, opinion, size, age, shape, color, origin, material, purpose.

Robin saw fifteen foresters seated beneath a huge oak tree.
It does not sound right to say *oak huge tree* or *huge and oak tree.*
The adjectives are cumulative and should not have a comma.

A **possessive adjective** is a noun functioning as an adjective in order to show ownership. See page G-28.

The vest belonged to Timmy (noun).

Timmy's (possessive adjective) vest had several pockets.

Adjective Test:
the _______ pen

Which pen?
the *first* pen
that pen

What kind of pen?
a *shiny* pen
the *green* pen

How many pens?
twenty pens
few pens

Whose pen?
the *teacher's* pen
my pen

Some words form irregular comparatives and superlatives. The most common of these are *good, better, best* and *bad, worse, worst.*

Only coordinate adjectives need to be separated with a comma.

Adjectives are coordinate if you can reverse their order or add *and* between them.

Adjectives are cumulative if they must be arranged in a specific order.

Adverb

An **adverb** modifies a verb, an adjective, or another adverb. An adverb tells how, when, where, why, or to what extent.

I dropped the pen there beside the book.
Dropped where? *there*

He seemed genuinely happy when he indicated that he would visit us later.
How happy? *genuinely* Visit when? *later*

An **-ly adverb** is an adverb that ends in -ly. Not all words that end in -ly are adverbs. Impostor -ly adverbs are adjectives like *chilly, ghastly, ugly,* and *friendly.* If the word ending in -ly describes a noun, it is an adjective and not an adverb.

Inadvertently Frederick touched Dorinda's omelet with his hind leg.
Touched how? *inadvertently* Inadvertently is an adverb.

Dorinda accidentally hurled him across the room.
Hurled how? *accidentally* Accidentally is an adverb.

Frederick uttered a ghastly sound when his leg broke.
What kind of sound? *ghastly* Ghastly is not an -ly adverb. It is an adjective because it describes the noun *sound.*

An **interrogative adverb** is an adverb used to begin a question. The interrogative adverbs are *how, when, where,* and *why.*

Why do bees sting, Baloo?

How will you collect the honey?

A **comparative** or **superlative** adverb is usually formed by adding the adverbs *more* or *most* in front of the adverb. If the adverb is short, the suffix *-er* or *-est* is used, as in faster or fastest. If in doubt, consult a dictionary.

Do not place *more* or *most* before the word with *-er* or *-est* after. Not *more faster* but *faster.*

Interjection

An **interjection** expresses an emotion.

When an interjection expresses a strong emotion, use an exclamation mark. The next word begins with a capital letter.

Help! My golden ball has vanished.

When an interjection does not express a strong emotion, use a comma.

Oh, I see it now.

The Sentence

Sentences are essential to writing. As the building blocks of sentences, clauses and phrases are the most important structural units of language. For the reader, the ability to recognize clauses and phrases results in greater comprehension. For the writer, the ability to organize clauses and phrases results in clearer communication. The writer must know enough about each to punctuate properly. This section defines these terms and explains the related commas rules.

Sentence

A sentence contains a subject and a verb and expresses one complete thought.

Every sentence must have a main clause.

A sentence begins with a capital letter and ends with an end mark. It contains at least one subject-verb pair, which is called a main clause. A **subject** is the noun or pronoun that tells who or what the clause is about. A **verb** tells what the subject is doing. Additional words, phrases, and clauses may be added.

A **run-on** occurs when a sentence has two main clauses that are not connected properly. There are two types of run-ons, which are always wrong.

A **fused sentence** is two main clauses placed in one sentence without any punctuation between them. **MC MC.**

Quinn glanced up the door slammed shut.

A **comma splice** is two main clauses placed in one sentence with only a comma between them. **MC, MC.**

Quinn glanced up, the door slammed shut.

There are four main ways to fix a run-on.

A period is usually the easiest solution for run-ons.

A semicolon is only used when both main clauses are closely related and usually parallel in construction.

1. Period: Quinn glanced up**.** The door slammed shut**.** **PATTERN MC. MC.**
2. Comma + cc: Quinn glanced up**,** *and* the door slammed shut. **PATTERN MC, cc MC.**
3. Adverb clause: Start one of the clauses with one of the www words.

   As Quinn glanced up**,** the door slammed shut. **PATTERN AC, MC.**

   Quinn glanced up *as* the door slammed shut. **PATTERN MC AC.**
4. Semicolon: Quinn glanced up**;** the door slammed shut. **PATTERN MC; MC.**

Of these options for this example, the adverb clause is the best solution because *as* explains how the two clauses are related.

A **fragment** occurs when a sentence does not contain a main clause. The group of words may contain a phrase and/or a dependent clause, but it is only part of a sentence.

Fragments that do not leave the reader hanging and that fit the flow of the paragraph are dramatic and effective. *Fix It!* stories permit such fragments, especially in dialogue.

Timmy saw his dear friend. (sentence)
Greeting him kindly. (unacceptable fragment)
"Hello, Johnny!" (acceptable fragment)

Phrase

A phrase is a group of related words that contains either a noun or a verb, never both.

A **prepositional phrase** begins with a preposition and ends with a noun. There might be other words between the preposition and the noun, but there is never a verb in a prepositional phrase.

PATTERN

preposition + noun (no verb)

To identify a prepositional phrase, find a word that appears to be a preposition and ask *what?* Answer with a noun, never a verb. See page G-8.

Through the glimmering twilight beamed the evening star in all its beauty.
Find a preposition. *through* through what? *through the glimmering twilight*
Find a preposition. *in* in what? *in all its beauty*

If a prepositional opener has five words or more, follow it with a comma.

Under the table (no comma) the tiny mouse hid.

*Under the heavy wooden table***,** the tiny mouse hid.

If two or more prepositional phrases open a sentence, follow the last phrase with a comma.

*Under the heavy wooden table in the kitchen***,** the tiny mouse hid.

If a prepositional opener functions as a transition, follow it with a comma.

*Of course***,** the cook was afraid of mice.

If a prepositional opener is followed by a main clause that has the verb before the subject, do not use a comma.

Under the heavy wooden table hid a tiny mouse.

Do not put a comma in front of a prepositional phrase unless the phrase is a transition.

The mouse hid (no comma) *under a table in the kitchen.*

The cook was**,** *of course***,** afraid of mice.

Prepositional phrases that function as transitions require commas.

in fact
in addition
by the way
by contrast
for example
for instance
of course
on the other hand

Recognizing the basic clause and phrase structure of a sentence will allow students to punctuate their sentences properly. Removing prepositional phrases helps reveal the underlying structure of the sentence.

When a prepositional phrase is misplaced, the meaning is distorted, often humorously. Revise the sentence by moving the prepositional phrase.

The mouse hid under a table with the long gray tail.

The mouse, not the table, has the long gray tail.

The mouse with the long gray tail hid under a table.

Advanced

When a preposition ends a sentence, it is not wrong. This is a carryover from Latin and not a true rule in English. Andrew Pudewa quips that Winston Churchill gave the definitive answer to this problem when he remarked, "That is a rule up with which I will not put!" If the sentence is more awkward to revise with the preposition placed earlier, it is better to have it at the end.

I have only a staff to meet you with.

The alternative is this stilted construction: I have only a staff with which to meet you.

A **verb phrase** is one main verb (action or linking) and one or more helping verbs. The helping verb indicates the tense, mood, and voice. Sometimes the helping verb(s) and the main verb are separated by other words. See page G-9.

Every clause must have an action or a linking verb, not a helping verb.

The Little Mermaid *could* (helping verb) not *forget* (action verb) the charming prince.
The verb phrase *could forget* functions as the verb.

A **participial phrase** begins with a participle (verb + -ing or -ed) and includes its modifiers and complements. A participial phrase functions as an adjective that describes a noun in the sentence.

A #4 -ing opener is a participial opener. See page G-44.

Springing to his feet, Robin Hood confronted the challenger.
Springing to his feet describes Robin Hood, the subject of the main clause.

Robin Hood, *thinking of Maid Marian,* whistled merrily.
Thinking of Maid Marian describes Robin Hood, the subject of the main clause.

Affronted by their mockery, Robin challenged the foresters.
Affronted by their mockery describes Robin, the subject of the main clause.

The path brought them to a broad stream *spanned by a narrow bridge.*
Spanned by a narrow bridge describes stream, the object of the prepositional phrase.

Use a comma after a participial opener (-ing), even if it is short.
PATTERN **-ing word/phrase, main clause**

Gathering their three gifts, the soldiers visited the king.
The thing after the comma is the thing doing the inging.

Place commas around a mid-sentence participial phrase if it is nonessential to the meaning of the sentence.

David, *playing on the beach*, saw a mermaid. (nonessential, commas)
The proper noun David defines which child saw a mermaid.

Use a comma when a participial phrase comes at the end of a sentence and describes a noun other than the word it follows.

Robin whistled, *thinking of Maid Marian.* (describes Robin, comma)

Do not place commas around a mid-sentence participial phrase if it is essential to the meaning of the sentence. See page G-26.

The child *playing on the beach* saw a mermaid. (essential, no commas)
The phrase is essential because it defines which child saw a mermaid.

Do not use a comma when a participial phrase comes at the end of a sentence and describes the word it follows.

Dorinda saw her ball rolling down the hill. (describes ball, no comma)

Clause

A clause is a group of related words that contains both a subject and a verb.

A **main clause [MC]** has a subject and a verb. A main clause, sometimes called an independent clause, can stand alone as a sentence because it expresses a complete thought.

The second solider took the road to the right. [main clause]

A **dependent clause** also has a subject and a verb. However, it cannot stand alone as a sentence because it does not express a complete thought. As a result, a dependent clause, sometimes called a subordinate clause, must be added to a main clause to make sense. Dependent clauses begin with a word that causes them to be an incomplete thought.

Although the second soldier took the road to the right. (dependent clause)

One of the keys to punctuating sentences properly is being able to identify dependent clauses accurately. Every dependent clause functions as either an adjective, an adverb, or a noun.

Identify the clause by 1) focusing on the word that begins the dependent clause and 2) checking the placement of the clause in the sentence. Once the clause function has been determined, properly punctuating the sentence is easy.

Contains:
subject + verb

stands alone

Contains:
subject + verb

cannot stand alone

Main Clause [MC]

subject + verb
stands alone

[The frog rescued her ball.]

Dependent Clause

subject + verb
cannot stand alone

Adjective Dependent Clause

[The frog, (who was actually a prince,) rescued her ball.]

who/which clause (*w/w*)
functions as an adjective
begins with *who, which, that*
use commas unless essential

Adverb Dependent Clause

(When her ball fell into the well,) [the frog rescued it.]

[The frog rescued her ball] (when it fell into the well.)

www.asia.b clause (AC)
functions as an adverb
begins with www word
use comma after but not before

Noun Dependent Clause

[Dorinda did not realize] (that the frog was a prince.)

that clause (that)
functions as a noun
often begins with *that*
no commas

An **adjective clause** is a dependent clause that functions as an adjective.

Because the adjective clause is a dependent clause, it must be added to a main clause. Most of the time it directly follows the noun or pronoun that it describes.

An adjective clause begins with a relative pronoun (*who, which, that*) or a relative adverb (*where, when, why*) and contains both a subject and a verb. The subject of the adjective clause is often the word it begins with (such as *who, which, where*). See page G-6.

> The *who/which* clause is an adjective clause that begins with *who* or *which*. See page G-39.

Robin, who lived among them, led the outlaws.
Robin led the outlaws is the main clause.
(*Robin* is the subject; *led* is the verb.)

Who lived among them is the adjective clause.
(*Who* is the subject; *lived* is the verb.)

> An adjective clause that begins with *that* is always essential. Thus, *that* clauses do not take commas.

Place commas around an adjective clause
if it is nonessential to the meaning of the sentence.

Robin**,** *who was happy and carefree***,** traveled through the forest. (nonessential, commas)

Do not place commas around an adjective clause
if it is essential to the meaning of the sentence. See page G-26.

The men *who followed Robin Hood* could be trusted. (essential, no commas) The clause is essential because it defines which men could be trusted.

Advanced

A relative pronoun introduces the adjective clause and connects it to the main clause. It functions as a pronoun because it replaces the noun or pronoun that precedes it.

which
The woman served brown bread, ~~bread~~ tasted delicious.

An **adverb clause** is a dependent clause that functions as an adverb.

Because the adverb clause is a dependent clause, it must be added to a main clause. An adverb clause may appear anywhere in a sentence.

An adverb clause begins with a subordinating conjunction (www word) and contains both a subject and a verb. See page G-13.

> **PATTERN**
>
> **www word + subject + verb**

Eden admired Quinn while she sang her solo.
Eden admired Quinn is the main clause.
(*Eden* is the subject; *admired* is the verb.)

While she sang her solo is the adverb clause.
(*She* is the subject; *sang* is the verb.)

Use a comma after an adverb clause that comes before a main clause.
PATTERN AC, MC

*When it rained***,** Timmy stayed indoors.

Do not use a comma before an adverb clause.
PATTERN MC AC

Timmy stayed indoors (no comma) *when it rained.*

> A comma is placed before *although*, *while*, or *whereas* when a strong contrast exists. See page G-26.

An adverb clause follows the pattern www word + subject + verb. If a verb is not present, the group of words is likely a prepositional phrase. See page G-18.

A **noun clause** is a dependent clause that functions as a noun.

A noun clause can do any function that a noun can do: subject, object of the preposition, direct object, indirect object, subject complement. See page G-7.

Like the other dependent clauses, the noun clause contains both a subject and a verb. Many noun clauses begin with *that,* but they can also begin with other words, including *how, what, when, where, whether, which, who, why.*

The advanced dress-up noun clause is a noun clause that begins with *that.* See page G-41.

What Dorinda said disappointed her father.
What Dorinda said is the subject of the main clause.

Dorinda did not realize *when her actions were unacceptable.*
When her actions were unacceptable is the direct object of the verb *realize.*

Dorinda's primary problem was *that she was self-centered.*
That she was self-centered is the subject complement.

An invisible noun clause occurs when the word *that* is implied, not stated directly.

Dorinda never seemed to understand [that] she was responsible.
She was responsible is the direct object of the verbal *to understand. That* is implied.

Frederick could tell [that] he would enjoy his stay.
He would enjoy his stay is the direct object of the verb *could tell. That* is implied.

Both noun clauses and adjective clauses can begin with the word *that.*

If *which* can be substituted for *that,* the *that* clause is an adjective clause.

Noun clauses do not take commas.

People felt (no comma) *that Robin Hood was like them.*

Robin Hood was pleased (no comma) *that he had escaped.*

Advanced

The first word of a dependent clause does not always indicate the type of clause. The word *that* can begin both adjective clauses and noun clauses. The words *where, when,* and *why* can begin adjective, adverb, and noun clauses. Accurate identification requires one to consider the way the entire clause is functioning in the sentence.

The Little Mermaid determined to look *where the prince now lived with his bride.*
The dependent clause begins with *where* and tells the location of where the Little Mermaid looked.
This is an adverb clause, so a comma is not needed.

The Little Mermaid noticed the sky, *where the rosy dawn glimmered more and more brightly.*
The dependent clauses begins with *where* and directly follows the noun *sky.*
This is a nonessential adjective clause, so a comma is needed.

Punctuation

End Marks . ? !

Period

Use a period at the end of a statement.

He bowed and walked away.

Use a period with some abbreviations.

ea. st. Mrs.

Question Mark

Use a question mark at the end of a question.

Did you ever hear the story of the three poor soldiers?

Exclamation Mark

Use an exclamation mark at the end of a sentence that expresses strong emotion.

No one calls me a coward!

Use an exclamation mark after an interjection that expresses strong emotion.

Yuck! I won't touch another bite.

Use only one end mark.

"You're sure?" "Hah!" he said. (correct)

"You're sure?!" "Hah!," he said. (incorrect)

Commas ,

Adjectives before a Noun

Use a comma to separate **coordinate adjectives.** Adjectives are coordinate if each adjective independently describes the noun that follows. The order is not important.

The woman had a pointed**,** protruding nose.
It sounds right to say both *protruding, pointed nose* and *pointed and protruding nose.*
The adjectives are coordinate and the comma is necessary.

Do not use a comma to separate **cumulative adjectives.** Adjectives are cumulative if the first adjective describes the second adjective and the noun that follows. Cumulative adjectives follow this specific order: quantity, opinion, size, age, shape, color, origin, material, purpose.

The soldiers reached the tall green gate.
It does not sound right to say *green tall gate* or *tall and green gate.*
The adjectives are cumulative and should not have a comma.

Only coordinate adjectives need to be separated with a comma.

Adjectives are coordinate if you can reverse their order or add *and* between them.

Adjectives are cumulative if they must be arranged in a specific order.

Noun of Direct Address (NDA)

Place commas around a noun of direct address. See page G-7.

*My friends***,** for fourteen days we have enjoyed no sport.

For fourteen days**,** *my friends***,** we have enjoyed no sport.

For fourteen days we have enjoyed no sport**,** *my friends.*

Items in a Series

PATTERN a, b, and c Use commas to separate three or more items in a series. Place the final comma before the coordinating conjunction. These items must be grammatically the same.

He *ran* to the window**,** *opened* it**,** and *jumped* out.

The cook removed the *tomatoes***,** *beans***,** and *cucumbers.*

PATTERN a and b Do not use a comma before a coordinating conjunction when it connects two items in a series unless they are main clauses.

The cook removed the *tomatoes* (no comma) and *cucumbers.*

The cook *yelled* (no comma) and *ran.*

The Oxford Comma is the comma before the coordinating conjunction in three or more items in a series. Although the Oxford comma is optional if there is no danger of misreading, writers do not always recognize potential confusion. It is wise to include it since the addition of the Oxford Comma is rarely wrong.

Compound Verb

PATTERN MC cc 2nd verb Do not use a comma before a coordinating conjunction when it connects two verbs (a compound verb) with the same subject. There is no subject after the cc.

The cook *yelled* (no comma) and *ran.*

He *ran* to the window (no comma) and *opened* it.

This is the same as pattern a and b.

Compound Sentence

PATTERN MC, cc MC Use a comma before a coordinating conjunction when it connects two main clauses (a compound sentence). There is a subject and a verb after the cc.

The *cook yelled***,** and the *mouse ran.*

He ran to the window**,** and *he opened* it.

The comma in the MC, cc MC pattern is optional when the clauses are short and there is no danger of misreading.

Mid-Sentence Prepositional Phrase

Do not put a comma in front of a prepositional phrase unless the phrase is a transition.

The mouse hid (no comma) *under a table in the kitchen.*

The cook was**,** *of course***,** afraid of mice.

Prepositional Phrase Opener (#2 Sentence Opener)

If a prepositional opener has five words or more, follow it with a comma.

Under the table (no comma) the tiny mouse hid.

Under the heavy wooden table, the tiny mouse hid.

If two or more prepositional phrases open a sentence, follow the last phrase with a comma.

Under the heavy wooden table in the kitchen, the tiny mouse hid.

If a prepositional opener functions as a transition, follow it with a comma.

Of course, the cook was afraid of mice.

If a prepositional opener is followed by a main clause that has the verb before the subject, do not use a comma.

Under the heavy wooden table hid a tiny mouse.

Prepositional phrases that work as transitions and require commas include

in fact
in addition
by the way
by contrast
for example
for instance
of course
on the other hand

Transition and Interrupter

Place commas around a transition and an interrupter.

Of course, Dorinda and Maribella lived in the castle.

As grown-up girls they could, *on the other hand*, leave when they pleased.

They rarely left the palace grounds, *however*.

When transitional words connect two main clauses, put a semicolon before and a comma after. See page G-29.

-ly Adverb Opener (#3 Sentence Opener)

Use a comma if an -ly adverb opener modifies the sentence.

Foolishly, Timmy bit into a hot pepper.
Test: It was foolish that Timmy bit ... makes sense. *Foolishly* modifies the sentence.

Do not use a comma if an -ly adverb opener modifies the verb.

Eagerly Timmy ate a ripe cucumber.
Test: It was eager that Timmy ate ... does not make sense. *Eagerly* modifies the verb *ate*.

Test:

It was ___ that ___.

End-Sentence Participial Phrase

Do not use a comma when the participial phrase (-ing) describes the word directly before it.

Dorinda saw her ball (no comma) *rolling down the hill.*

Robin Hood whistled, *thinking of Maid Marian.*

Participial Phrase Opener (#4 Sentence Opener)

Use a comma after a participial opener (-ing), even if it is short.

Excusing herself from the table, Dorinda hurried away.

Adverb Clause Opener (#5 Sentence Opener)

PATTERN AC, MC Use a comma after an adverb clause opener.

When the cat prowled at night, the mice hid.

Mid-Sentence Adverb Clause

PATTERN AC, MC Use a comma after an adverb clause that comes before a main clause.

Early that morning *when Timmy saw the cat*, he was aghast.

PATTERN MC AC Do not use a comma before an adverb clause.

Early that morning Timmy was aghast (no comma) *when he saw the cat.*

Quotation

Use a comma to separate an attribution from a direct quote.

A throaty voice offered, "I should be honored to find your ball."

"I should be honored," a throaty voice offered, "to find your ball."

"I should be honored to find your ball," a throaty voice offered.

The attribution is the narrative that includes the person speaking and the speaking verb (*he said*).

Comparing Items

Do not use a comma when making a comparison.

Robin was a better shot (no comma) *than the other archers.*

Contrasting Items

Use a comma to separate contrasting parts of a sentence.

The ideas in this story are the rooster's thoughts, *not mine.*

Use a comma to contrast, not compare.

Use a comma even if the contrasting part begins with www words *although, while,* or *whereas.* This rule applies only when there is an extreme contrast and is an exception to **MC AC**.

He seemed interested, *whereas* she did not.

Timmy favored the country, *while* Johnny preferred the city.

Appositive, Adjective Clause, Mid-Sentence Participial Phrase

A nonessential appositive, adjective clause, or mid-sentence participial phrase adds information to a sentence.

Use commas to separate nonessential elements from the rest of the sentence.

Robin Hood, *the archer*, led his men through the forest.

Little John, *who liked a challenge*, readily followed Robin.

The men, *laughing at each other*, hiked through the forest.

An appositive is an invisible *who/which* clause. See page G-39.

A *who/which* clause is an adjective clause.

A participial phrase is an -ing phrase.

An essential appositive, adjective clause, or mid-sentence participial phrase defines the noun it follows. If the essential information is removed, the overall meaning of the sentence changes.

Do not use commas with essential elements.

The archer *Robin Hood* led his men through the forest.

The men *who followed Robin Hood* could be trusted.

The man *walking across the bridge* was a stranger.

To determine if a phrase or clause is essential, remove it from the sentence to see if it changes the meaning of the sentence.

Little John, *who liked a challenge*, readily followed Robin.
Remove the *who/which* clause: Little John readily followed Robin. This does not change the meaning of the sentence. This *who* clause is nonessential. Use commas.

The men *who followed Robin Hood* could be trusted.
Remove the *who/which* clause: The men could be trusted. This changes the meaning because the reader does not know which men could be trusted. This *who* clause is essential. Do not use commas.

Nonessential items need commas.

Essential items eliminate commas.

In some cases, the commas determine the meaning of the sentence.

Even the footmen, *who once obeyed her*, snubbed her.
With commas this sentence indicates all footmen snubbed her and all once obeyed her.

Even the footmen *who once obeyed her* snubbed her.
Without commas this same sentence now indicates that only those footmen who once obeyed her now snubbed her.

Quotation Marks " "

Direct Quotation

Use quotation marks to enclose direct quotations.

"I want to live above the sea," said the Little Mermaid.

There should not be a space between the quotation mark and the word or punctuation it encloses.

Indirect Quotation

Do not use quotation marks with indirect speech, which usually begins with *that.*

The Little Mermaid said that she wanted to live above the sea.

Thoughts

When typing, place thoughts in italics. When handwriting, use quotation marks.

I do not want a fish's tail, thought the Little Mermaid.

Punctuating a Quotation

Use a comma to separate an attribution from a direct quote. If a direct quote is an exclamation or question, follow it with an exclamation or question mark.

The attribution is the narrative that includes the person speaking and the speaking verb (*he said*).

Attribution**,** "Quote."	Attribution**,** "Quote!"	Attribution**,** "Quote?"
"Quote**,**" attribution.	"Quote**!**" attribution.	"Quote**?**" attribution.

Commas and periods always go inside closing quotation marks.

"I want to live above the sea**,**" said the Little Mermaid.

Hans Christian Andersen wrote "The Little Mermaid**.**"

Exclamation marks and question marks go inside closing quotations when they are part of the quoted material; otherwise, they go outside.

"Can humans live forever**?**" the Little Mermaid asked.

Did Grandmother say, "Humans can live forever"**?**

When a spoken sentence is interrupted, close the first part and begin the second with quotation marks. Do not capitalize the first letter of the continuation.

"Human beings have a soul," explained Grandmother, "**t**hat lives eternally."

In conversation, if someone speaking changes topic, start a new paragraph. Close the first paragraph without a quotation mark to signal the speaker has not finished speaking. Open the new paragraph with a quotation mark to indicate that someone is still speaking.

The prince responded, "You remind me of a girl I once met.

"Long ago, my ship wrecked, and the waves cast me ashore. A maiden saved my life."

Referencing Words

When typing, place words referred to as words in italics or quotation marks. When handwriting, use quotation marks.

Insert "the word(s)" or "the name" before the word in question to tell if this rule applies.

The king believed *sir* and *madam* should be used when addressing one's elders.

Single Quotation Marks

Use single quotation marks for quotations within quotations.

The maid said, "Strip the mattresses since, as the queen put it, 'They might be unclean.'"

This is the only reason to use single quotation marks.

Apostrophes ’

Contraction

Use an apostrophe to show where a letter or letters have been removed.

I’ll figure out how to trick them.

It’s too bad, but we’d better go our separate ways.

Possessive Adjective

Use an apostrophe to show possession.

To form singular possessives, add an apostrophe + *s*.

the second soldier’s turn

To form plural possessives, make the noun plural; then add an apostrophe.

the soldiers’ last night at the palace (the last night of all three soldiers)

An exception is irregular plural possessives.

the children’s mittens and the women’s scarves

Plural Noun

Do not use an apostrophe to make a word plural.

The *soldiers* each took a turn.

The *princesses* received whatever they requested.

Possessive Pronoun

Do not use an apostrophe with possessive pronouns.

his, hers, its, theirs, ours, yours

Possessive Pronouns	Contractions
its	it’s (it is)
their	they’re (they are)
theirs	there’s (there is)
whose	who’s (who is)

Ellipsis Points ...

Fictional Writing

Use ellipsis points to signal hesitation or a reflective pause, especially in dialogue.

“Ahem ... ” Lord Ashton cleared his throat conspicuously.

“Um ... certainly ... the mattress test,” the king sighed.

Nonfictional Writing

Use ellipses only when omitting words from a direct quotation.

Semicolons ;

Main Clauses

PATTERN MC; MC Use a semicolon to join main clauses that are closely related and parallel in construction.

The Little Mermaid pondered golden sunsets**;** she dreamed of twinkling stars.

Conjunctive Adverb

PATTERN MC; ca, MC. If a conjunctive adverb is used to connect two main clauses that express similar ideas, put a semicolon before the conjunctive adverb and a comma after.

Conjunctive adverbs are transition words.

Years of indulgence had spoiled her beyond recognition**;** *however***,** Lady Constance recalled a time in Dorinda's childhood when she had been a lovable child.

Items in a Series

Use semicolons to separate items in a series when the items contain internal commas.

Highborn women lamented when Troy, that noble city celebrated by Homer, fell through trickery**;** when Pyrrhus, ancient Greek ruler, seized King Priam by the beard**;** and when the Romans, ruthless and crazed, torched Carthage to the ground.

Colons :

List

PATTERN MC: list Use a colon after a main clause to introduce a list when a phrase like *for example* is not included.

Colons follow a complete thought and mean *see what follows* or *an example follows.*

Robin Hood had two choices**:** run away or fight.

Explanation

PATTERN MC: explanation Use a colon after a main clause to introduce an explanation when a phrase like *for example* is not included.

One other thing I ask**:** please accept this simple souvenir from me.

Quotation

PATTERN MC: quotation Use a colon when a complete thought sets up a quotation.

Contrast this with an attribution. The innkeeper answered, "Sir, your friend left town at dawn."

The innkeeper answered him straightaway**:** "Sir, your friend left town at dawn."

Titles with Subtitles

PATTERN Title: Subtitle Use a colon to separate a title from a subtitle.

Charles Dickens wrote *Oliver Twist***:** *The Parish Boy's Progress* and *A Christmas Carol***:** *A Ghost Story of Christmas.*

Hyphens -

Numbers

Use a hyphen with compound numbers from twenty-one to ninety-nine and with fractions.

thirty-seven; one-fourth

Compound Nouns

Use hyphens with some compound nouns.

lady-in-waiting; mother-in-law; self-restraint

Compound Adjectives

Use a hyphen when two or more words come before a noun they describe and act as a single idea.

The *nineteenth-century* author enjoyed his fame.

The *five-year-old* boy cried.

When a compound adjective follows the noun it describes, the adjective may or may not be hyphenated. If in doubt, consult a dictionary.

The boy was *five years old.*

Mowgli was *self-confident.*

Em Dashes and Parentheses — ( )

Emphasis

Use em dashes to emphasize something.

Your word—of all people's—must be trustworthy.

Interruption

Use em dashes to indicate an interruption in speech or a sudden break in thought.

His younger daughter—now there was another topic that brought red to his face—embarrassed him in front of the guests.

Nonessential Elements

Use em dashes to set off nonessential elements that have commas inside them.

The poor widow owned a few farm animals—three hefty sows, three cows, and a sheep dubbed Molly—with which she attempted to eke out a living.

Extra Information

Use parentheses to provide extra information.

"Oh, yes, benevolent frog!" (Notice that in fairy tales, characters don't have great curiosity about such oddities as talking frogs.)

Use em dashes in place of commas when you want to draw attention to something.

Use parentheses in place of commas when you want to offer an aside.

Additional Concepts

Indentation

In copy work, indent by doing two things: 1) start on the next line, and 2) start writing ½ inch from the left margin.

The paragraph mark (¶) is called a pilcrow.

To mark indentation, add the ¶ symbol or an arrow (➔) in front of each sentence that should start a new paragraph.

In fiction (stories), there are four reasons to start a new paragraph.

New Speaker

Start a new paragraph when a new character speaks. Include the attribution with the quotation.

> She cried loudly, "Thieves!"

If a narrative sentence sets up the quotation, it should go in the same paragraph as the quoted sentence.

> The stranger came right to the point. "It is cowardly to stand there with a lethal arrow aimed at my heart."

If a narrative follows a quotation in a separate sentence but points directly back to the quotation, it can also go in the same paragraph.

> "It is cowardly to stand there with a lethal arrow aimed at my heart." The stranger did not mince words.

New Topic

Start a new paragraph when the narrator or a character switches topic or focus.

New Place

Start a new paragraph when the story switches to a new location. If several switches are made in quick succession, such as a character's journey to find something, it may be less choppy to keep in one paragraph.

New Time

Start a new paragraph when the time changes unless there are several time shifts in close succession that make sense together in a single paragraph.

Capitalization

Sentence

Capitalize the first word of a sentence and of a quoted sentence, even when it does not begin the full sentence.

The princess cried, "**M**y nose has grown too long."

Do not capitalize the first word of an attribution when it follows the quoted sentence.

"My nose has grown too long," **t**he princess cried.

"You must be content!" **u**rged grandmother

Quotation Continues

When a spoken sentence is interrupted, do not capitalize the first letter of the continuation.

"**M**y nose," the princess cried, "**h**as grown too long."

Proper Nouns and Adjectives

Capitalize proper nouns and adjectives derived from proper nouns.

Sherwood Forest; Robin Hood; English flag

Titles

Capitalize titles that precede a name. Do not capitalize titles that are not used with a name.

In 1952 *Queen Elizabeth II* became the *queen* of England.

Capitalize titles that substitute for a name in a noun of direct address.

"Can you clean his wound, *Doctor*?"

Do not capitalize family members unless used as a substitute for a name or with a name.

He succeeded his *father* as king.

Did *Father* say that we could play outside?

An exception is *sir* or *madam* as a noun of direct address: "Stand back, sir," demanded Robin.

Calendar Words

Capitalize days of the week and months of the year. Do not capitalize seasons: spring, summer, fall, winter.

Timmy enjoyed peas on a hot *summer Wednesday* evening in *June*.

Directions

Capitalize compass directions when they refer to a region or proper name. Do not capitalize these words when they indicate direction. Do not capitalize words like *northward* or *northern*.

On her journey *north* Eden encountered few obstacles.
Eden is heading in a *northward* direction but not traveling to a region known as the *North*.

Literary Titles and Subtitles

Capitalize the first word and the last word of titles and subtitles. Capitalize all other words except articles, coordinating conjunctions, and prepositions.

A young girl recited "Mary Had a Little Lamb."

Read *Mozart: The Wonder Boy* by next week.

Numbers

Words

Spell out numbers that can be expressed in one or two words.

twenty; fifty-three; three hundred

Dorinda had racked up *one thousand* text messages on her cell phone in one month.

Spell out ordinal numbers.

first, second, third

The next year the *second* sister was permitted to rise to the surface.

Numerals

Use numerals for numbers that use three or more words.

123; 204

That evening 250 rockets rose in the air.

Never begin a sentence with a numeral.

1492 is a famous year in history. (incorrect)

The year 1492 is a famous year in history. (correct)

Use numerals with dates. Do not include *st, nd, rd,* or *th.*

December 25, not December 25th

Meet me at the Green Chapel in one year and one day on January 1, 1400.

Use numerals when numbers are mixed with symbols.

We received $500 in donations last month.

We can expect at least 40% of those invited to attend.

Homophones and Usage

Homophones

Homophones are words that sound alike but are spelled differently and have different meanings.

there
their
they're

There is an adverb pointing to a place or point: *over there* (there is the spot).
Their is a possessive pronoun: *their house* (the house belongs to them).
They're is a contraction: *they're finished* (they are finished).

Although less common, *there* can function as a noun, pronoun, or adjective.

your
you're

Your is a possessive pronoun: *your weapon* (the weapon belongs to you).
You're is a contraction: *you're finished* (you are finished).

to
two
too

To is a preposition or part of an infinitive: *to the left* (preposition); *to rush* (infinitive).
Two is a number: *two women* (2 women).
Too is an adverb meaning also or to an excessive degree: *I'll go too; too far.*

its
it's

Its is a possessive pronoun: *its wing* (the wing belongs to the bird).
It's is a contraction: *it's too bad* (it is too bad).

then
than

Then is an adverb meaning next or immediately after: *wake and then eat.*
Than is a word used to show a comparison: *Sam is shorter than Bob.*

affect *Affect* is a verb that means to have an influence or to cause:
Dorinda was too self-centered for anyone else to *affect* her deeply.

effect *Effect* is a noun that refers to the result of some action:
Years of indulgence had the obvious *effect* of spoiling Dorinda.

The definitions given for *affect* and *effect* are the most commonly used.

Usage

Usage errors occur when a word is used incorrectly.

between
among

Between is a preposition that refers to two items: She stood *between* the (two) trees.
Among is a preposition that refers to three or more items: She walked *among* them.

like
as

Like is a preposition that compares a noun to a noun: Waves rose *like* mountains.
As is a subordinating conjunction that compares a noun to an idea (subject + verb).
The waves rose suddenly *as* the storm swelled.
As is a preposition when it means in the role of: They traveled *as* adults.

farther
further

Farther refers to measurable distance: I jumped *farther* than I did yesterday.
Further refers to a figurative distance: We want to avoid *further* delays.
Further functions as a verb when it means to promote: He will *further* the agenda.

Use *farthest* like *farther*, *furthest* like *further*.

lie
lay

Lie is a verb that means to recline or remain: The hen rarely *lies* down.
Lay is a verb that means to put something down: Daily, the hen *lays* an egg.

The past tense of *lie* is *lay*, which is the same as the present tense of *to lay*.

infinitive	present	past	past participle
to lie	*lie*	*lay*	*lain*
to lay	*lay*	*laid*	*laid*

Present: The hens *lie* down (recline) after they *lay* eggs (put eggs down).

Past: Yesterday the hens *lay* down (reclined) after they *laid* eggs (put eggs down).

Stylistic Techniques

Fix It! stories teach the stylistic techniques of the Institute for Excellence in Writing. Dress-ups are placed within sentences to strengthen vocabulary and add complex sentence structures. Sentence openers are different ways to begin sentences, encouraging sentence variety. Decorations are stylistic devices that embellish prose.

Dress-Ups

Dress-ups are descriptive words, phrases, and clauses that are placed within a sentence.

Three of the dress-ups encourage stronger vocabulary: -ly adverb, strong verb, quality adjective. The other dress-ups encourage more complex sentence structure: *who/which* clause and *www.asia.b* clause.

-ly Adverb Dress-Up

An -ly adverb is an adverb that ends in *-ly*. Adverbs are words that modify verbs, adjectives, or other adverbs. Most often they tell *how* or *when* something is done. The -ly adverb dress-up is used to enhance the meaning of a word. See page G-15.

See a list of -ly adverbs on page G-43.

Notice how the meaning of this sentence changes when different -ly adverbs are added:

She masqueraded as a poor girl.

She *cleverly* masqueraded as a poor girl.

She *arrogantly* masqueraded as a poor girl.

She *deceptively* masqueraded as a poor girl.

Not all words that end in -ly are adverbs. Impostor -ly adverbs are adjectives. If the word ending in -ly describes a noun, it is an adjective and not an adverb.

Adjective Test:

the ______ pen

To find -ly adverbs to use in your writing, use a thesaurus or vocabulary words. Alternatively, look at -ly adverb word lists on the *Portable Walls for Structure and Style Students®* or the IEW Writing Tools App.

Common Impostors
These -ly words are adjectives.

chilly	holy	lovely	queenly
friendly	kingly	lowly	ugly
ghastly	knightly	orderly	worldly
ghostly	lonely	prickly	wrinkly

Strong Verb Dress-Up

A strong verb is an action verb that creates a strong image or feeling. It helps a reader picture what someone or something is doing. See page G-9.

Verb Test:

I ______.

It ______.

Challenge students to distinguish between strong verbs and vague ones.

The mermaids often *went* to the castle.
The mermaids often *visited* the castle and *toured* its opulent halls.

The horse *was* in the barn.
The horse *buried* itself in the hay.

The mermaids' hands *were nibbled* on by the fish.
The fish *nibbled* the mermaids' hands.

Quality Adjective Dress-Up

A quality adjective is a descriptive word that provides specific details about a noun or pronoun. Like a strong verb, a quality adjective provides a strong image or feeling. See page G-14.

Adjective Test:

the ______ pen

Notice how the image of *brook* changes with the use of different adjectives. In both examples, the first suggested adjective is weak, whereas the other two provide a stronger image or feeling.

He hurdled the *small* brook.
He hurdled the *narrow* brook.
He hurdled the *babbling* brook.

The *big* stranger greeted Robin.
The *confident* stranger greeted Robin.
The *disagreeable* stranger greeted Robin.

To find strong verbs and quality adjectives to use in your writing, use a thesaurus or vocabulary words. Alternatively, look at word lists on the *Portable Walls for Structure and Style Students* or the IEW Writing Tools App.

Advanced

Deliberate use of dual -ly adverbs, strong verbs, or quality adjectives, especially when the words add a different nuance, enriches prose and challenges students to be precise with words chosen. Classic writers of the past like Charles Dickens and persuasive essayists like Winston Churchill have used duals and triples to convey their meaning most powerfully.

The ship glided away *smoothly* and *lightly* over the tranquil sea.

The wind *filled* and *lifted* the ship's sails.

All who beheld her wondered at her *graceful, swaying* movements.

To punctuate dual adjectives properly, see page G-24.

Who/Which Clause Dress-Up

A *who/which* clause is a dependent clause that provides description or additional information about the noun it follows.

The *who/which* clause immediately follows the noun it describes.

Robin Hood cut a staff, *which measured six feet in length.*
Which measured six feet in length describes the staff.

Frederick hoped to make friends with the princess, *who frequently visited the garden.*
Who frequently visited the garden describes the princess.

A *who/which* clause is a dependent clause that begins with the word *who* or *which.*

Forms of *who* include *whom* and *whose*. See page G-6.

Use *who* when referring to people, personified animals, and pets.
Use *which* when referring to things, animals, and places.

Because the *who/which* clause is a dependent clause, it must be added to a sentence that is already complete. If only the word *who* or *which* is added, a fragment is formed.

The noise alerted Sam. (sentence)
The noise, *which alerted Sam.* (fragment)
The noise alerted Sam, *who drove to safety.* (sentence)
The noise, *which alerted Sam,* alerted him to drive to safety. (sentence)

If the *who/which* clause is removed, a sentence must remain.

Place commas around a *who/which* clause if it is nonessential to the meaning of the sentence.

William**,** *who had little***,** shared with his neighbors. (nonessential, commas)

Do not place commas around a *who/which* clause if it is essential to the meaning of the sentence. See page G-26.

The students *who finished the test* left early. (essential, no commas)
The clause is essential because it defines which students left early.

Although the word *that* may begin an adjective clause, a *that* clause is not a *who/which* clause dress-up.

Advanced

A *who* clause always describes a single noun.

A *which* clause can describe a single noun, or it can describe the entire idea that comes before *which.*

You have killed the king's deer, *which is a capital offense.*
It is not the *deer* (noun before *which* clause) that is the offense but killing it—
the entire idea expressed in the main clause.

If a *who/which* clause contains a *be* verb, the *who* or *which* and the *be* verb can be removed to form an invisible *who/which* clause. An invisible *who/which* clause is called an appositive or appositive phrase, not a clause because the subject (*who* or *which*) and the be verb have been removed from the written sentence. Follow the same comma rules.

Dorinda frustrated Lady Constance, ~~who was~~ her companion since childhood.

All had come to Sherwood Forest, ~~which was~~ a vast, uncharted wood.

www.asia.b Clause Dress-Up

A *www.asia.b* clause is a dependent clause that usually functions as an adverb. It begins with a subordinating conjunction (www word) and contains both a subject and a verb.

Robin Hood and his band guffawed loudly *until the stranger showed irritation.*
Remain on the other side *while I make a staff.*

There are many subordinating conjunctions. The most common are taught using the acronym *www.asia.b*: when, while, where, as, since, if, although, because. Other words function as subordinating conjunctions: after, before, until, unless, whenever, whereas, than. See page G-13.

Because the *www.asia.b* clause is a dependent clause, it must be added to a main clause. Although an adverb clause may appear anywhere in a sentence, the *www.asia.b* clause dress-up should not begin a sentence because only sentence openers begin sentences.

PATTERN

www word + subject + verb

Memorize the most common www words using the acronym *www.asia.b:* when, while, where, as, since, if, although, because.

Use a comma after an adverb clause that comes before a main clause.
PATTERN AC, MC

That morning *while it rained*, Timmy stayed indoors.

Do not use a comma before an adverb clause.
PATTERN MC AC

Timmy stayed indoors (no comma) *when it rained.*

An adverb clause follows the pattern www word + subject + verb. If a verb is not present, the group of words is likely a prepositional phrase and not an adverb clause.

Dorinda prepared the guestroom *after supper.*
After supper is not a clause because it does not contain a subject and a verb.
After supper is a prepositional phrase.

Dorinda prepared the guestroom *after they ate supper.*
After they ate supper is a clause because it contains both a subject (they) and a verb (ate).

Two tricks help tell the difference between a phrase and a clause.

Look for a verb. A clause must have a verb. A prepositional phrase will not have a verb.

Drop the first word of the phrase or clause in question and look at what is left.

If it is a sentence, the group of words is an adverb clause; if it is not, the words form a prepositional phrase.

~~after~~ supper
This does not have a verb. This does not form a sentence. This is a phrase.

~~after~~ they ate supper
This has a verb (ate). This forms a sentence. This is a clause.

Advanced

When the www words *as, where, when* begin a clause that follows and describes a noun, the clause is probably an adjective clause. Test by inserting *which is* between the noun and www word. If it sounds correct, the clause is an adjective clause, not an adverb clause. Punctuate accordingly. See pages G-21 and G-26.

King Arthur decided to climb to the top of the cliff, *where he could drink from the pool of water.*
King Arthur decided to climb to the top of the cliff, [which is] *where he could drink from the pool of water.*
This is an adjective clause beginning with the word *where.* Because it is nonessential, it requires commas.

When the www words *although, while,* and *whereas* present an extreme contrast to the main clause in the sentence, insert a comma. This is an exception to the more common rule **MC AC**. See page G-26.

Timmy favored the country, *while* Johnny preferred the city.

Advanced Dress-Ups

Dual -ly Adverbs, Strong Verbs, Quality Adjectives

Deliberate use of dual -ly adverbs, strong verbs, or quality adjectives, especially when the words add a different nuance, enriches prose and challenges students to be precise with words chosen. Classic writers of the past like Charles Dickens and persuasive essayists like Winston Churchill have used duals and triples to convey their meaning most powerfully.

The ship glided away *smoothly* and *lightly* over the tranquil sea.
The wind *filled* the ship's sails and *propelled* the ship through the sea.
All who beheld her wondered at her *graceful, swaying* movements.

Invisible *Who/Which* Clause

An invisible *who/which* clause is formed when the word *who* or *which* is followed by a *be* verb. Removing *who* or *which* and the *be* verb that follows allows for a more elegant construction. Follow the same comma rules.

Not all *who/which* clauses can be made invisible.

Dorinda frustrated Lady Constance, ~~who was~~ her companion since childhood.

All had come to Sherwood Forest, ~~which was~~ a vast, uncharted wood.

Teeter-Totters

The adverb teeter-totter uses a verb as a fulcrum with dual -ly adverbs preceding the verb and a *www.asia.b* clause following it. Both the -ly adverbs and the *www.asia.b* clause modify the same verb. **PATTERN -ly -ly verb *www.asia.b***

dual -ly adverbs | verb | *www.asia.b*

The tortoise *slowly* yet *steadily* finished the race *as the crowd watched in awe.*

The adjective teeter-totter uses a noun as a fulcrum with dual quality adjectives preceding the noun and a *who/which* clause following it. Both the quality adjectives and the *who/which* clause describe the same noun. **PATTERN adjective adjective noun *w/w***

dual adjectives | noun | *w/w* clause

The Little Mermaid placed the prince on the *fine white* sand, *which the sun had warmed.*

Noun Clause

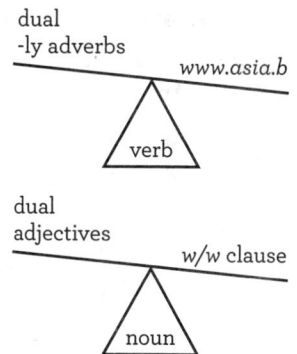

A noun clause dress-up is a dependent clause that functions as a noun and begins with the word *that.* It typically follows a verb and answers the question *what.*

If the *that* clause is an adjective clause and not a noun clause, the word *which* can replace *that.*

The king of the beasts never imagined *that* a puny rodent could help him.
The king of the beasts never imagined *which* a puny rodent could help him.
This does not make sense. This is not an adjective clause but a noun clause.

The king of the beasts was freed from a net *that* a mouse had persistently gnawed.
The king of the beasts was freed from a net *which* a mouse had persistently gnawed.
This makes sense. This is an adjective clause. See page G-21.

An invisible noun clause occurs when the word *that* is implied, not stated directly.

Dorinda never seemed to understand [that] *she was responsible.*

Frederick could tell [that] *he would relish his palace stay.*

Noun clauses do not take commas.

People felt (no comma) *that Robin Hood was like them.*

Robin Hood was pleased (no comma) *that he had escaped.*

Sentence Openers

Sentence openers are descriptive words, phrases, and clauses that are added to the beginning of a sentence.

There are six openers—six ways to open or begin a sentence. Using various sentence openers forces sentence variety, which will improve writing quality. Learning the sentence opener patterns and their related comma rules will result in sophisticated writing skills.

#1 Subject Opener

A subject opener is simply a sentence that begins with its subject. This is the kind of sentence one most naturally writes. A subject opener begins with the subject of the sentence.

Fish glide among the branches.

There may be an article or adjectives in front of the subject, but that does not change the sentence structure. It is still a #1 subject opener.

The colorful fish glide among the branches.

#2 Prepositional Opener

A prepositional opener is a prepositional phrase placed at the beginning of a sentence. See pages G-8 and G-18.

If a prepositional opener has five words or more, follow it with a comma.

Under the table (no comma) the tiny mouse hid.

Under the heavy wooden table, the tiny mouse hid.

If two or more prepositional phrases open a sentence, follow the last phrase with a comma.

Under the heavy wooden table in the kitchen, the tiny mouse hid.

If a prepositional opener functions as a transition, follow it with a comma.

In fact, the cook was afraid of mice.

If a prepositional opener is followed by a main clause that has the verb before the subject, do not use a comma.

Under the heavy wooden table hid a tiny mouse.

PATTERN

preposition + noun (no verb)

Because of begins prepositional phrases.

Because begins clauses.

Advanced

An invisible prepositional opener is formed when some kind of time is followed by the main clause. The preposition *on* or *during* is implied.

~~On~~ *Wednesday* we will go to the beach.

~~On~~ *The day before yesterday* we visited the park.

~~During~~ *That afternoon* she visited friends.

#3 -ly Adverb Opener

An -ly adverb opener is an -ly adverb placed at the beginning of a sentence. Beginning the sentence with an -ly adverb changes the rhythm of the sentence.

Test:

It was ____ that ____.

Use a comma if an -ly adverb opener modifies the sentence.

Foolishly, Timmy bit into a hot pepper.
Test: It was foolish that Timmy bit ... makes sense.
Foolishly modifies the sentence. A comma is required.

Do not use a comma if an -ly adverb opener modifies the verb.

Eagerly Timmy ate a ripe cucumber.
Test: It was eager that Timmy ate a ripe cucumber ... does not make sense. *Eagerly* modifies the verb *ate*. A comma is not needed.

Advanced

In some cases, the comma indicates the meaning of the sentence.

Sorrowfully Timmy acceded to the counsel of Johnny.
He acceded, but he did so sorrowfully, with regret.

Sorrowfully, Timmy acceded to the counsel of Johnny.
This opener indicates that Timmy made a mistake in acceding to Johnny's advice.
It is sorrowful that Timmy acceded to his Johnny's counsel.

-ly Adverbs List

angrily	critically	historically	mournfully	sleepily	unhappily
annoyingly	deceptively	hopefully	oddly	slyly	usually
boredly	disappointingly	horribly	proudly	sneakily	viciously
busily	discouragingly	joyfully	rapidly	strangely	vigorously
commonly	excitedly	kindly	repeatedly	suddenly	violently
completely	finally	meanly	sadly	tragically	warmly
constantly	greedily	miraculously	seriously	uncomfortably	willfully
continuously	happily	mostly	shamefully	unexpectedly	wisely

#4 -ing Opener

An -ing opener is a participial phrase placed at the beginning of a sentence.

A #4 -ing opener is a participial opener.

Taking up his bow, Robin Hood shot with unparalleled skill.

PATTERN -ing word/phrase, main clause. This is the most sophisticated sentence pattern. It is easily written when the pattern is followed. The sentence must begin with an action word that ends in -ing. This is called a participle. The -ing word/phrase and comma are followed by a main clause. The thing (subject of main clause) after the comma must be the thing doing the inging.

The thing after the comma must be the thing doing the inging.

Gathering their three gifts, the soldiers visited a neighboring king. The sentence begins with an action word that ends in -ing: *Gathering*
The -ing word/phrase and comma are followed by a main clause: *the soldiers visited a neighboring king.*
The thing (subejct of main clause) after the comma must be the thing doing the inging: *soldiers* (subject) *are gathering.*

An illegal #4 opener is grammatically incorrect. If the thing after the comma is not the thing doing the inging, the sentence does not make sense. This is known as a dangling modifier.

Hopping quickly, Dorinda let the frog follow her to the dining hall.
Who was hopping quickly? *Dorinda.* This is incorrect because the frog was hopping quickly.

An impostor #4 opener begins with an -ing word but does not follow the pattern. There are two types.

Living at the splendid castle cheered the soldiers.
This is a #1 subject opener. There is neither a comma nor a subject doing the inging. *Living* is the subject.

During the dance she twirled him around.
This is a #2 prepositional opener. *She* (the subject) is not doing the *during.*

Prepositions ending in -ing include *concerning, according to, regarding, during.*

Advanced

An invisible -ing opener is formed when *being* is implied before the first word of the sentence. Removing the word *being* allows for a more elegant construction. Follow the same comma rules.

~~Being~~ Quick-witted and agile, Robert compensated for his limitation with an eagerness to please.

~~Being~~ Relaxed and untroubled, the stranger genially waited for him.

~~Being~~ Encouraged by Samuel's speech, William stepped onto the stage.

#5 Clausal Opener

A clausal opener is an adverb clause placed at the beginning of a sentence. This opener is the same as the *www.asia.b* dress-up. The only difference is placement in the sentence. The opener begins a sentence.

PATTERN AC, MC Use a comma after an adverb clause opener.

If possessions were plundered, Robin and his men would recapture the goods and return them to the poor.

As he approached, Robin Hood noticed a tall stranger on the other side of the stream.

When Robin attempted to cross the river, the stranger blocked his way.

PATTERN

www word + subject + verb

Because begins clauses.

Because of begins prepositional phrases.

An adverb clause follows the pattern www word + subject + verb. If a verb is not present, the group of words is likely a prepositional phrase and not an adverb clause.

After supper, Dorinda prepared the guestroom.
After supper is not a clause because it does not contain a subject and a verb.
After supper is a prepositional phrase.

After they ate supper, Dorinda prepared the guestroom.
After they ate supper is a clause because it contains both a subject (they) and a verb (ate).

Two tricks help tell the difference between a phrase and a clause.

Look for a verb. A clause must have a verb. A prepositional phrase will not have a verb.

Drop the first word of the phrase or clause in question and look at what is left. If it is a sentence, the group of words is an adverb clause; if it is not, the words form a prepositional phrase.

~~After~~ supper
This does not have a verb. This does not form a sentence. This is a phrase.

~~After~~ they ate supper
This has a verb (ate). This forms a sentence. This is a clause.

#6 Vss Opener

A very short sentence (vss) is simply a short sentence. It must be short (two to five words), and it must be a sentence (subject + verb and be able to stand alone). It is not a fragment.

Remember that variety in sentence structure is important in good writing. Purposefully adding a very short sentence can help break up the pattern of sentences in a stylish way. It catches the reader's attention. As a result, place it in a spot that needs emphasis.

Robin Hood left.

The blow inflamed him.

King Morton esteemed values.

As an added challenge, include a strong verb so that the very short sentence packs a punch.

Advanced Sentence Openers

#F Fragment Opener

A fragment that does not leave the reader hanging and that fits the flow of the paragraph can be dramatic and effective. This opener is often used in fictional writing.

Timmy saw his dear friend. (sentence)

Greeting him kindly. (unacceptable fragment)

"Hello, Johnny!" (acceptable fragment)

#Q Question Opener

A question is a complete sentence. It must contain a subject and a verb and make sense.

Where could he take a nap?

#T Transitional Opener

The transitional opener may be an interjection or a transitional word or phrase.

Place commas after a transitional expression.

Meanwhile, Robin's men rested near the river.

Of course, Dorinda and Maribella lived in the castle.

When an interjection expresses a strong emotion, use an exclamation mark. When an interjection does not express a strong emotion, use a comma.

Help! My golden ball has vanished.

Oh, I see it now.

List of Common Transitions

however	first
therefore	next
then	also
thus	moreover
later	hence
now	furthermore
otherwise	henceforth
indeed	likewise

Decorations

Used sparingly, as an artist might add a splash of bright color to a nature painting, these stylistic techniques daringly or delicately decorate one's prose.

Alliteration Decoration

Alliteration is using three or more words close together that begin with the same consonant sound. Our ear likes the repetition of sound. The alliterative words may be separated by conjunctions, articles, short pronouns, or prepositions.

Samuel was *seeking some* shady relief from the *sweltering sun.*
Shady is not part of the alliteration because it does not have the same initial sound as the other *s* words. It is not the letter that matters but the sound. Thus, *celery* and *sound* are alliterative, but *shady* and *sound* are not.

Question Decoration

The question may be a rhetorical question, which means the answer is understood and does not need to be given, or it may be a question that the writer answers soon after asking. If a character in the story asks a question of another character, that is simply conversation. The question decoration is directed towards the reader, causing the reader to stop and think.

Someone suddenly appeared on the path. *Who was it?* It was Johnny!

Conversation/Quotation Decoration

Conversation appears in narrative writing when characters talk.

"You're finally here, Johnny!" exclaimed Timmy.

A quotation appears when the writer uses the exact words that someone else has used. A quotation includes a well-known expression, words stated by a famous person, or words found in another source. When a quotation is used as a decoration, it does not require a citation, but the source should be included as a lead-in. Punctuate correctly. See page G-27.

As Mark Twain noted, "History may not repeat itself, but it sure does rhyme."

3sss Decoration

3sss stands for three short staccato sentences. The 3sss is simply three #6 very short sentences in a row. Using short sentences together, especially among longer sentences, can be a powerful stylistic technique because the short sentences will draw attention to themselves.

A 3sss will have the most impact when the number of words in each of the sentences is the same or decreasing. Increasing patterns have less impact.

4:3:2 Killer bees invaded America. Viciously they attacked. Humans suffered.

3:3:3 Savage bees attacked. Violently they killed. Nobody was spared.

2:2:2 Bees invaded. They marauded. Humans perished.

Simile/Metaphor Decoration

Both a simile and a metaphor are figures of speech which compare two items that are very different from each other. The well-known simile *her cheeks are like roses* compares cheeks to roses, two very different things. A simile makes the comparison by using the words *like* or *as*. A metaphor does not use *like* or *as*. It simply refers to one thing as if it is another.

The key to recognizing these figures of speech is that they compare unlike things. For example, to say that a cat is like a tiger is a comparison but not a simile.

The ship dove like a swan between them. (simile)

The waves rose mountains high. (metaphor)

Dramatic Open-Close Decoration

The vss open-close decoration frames a single paragraph. The vss open-close decoration contains two very short sentences two to five words long. One is placed at the beginning of the paragraph, and the other is placed at the end.

Hungry flames roared. (vss open) The farm lay in ashes. (vss close)

Peter sighed. (vss open) Peter had an idea. (vss close)

The mystery was solved! (vss open) The truth was told. (vss close)

The anecdotal open-close decoration frames a composition or essay that includes an introduction and conclusion. An anecdote is a very short story meant to amuse or teach. To use this decoration, begin the introduction with a story to draw in the reader. Revisit the story somewhere in the conclusion.

Anecdotal open (beginning of introduction):

With a bushel of cranberries slung over her shoulder, eight-year-old Jennie Camillo trod through the cranberry bog toward the bushel man who would collect her load. When the infamous photographer Lewis Hine asked her to stop so he could take a picture, she stopped for a brief moment to humor the man. Concernedly Jennie glanced toward her toiling father, who was regarding her stop with annoyance.

Anecdotal close (in the conclusion):

Working during the harvest season, Jennie missed the first six weeks of school. Due to her family's financial struggles, the Camillos were forced to take the whole family to Theodore Budd's bog near Philadelphia before returning home to New Jersey after the harvest.

Triple Extensions

Classic writers of the past have used duals and triples to convey their meaning most powerfully. The trick is to remember "thrice, never twice."

Repeating Words (same word)

Fearing for his sheep, *fearing* that the villagers would not arrive in time, and ultimately *fearing* for his own life, Peter screamed, "Help!" as he bolted down the hill.

Never in the field of conflict was *so* much owed by *so* many to *so* few (Churchill).

Villainy is *the matter*; baseness is *the matter*; deception, fraud, conspiracy are *the matter* (Dickens).

With a *common* origin, a *common* literature, a *common* religion and *common* drinks, what is longer needful to the cementing of the two nations together in a permanent bond of brotherhood (Mark Twain)?

Repeating Clauses

They lived in a land *where* the winter was harsh, *where* food became scarce, and *where* provisions had to be stored.

Repeating Prepositional Phrases

We have not journeyed all this way *across* the centuries, *across* the oceans, *across* the mountains, *across* the prairies, because we are made of sugar candy (Churchill).

Repeating -ings

Gnawing, jerking, and *yanking,* the mouse freed the lion from the thick rope.

The Little Mermaid could be seen *holding* the prince while *kissing* his brow and *stroking* his hair.

Repeating -ly Adverbs

Robin Hood *cheerfully, boldly,* and *fearlessly* led his men.

The mouse *vigorously* gnawed at the tough fibers and *tenaciously* jerked at the rope while he *continuously* assured the lion of escape.

Repeating Adjectives

The *patient, persistent,* and *personable* tortoise determined that at least he would have a chance.

Repeating Nouns

Peter's deceptive cries for help finally determined the *attitude, behavior,* and *actions* of the village people.

Repeating Verbs

With all his might, the mouse *gnawed, jerked,* and *yanked* at the thick rope.

What's next 

Mowgli and Shere Khan LEVEL 4

IEW.com/FIX-L4